Knitting

For Fun & Profit™

Shirley MacNulty

PRIMA HOME
An Imprint of Prima Publishing

Special thanks to Renee Chase for her editorial help.

Library of Congress Cataloging-in-Publication Data

MacNulty, Shirley.
   Knitting for fun & profit / Shirley MacNulty.
      p.   cm.
   Includes index.
   ISBN 0-7615-2108-9
   1. Knitting.   I. Title. II. Title: Knitting for fun and profit.
TT820.M23 1999
746.43'2—dc21

99-39230
CIP

99 00 01 02 ii 10 9 8 7 6 5 4 3 2 1

How to Order

Single copies may be ordered from Prima Publishing,
P.O. Box 1260BK, Rocklin, CA 95677; telephone (916) 632-4400.
Quantity discounts are also available. On your letterhead, include
information concerning the intended use of the books and
the number of books you wish to purchase.

Visit us online at www.primalifestyles.com

Contents

Introduction

I CAN'T REMEMBER LIFE before knitting. In fact, I may have been born with knitting needles in my hands. This wonderful craft has given me many hours of pleasure throughout the years, and I'm very excited about sharing it with you. Welcome to the world of knitting!

Why Knitting Is a Perfect Combination of Hobby and Income

If you enjoy being creative, love fashion, and also like working with your hands then almost certainly, you will enjoy knitting. Knitting ranks as a favorite among thousands of people for many reasons: It's fun, relaxing, extremely portable, and, you can profit financially from it. What more can you ask from a hobby?

Knitting is a flexible craft with infinite possibilities. Everyone in the industry is constantly developing new and creative ideas, and today's knitters enjoy an endless supply of new patterns and designs. Believe me, you'll never run out of inspiration for knitting projects!

Fashion knitwear is extremely popular and enjoyed by men, women, and children alike. As a knitter, you will create beautiful, designer-quality garments for yourself or for your relatives and friends, or you can simply sell your garments for a profit. Once you're proficient at knitting and have learned how to incorporate a few design basics, you will be able to duplicate virtually any knitted garment you see. Imagine the pride you'll feel when you can say, "I designed and knitted it myself!"

Knitting is equally useful for interior decorating and creating your own accessories. Today, knitting produces everything from afghans, pillows, throws, bedspreads, and lace curtains, to pocketbooks, doilies, place mats, and tablecloths. You are limited only by your imagination.

Another great thing about knitting is its portability. Unlike the majority of craft projects, you can carry knitting with you. I knit everywhere: on airplanes and buses, at the doctor's office, in meetings, and even at the gas station!

Knitting in public is a great conversation starter, too. It never fails: Someone always asks me what I'm making. I have met some very special people this way. It really is a lot of fun to show off your new sweater while getting acquainted with a new friend. This type of chance meeting can also present a sales opportunity. On several occasions, I have taken special orders from people I've met this way. Imagine that! Knitting allows you to advertise your creative ability effortlessly.

Knitting also creates fantastic opportunities that you would never expect. In addition to creating and selling beautiful hand-crafted items, my experience with knitting has allowed me to lead various workshops, teach classes, and judge all levels of knitting and needlework competitions. I have written numerous magazine articles about knitting and I have edited my own knitting newsletter, *Knitting News,* since 1988.

I now have the distinct pleasure of writing this knitting book. Knitting has been a very exciting and satisfying career choice for me, especially because it stems from sheer love. I hope you will enjoy it as much as I do.

History of Knitting

Knitting is one of our oldest crafts. According to Mary Thomas, who first started writing about knitting in 1938, knitting originated in the East, around the Arabian peninsula, sometime between the seventh and ninth centuries, but the actual date when knitting began is much debated. For example, some of the earliest pieces of knitted cloth are sock fragments found in Egypt. You can find many fabrics that suggest knitting techniques in museums around the world. A true "folk art," it has been developed over the centuries by ordinary people like you and me.

In the Middle Ages, the knitters' guilds were composed entirely of men, as were most guilds of that day. To become a member of these guilds, a young man had to serve as an apprentice for approximately three years, followed by additional time spent studying and traveling. Because of this fact, it is believed that men developed the early forms of knitting.

Old knitting patterns have been handed down from generation to generation without any written records. In fact, quite often, knitters couldn't read or write, despite the beautiful works of art they created.

American Knitting

In her book, *No Idle Hands, The Social History of American Knitting*, Anne L. Macdonald presents a wonderful, comprehensive history of American knitting. The book tells the interesting story of how Martha Washington carried her knitting with her during the Revolution. In fact, historical records from Mt. Vernon reflect the purchase of "knitting pins of different sizes" (knitting needles used to be called "pins"). Another story from the book takes place during World War II, when the FBI detained a woman entering the U.S. because she was carrying a code, *k2.p4.k6,* for which the State Department Library had no key. They were later embarrassed to discover their "spy" was actually an innocent, patriotic knitter. This fascinating book also discusses Eleanor Roosevelt's penchant for knitting, and how she encouraged the nation to knit for the troops. Her knitting bag was often seen in pictures, both on the campaign trail, and in the White House.

Knitting for the War Effort

As World War II approached, women and schoolchildren knitted for the war effort. Even the November 24, 1941 cover of *Life* magazine depicts a college student knitting. Pattern leaflets called, "Knitting for Servicemen," were also distributed during this time, according to Ellen Keating who found one among her mother-in-law's knitting supplies.

"When I was in the sixth grade, World War II broke out, and to do our patriotic duty, we took class time to knit six-inch squares," recalls my good friend Sally Crandall. "Even the boys had to knit. I spent my summer that year, spread out on the school hall floor, sewing the squares together for an afghan. That summer, I also went to a lady's house every Saturday, and helped knit olive drab-colored sweaters for the Russians." The colors used for war clothing were usually dull and pale because these were the only colors available at the time.

For school-age children, *garter stitching* was, and continues to be, the first type of stitch learned, thus its prevalence made it the perfect stitch for many projects during the war effort. Professional knitwear designer, teacher, and knitting history expert, Janet Johnson Stephens, remembers knitting as a part of school projects for the war: "I learned to knit in the third grade when we were making blankets during the war," she says. "Even though I didn't like [knitting] at the time, it was mandatory."

Modern Knitting

Knitting has come a long way in the past 20 years. Up-to-date production methods have given us a wide range of beautiful yarns to choose from. New techniques and patterns are constantly being developed.

Many of the knitwear designers of today are from the British Isles and Australia. Recently, many ethnic knitting books covering Latvian, Aran, Swedish, Danish, Shetland, Austrian, Indian, Japanese, Russian, Icelandic, and African forms of knitting, have hit the market. In addition, many nineteenth-century lace patterns have been translated and printed for modern-day use.

There is a healthy consumer demand for knitting, and the market for luxury clothing is thriving. Casual knitwear is popular, and innovative sweater designs are in demand. Magazines and department store catalogues are full of the latest knitwear trends, from casual styles to fancy evening wear.

How to Use This Book

This book can help you reach any and all of your knitting goals, no matter what they may be. Are you are a crafter interested in knitting and want to take it up as a hobby? Do you know some of the basics of knitting and want to expand your knowledge? Are you an experienced knitter who wants to earn a living from your knitting? Whatever your circumstances are, the information you need is in this book.

The chapters are arranged in two parts. Part One covers the basics of knitting, in which you will learn about various types of yarn, how to choose the appropriate yarn for your pattern, and how to care for knitted garments. Detailed instructions about how to knit are also included. Experienced knitters can review basic knitting techniques, and revisit topics such as knitting tools, How-to's, finishing, recognizing and correcting errors, and the importance of following directions. You will find answers to some of your questions in the section Tips Grandma Never Taught You in chapter 4. In addition, there are four, fun and simple, noncopyrighted projects for you to make and sell, if you wish.

Part Two of *Knitting for Fun and Profit* includes valuable information about how to profit from your love of knitting, and what you need to know about selling your products. You'll enjoy the personal anecdotes about knitters who design, sell, teach, or otherwise profit from their knitting. Their stories will educate and amuse you. You will certainly discover that knitters are wonderful, fun people!

The Resource section lists recommended books, magazines, Web sites, educational opportunities, yarn and notion suppliers, craft shows, and malls. An extensive knitting Glossary, which is important for every knitter, is also provided.

Be sure to look through the table of contents, and browse through the different chapters for an overview. I'm sure you'll agree that this book is exactly what you're looking for. Read on and enjoy!

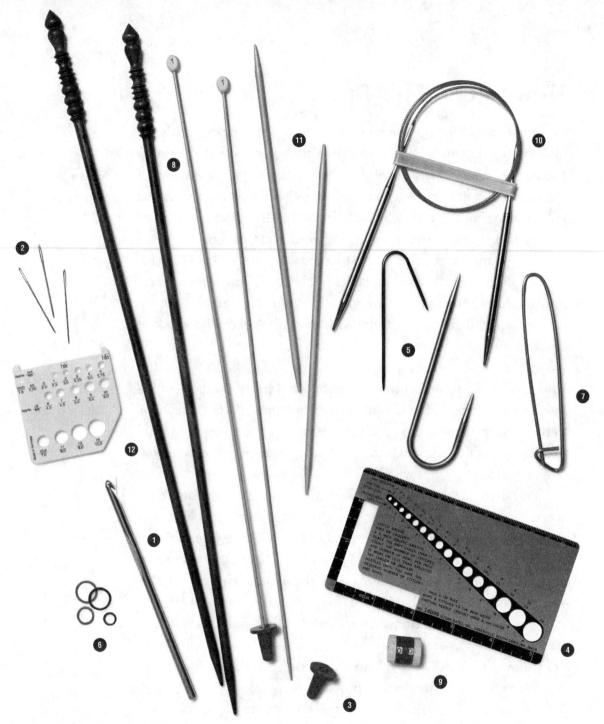

Basic Tools for Knitting

1 Crochet hook
2 Tapestry needles
3 Point protector
4 Stitch gauge
5 Cable needles
6 Markers
7 Stitch holder
8 Single point knitting needles
9 Row counter
10 Circular knitting needle
11 Double pointed needles
12 Needle gauge

Part One

For Fun

The Joy of Knitting

▼▼▼

KNITTING IS A FUN CRAFT that lets you actually create your own unique fabric with yarn and needles. Choosing your yarn is probably the funnest part of knitting; however, if you're like most knitters, you'll want to buy every style and color! Today's yarn is absolutely beautiful and comes in a multitude of colors and textures.

You can knit almost any type of fabric, from the most delicate lace to heavy-duty blankets. You'll be pleased to know that, although some of the most beautiful knitting looks difficult, it really is very simple to make.

Knit and *purl* are the two major stitches used in knitting. Have you ever noticed that the front side (also called the right side) and back side (also called the wrong side) of a knitted object are completely different? This occurs because the knit stitch shows on one side, and the purl stitch shows on the other. These two stitches, along with the *cable* and *yarn-over* stitches, form the four basic knitting techniques. You'll learn everything you need to know about these stitches in chapter 4.

DIANE'S STORY

Diane Zangl can't remember a time when she didn't have thread, yarn, and needles in her hands. At six years old, her mother taught her to embroider, and even though she can't remember doing it, she still owns her first project: a small dish towel with a little kitten stitched on one corner.

A cousin tried to teach eleven-year-old Diane to knit, but she couldn't quite catch on and discarded the idea in a fit of frustration. Diane didn't pick up a knitting needle again for about ten years, when a future sister-in-law finally showed her how to knit—successfully. Diane bought a small, "Learn How" book for twenty-nine cents that contained a twenty-two-page section about knitting. The book became her "bible" for many years.

Writing and art often inspire Diane: "I like to visit museums because they are my major source of inspiration," she explains. "My most successful designs are those that are inspired by ethnic garments, or the ones that incorporate the colors found in the nature preserve near my home. The least successful ones are those that I rush through."

Diane loves using natural fibers with unique textures such as heather, tweeds, or color blends. She often plays with combinations of color and texture and incorporates sewing or embroidery techniques into her work.

Diane's designs lean more toward the classic-style end of fashion design. She usually avoids high-end fashion, because she feels that a knitted garment should stay in style for a very long time. Lately she has also developed a strong interest in ethnic and historic techniques.

"Being from Wisconsin, I have a tendency to knit warm wooly things," says Diane. "Our summers are rather short, and by the time I'm into the summer mode, we're back into the snow season again. Whatever the geographic region, people seem to be in more of a knitting mode in the fall and winter months, and the winter styles seem to sell best."

Diane traces her needlework skills back to her Italian grandmother. She says that her grandmother could look at a picture of a sweater and duplicate it perfectly. In fact, Diane still owns a sweater that was knitted for her father almost seventy years ago.

Diane has taught all three of her daughters to knit, sew, embroider, and crochet. Their interests waver, but they do one or more of these crafts at varying levels of success. Diane has also taught knitting to kindergarten students, 4-H members, and octogenarians at a local community college. In addition to teaching at local guilds and yarn shops, Diane has also conducted workshops and seminars for The National Needlework Association (TNNA), The Knitting Guild of America (TKGA), and Stitches (sponsored by *Knitter's* magazine).

Elizabeth Zimmermann (from the PBS series, *Busy Knitter*) really encouraged Diane to design, so she submitted one of her designs to *Knitter's* magazine. Since then, Diane has had designs or articles published in almost every nationally recognized knitting publication, and has also designed pattern books and leaflets for major yarn manufacturers and distributors such as Brown Sheep Company, Cascade Yarns, Coats Patons, and Tahki Yarns. Now Diane works 8 to 10 hours a day developing ideas, sketches, swatches, patterns, and models, and creating freelance knitwear at her business, Stitch Witch Designs.

(continues)

"I believe that both small and large projects are in demand today," she explains. "People's lives are so involved that they need small projects they can complete quickly. The recent popularity of sock knitting is a good example of this." Diane also believes that people enjoy the more complicated patterns like the Fair Isle or Nordic-styled sweaters. "Working on something more detailed provides people with a feeling of accomplishment," she says.

As a pastime, Diane enjoys prairie and wildflower gardening and nature watching. "We live at the edge of a large national wildlife refuge, and

Creating Special Handknitted Gifts

Who doesn't love to receive a handmade gift? We live in a very fast-paced world and most people can't, or won't, take the time to create handmade items. This is why handcrafted gifts are appreciated more today than ever before.

After you've been knitting for a while, you will find knitting projects that are ideal for gift giving. One of my longtime favorite projects is knitting argyle socks. I'll never forget the first time I knitted them. I was 12 years old and knitted a pair for my father's Christmas present. The look on his face when he opened that gift will remain forever in my heart. It fills me with pride each time I give a handknitted gift to a friend or loved one. As soon as you learn how to knit, I'm sure you'll want to knit something special for someone close to you. (Directions about how to knit socks are included in chapter 5. I hope you enjoy knitting them as much as I have over the years.)

Exchanging handmade gifts with friends is so much fun and extremely personal. My good friend Joan (a ceramist) and I exchange

the changing colors and scenes often have a great effect on the colors I choose for my designs," says Diane. "I also enjoy listening to Celtic music and reading Celtic and Scandinavian lore, which probably explains why I design things with an ethnic twist."

Christmas presents every year. Each fall I pick out a ceramic piece I like, and she tells me what handknitted item she wants. So far, I have knitted her a "fur" scarf, a lace shawl, and a hat. I encourage you to start your own special tradition of gift giving with your crafting friends and family members. It is something you will greatly anticipate every year.

"Knitting a gift pleases both the giver (me) and the recipient (I hope)," says Nancy Davenport, a cardiologist in Washington, D.C. She loves to knit, and even knits at medical conventions. "I've never sold my knitting, I tend to give it away," she says. "I probably save money by making gifts, but I must be honest, I have so much knitting stuff that I probably don't save anything. It reminds me of the old adage, 'Chopping wood warms you twice.'"

Making Friends Through Knitting

You're going to love the people you meet through knitting. I have knitting friends all over the U.S., in England, and in Australia. I met

Thanks for My Boogie!

When Sally Crandall's grandson was born, she knitted him a baby blanket (his very own "Boogie"). He is now an active, 11-year-old boy who still dearly loves his Boogie. He even tried to sneak it into camp by hiding it in his pillowcase.

Boogie has been loved to pieces, and when the boy comes to visit his grandmother, she inspects Boogie and makes the necessary repairs. Her grandson enjoys watching as she mends Boogie with the same tender care that she gave it so many years before.

One day he looked up at her with a grin and said, "Grandma, this is the best present you have ever given me. I will probably take it to college with me!" Sally's eyes filled with tears of joy, and she gave him an extra big hug. She then watched him run off to play and returned to the *very* important task of mending Boogie.

them in various ways such as knitting classes; conventions; through my knitting newsletter; and most recently, via the Internet. E-mail is a great way to communicate—this is one way I keep in touch with several of my knitting friends. The Internet offers a great opportunity to meet knitters from around the world and discuss your crafts. Online knitters are very generous and more than willing to share information, including an occasional humorous knitting experience that will put a smile on your face. These friendships, formed from a mutual love of knitting, are very special. In fact, several of my friends are profiled in this book.

Knitting as Relaxation and Therapy

Knitting is easy to learn and, once you get started, you will find that it is a relaxing and enjoyable way to express yourself. Very few crafts allow you to make so much with so little. The only materials you'll need are yarn, a pattern (either your own design or a commercial one), knitting needles, a ruler or tape measure, a tapestry needle, and maybe a cable needle or other knitting tools you'll learn about later. In hardly any time at all you will have a finished work of art.

One of my knitting friends, Poochie Myers, feels that yarn shops should be more like clubs in which people gather weekly for "their yarn art therapy." I have met many people in my knitting classes who were dealing with a stressful lifestyle, a life crisis, or a serious illness. It's amazing how many people find comfort in knitting (see the sidebar Creative Creations in this chapter, for more information about Poochie).

> "I am a psychiatric nurse," says Ellen Keating. "I work on a crisis line and do emergency assessments for admission or referral. It is a very high-stress job, and I find the rhythm of the needles, and the feel of the yarn through my hands, to be very soothing. Because I have a two-hour commute each day, I frequently use my driving time to draft pattern ideas and plan projects in my head."

When Virginia Bingham was a child, her mother took her to a yarn store and said, "I've tried to teach her to crochet and she doesn't like it, so you teach her to knit. Then she won't need a psychiatrist when she is old."

"It must have worked," says Virginia. "I am still knitting 67 years later and haven't seen that kind of doctor yet."

Tips for Relaxing While Knitting

Janet Rehfeldt, a frequent knitter, knows what it's like to tense up after a long knitting session: "For the longest time, I had problems with

Did you know???

Doctors, especially psychiatrists and psychologists, sometimes prescribe knitting as a means of therapy.

painful hands, neck, and shoulders while working on my knitting projects, and watching television," explains Janet. "Looking up and down, between the television and my work, really irritated the already herniated disks in my neck."

After consulting a physical therapist, Janet discovered some basic tips that relieved her pain:

- Avoid eye strain. Keep your work area well lit. If working with dark colors, place a white pillowcase under your work to maximize your vision.

- Sit with a small pillow behind you to keep your back supported and straight. Rolling a hand towel and placing it behind your lower back can help.

- A cervical neck pillow works wonders for supporting the neck while sitting on the couch. (Janet finds that buckwheat-filled neck and back pillows work best for her.)

- Try placing one or two pillows on your lap to raise your work and ease the strain of looking up-and-down. The constant strain on the neck from the up-and-down motion is very hard on the cervical spine. Try one pillow first, or use one of those padded pillow lap desks with the hard surface facing down.

Just Enjoying It

Rona Smith is from England, where she knits not only for herself, but for family members and friends as well. "I never knit for financial reward," says Rona. "I work full time, and knitting is a leisure activity, a means of relaxation. Although I would dearly love to make it more of a full-time occupation, I'm afraid that if I turn it into a business, it might take away some or all of the enjoyment. I have always wanted to try designing, but I never seem to find the time."

If one pillow is not enough, try two pillows. Try not to raise your arms too high because it cuts off the blood circulation to the arms and hands.

- Use therapeutic gloves. These gloves work very well for aching and stiff hands. Wristbands are available to prevent damage to your wrists by keeping them from moving too much.

- Don't work for more than 20 to 30 minutes at a time without taking a break. Get up, walk around, and then go back to work.

- Do some simple stretching exercises. If you start to feel tightness in your neck and shoulders, try these simple stretches to relieve the tension:

  Head turns
  Head tilts
  Shoulder rolls
  Wrist flexes
  Shaking your hands
  Opening and closing your hands into soft fists

Janet advises a little common sense: "If you begin to ache and hurt, your body is telling you that you've overdone it," she says. "Relax, take a break. Your knitting will be there when you return."

You can find these tips and other interesting knitting items at Janet's Web site: home.earthlink.net/~kthreads/tipmisc4.htm.

Knitting as a Means of Self-Expression

Poochie Myers is a knitting teacher and designer, but she is first and foremost an artist. She started designing doll clothes by sewing, knitting, and crocheting when she was in first grade. "Nothing inspired me to become a designer—everything inspires me to design."

Creative knitting, which Poochie is known for, does not mean "throw away your patterns"; rather, it means having an option to use or not to use a pattern.

> "My garments are not usual, therefore I enter them into museum shows and art-to-wear galleries. I use wool, silk, cotton, and old clothes, together with our human form, to make my audience's eye move in a sensuous flow of in and out, over and around. I like to travel into the magical world of my subconscious, and perhaps discover my own atavistic tendencies to bring them to the modern world."

Ellen Keating's mother taught her everything she knows about knitting. "As a child in Denmark, my mother had to attend compulsory stitchery classes and hated every minute of it." Ellen cannot relate to her mother's, or anyone's, lukewarm approach to knitting or stitchery.

> "I must be a throwback to an earlier generation. Knitting is my joy, my creative outlet, and my stress reducer. I wind all my yarn by hand, as I love the feel of the yarn running through my hands. Building on prior sewing and tailoring skills, I started knitting, in earnest, when I was in high school. I have read avidly about techniques, and try to learn something with each project.

> "I always have several projects going at once, a sit-in-the-closet-and-concentrate one, a mindless project that I carry around with me, and usually something lacy.

> "I used to send my sweaters out for blocking and finishing, but now I find satisfaction in planning the finishing before I commence my project. Although I often use commercial patterns, I usually have to rewrite them to accommodate my size and customize the features. I particularly enjoy working on lace and shawls."

Stitching Your Moods

The great thing about knitting is, whatever my mood, there is a knitting project to fit it. On the days I'm feeling especially energetic, I can't wait to jump into a challenging knitting project. Yet there are times when I can barely think, much less work on something that requires intense concentration.

Like many knitters, I keep several projects going simultaneously. These projects vary in difficulty and usually consist of at least one complicated project, one or two simple projects, plus something personal. In this way, I can grab whatever project best suits my energy level and circumstance.

I also try to have a "power failure project" and a "knit in the car" project ready at all times. In fact, I never leave the house without my knitting bag. I call this my insurance against car breakdown and so far it has worked. You never know what life will throw you, and a knitter certainly wouldn't want to be caught unprepared!

Knitting helped me through an especially scary experience when I lived on the coast of southeastern North Carolina several years ago. The eye of a hurricane passed over the area twice in 1996 and once in 1998. Somehow, I kept my presence of mind and remembered to pack my knitting with the other necessary hurricane supplies. As the storm raged outside, I sat behind boarded-up windows, and knitted by candlelight while listening to the battery-operated radio. My knitting was such a comfort to me and helped pass the tension-filled hours.

The Popularity of Knitting

Knitting is very much alive and thriving, which is evidenced by the many new knitting publications and Web sites available.

Fashion knitwear is definitely "in," you can find it on the racks of almost every department and specialty store. Today's knitted designs are absolutely gorgeous and when you know how to knit, you will want to create dozens of styles for yourself. Designing and making your own clothes is very exciting and fun, but trust me, you will have a hard time finding the time to knit everything you want to!

Enjoying the Passion!

If you are like most knitters, you will enjoy an incredibly long and loving "relationship" with yarn. From a knitter's viewpoint, there is nothing more enjoyable than shopping for yarn. Have you ever watched a knitter in a yarn shop? If not, you should observe sometime—it can be quite amusing. You will notice how slowly they touch the yarn, reveling in the colors and textures until their senses are full, and their minds are literally exploding with creative ideas. The decision-making process is agonizing, and the energy and excitement grow as they wait to purchase their yarn. They drive home in anticipation, exercising extreme self-control in order to maintain the speed limit. Their families, bless their hearts, know that when the knitter arrives home with a new bag of yarn, everyone better step back because they're heading for the needles!

▼▼▼▼▼▼▼▼▼▼▼▼▼▼▼▼▼▼▼▼▼▼▼

Did you know???

Consumers are turning to mail order and the Internet to purchase their knitting supplies, and sales reports are very good.

▲▲▲▲▲▲▲▲▲▲▲▲▲▲▲▲▲▲▲▲▲▲▲

Making Original Garments

Have you ever wished that you could own one of those expensive, beautifully knitted garments that you find in the high-end clothing stores? Beginning now, with a little knitting knowledge, you can own as many of these unique garments as you want—made especially by you!

Creative Creations

Poochie Myers has been knitting since she was eight and began knitting professionally at age twelve. "I have been a painter for fifty years," she says. "Art is my first love, and I have entered my work into many museum shows." After many years of study, painting, and exhibiting, Poochie eventually developed the knowledge and nerve to design some very crazy sweaters. "I have developed the eye to know what designs will pass with the judges," she explains. I enter [my garments] into museum shows and art-to-wear galleries where the artist has a chance to win prize money."

Poochie's garments sell for $700 to $3,000 in galleries. One specific garment won "Best in Show" at the Sunrise Museum, and the "Governor's Award of Excellence" in West Virginia.

Not only will you make garments from patterns, but you will also design your very own styles. Designing is something that you will learn from experience by reading and experimenting. Your talent for designing will develop slowly, as you become more familiar and comfortable with the different stitches.

Over the years, I have designed many knitted items. I actually started designing when I was very young. My first projects were doll clothes, and because of the minimal patterns available, I just made up my own as I went along. Soon I was making pastel pullovers and cardigan sweaters with matching socks.

Even if you choose to use a pattern in your knitting, you still don't have to make the finished product exactly like the original. Make your own simple or elaborate changes to an existing pattern, and create a totally unique design that is yours alone. An advantage to being a knitter is the ability to make every garment your very own. You might want to change the color to complement your complexion, or you might want to use a completely different stitch. Several designers who work for magazines such as *Vogue, Knitter's,*

Interweave Knits, and *Knit 'n Style,* started out in other full-time careers, and now devote all of their time to their knitting careers.

Before you know it, you'll be ready for your first project. I recommend something simple and small so you can practice the basic stitches. Then, I recommend that you take on something more challenging, like one of the projects suggested in chapter 5. Any of those projects are suitable for selling.

For fashion knitwear, such as those lovely designer sweaters you see in clothing stores and magazines, I suggest you first practice some of the fancy stitches in chapter 4, and then keep your swatches for further reference. Decide what you would like to make, and either develop your own pattern, or purchase one along with the required yarn. (Be sure to check the supply sources listed in the back of this book.)

One of the first things you'll want to do is treat yourself to a yarn-shopping trip. You'll have great fun checking out the yarn and patterns. If this is your first yarn-shopping trip, don't forget to warn your family about what to expect when you return!

Getting Started

▼▼▼

YOU HAVE A LOT TO learn before diving into your first knitting project. This chapter examines the basic aspects of knitting and introduces you to the following issues:

- The sizeable selection of yarns available
- How to select your yarn
- The generous assortment of supplies and tools available to knitters
- How to care for your finished knitted garments
- Where to purchase your knitting supplies

Knitting Terms Used in This Book

Because this chapter contains several words and terms that you may not be familiar with, I have provided this mini-glossary. When you come across a new word or term, simply refer to these explanations. See the Glossary in the back of the book for a more extensive and complete set of terms.

- **Blocking:** A technique for knitting a piece into its desired shape.
- **Boucle:** Two yarns plied at different tensions, held in place by another yarn, forming small loops.
- **Cable stitches:** Selected stitches that have been twisted around each other to make a rope-like design.
- **Circular needles:** Two knitting needles attached by a cord.
- **Dye lots:** The number assigned to a color made from yarn colors that were dyed together.
- **Elasticity:** The ability to retain size and shape after stretching.
- **Intarsia:** A multiple-color technique in which blocks of color are worked using separate balls of yarn or bobbins.
- **Knitting in the round:** The process of knitting tubular-shaped items, such as socks.
- **Natural fibers:** Fibers that come from either animals or plants.
- **Pilling:** The matting of yarn or formation of yarn into little balls.
- **Plied:** When strands of yarn are joined together by twisting.
- **Ply:** The number of strands that a yarn is composed of.
- **Skein:** Yarn that has been wound so the inner strand can be pulled from the center.
- **U.S. size:** United States needle sizes that range from a very thin 0000 to very thick 35.
- **Weight:** The actual weight of a skein or ball of yarn, usually given in grams.
- **Worsted:** Yarn spun from longer fibers that have been combed to lie parallel. Often in the United States, worsted yarn refers to a medium weight yarn.

Selecting Yarn

Today's yarn is some of the finest yarn ever made. Many years ago there were only a few types of yarn for knitting—mainly wool, cotton, and silk. Modern spinning methods have fashioned many new and exciting yarns that you can divide into two basic groups— *natural* and *man-made* fibers.

Natural Fibers

Natural fibers, which you can either combine or use independently, come from animals or plants. This section covers some of the more popular varieties.

Wool

Considered one of "nature's miracles," wool is an amazing fiber that has been part of our culture for centuries. Wool yarn is so popular that some people mistakenly believe that all yarn is wool. It's spun from the fleece of sheep; in one year a single sheep can produce enough fleece to make three suits or a dozen sweaters. Moreover, sheep shearing is environmentally friendly and doesn't harm the sheep.

Several varieties of sheep exist, and some varieties of fleece are more desirable than others. *Merino* is considered the best. The natural color of fleece can be white, gray, brown, or black. White fleece is preferred for dyeing, because you can dye it any color. The dye soaks into the wool, giving it luster and depth.

Warm, durable, and elastic, wool has excellent insulating properties and keeps you toasty warm on a cold winter day. It allows your body to quickly adjust to room temperature, and absorbs moisture without seeming wet. It's easy to clean, keeps its shape after numerous washings, and resists staining because spills are apt to bead up on its surface, rather than soak in. With special care, a wool garment should last years. (See Caring for Your Handknits later in this chapter for suggestions about caring for your woolen garments.)

Mohair

A soft, durable, and luxurious fiber, mohair has been highly desired throughout the ages. Garments made from mohair last season after season. Yarn makers frequently blend mohair with other fibers to help them cling together, which make them easier to work with. A garment made with mohair yarn is warm in the winter, yet breathes in the summer (if the garment is loosely knit).

Angora

Angora is an expensive fiber that comes from the Angora rabbit. Harvesters comb the rabbits to glean the fur, yet a harvester only gathers one ounce of fur from each rabbit every 10 weeks. Because the fibers are only 3 to 5 inches long, angora is difficult to spin, thus it's usually combined with other fibers during the spinning process.

Cashmere

Cashmere is a luxury yarn that comes from the fleece of the Kashmir (cashmere) goat. These goats are found in the mountains of China, Mongolia, India, and Tibet. Harvesters obtain only a few ounces of this valuable fleece from each goat during an annual harvest. Cashmere yarn is extremely soft, receptive to dye, and resilient. The demand for cashmere far outweighs the supply. It's expensive, but because it's so light, a generous amount of yardage (between 150 and 200 yards) makes up one ounce.

Alpaca

Alpaca yarn comes from the alpaca, an animal found in parts of South America. A member of the camel family, and related to the llama, the alpaca possesses a fine, soft, and lustrous fleece.

The Evolvement of Design

"Knitting has come a long way in becoming more artistic," says knitting historian Janet Johnson Stephens. "We're seeing more fancy yarns and unusual shapes and colors in knitted garments. It wasn't too long ago that high fashion consisted of a few cables and a couple of stripes."

As Janet explains, designers need computer skills in today's world because their trade has become much more technical: "Designing is considered a profession and therefore requires a résumé, schematics, sketches, and floppy disks."

Silk

Silk is spun by the silkworm, and, much like wool, insulates but does not conduct heat. Silk yarns, when used in knitting, tend to stretch, thus yarn makers usually combine them with other fibers such as wool or acrylics.

Cotton

One of the oldest and most readily available plant fibers, cotton, grows in warm climates worldwide. Like most plant fibers, cotton differs greatly from wool. It conducts heat away from the body and keeps you cool. Cotton absorbs moisture, dries quickly, washes easily, and is nonallergenic. Because it has little elasticity, you will need to check your gauge often when knitting with 100% cotton yarn. (We will cover gauge, in detail, in chapter 4.) Yarn makers spin cotton into many different types of yarn. For example, *mercerized* cotton yarns are treated with a special process that makes them stronger, smoother, and less apt to shrink. Yarn makers combine some cotton yarns with other yarns to increase elasticity and decrease weight.

Linen

Produced from the flax plant, linen requires a great deal of processing before it can be made into yarn. Pure linen yarn tends to be stiff; therefore, yarn makers usually combine it with other fibers before spinning it into yarn.

Man-Made Fibers

The DuPont company introduced man-made yarn, also known as *synthetic* yarn prior to World War II. Knitters love these yarns because of their elasticity, their price, and because you can machine-wash (and dry) them. On the other hand, some knitters insist on natural fibers and refuse to knit with synthetics of any kind. With the advances in yarn production, many synthetic yarns now greatly resemble the texture of natural fiber yarns.

Nylon

The strongest synthetic fiber available—nylon—is sometimes used independently or as a reinforcement for sock heels. Because of its strength, yarn makers usually combine it with other fibers.

Acrylics

Developed as a substitute for wool, acrylic yarns look like wool and are as easy to care for, but lack the insulating, water-resistant qualities of wool. You will often find acrylic yarns blended with other fibers, which make the acrylic yarns more appealing.

Microfiber

A newly developed fiber, microfiber, is thin, lightweight, and resilient in comparison to other fibers. Microfiber also resists pilling and holds its shape very well. Cotton is more resilient when combined with microfiber.

Man-made fibers enhance the properties of natural fibers. An acrylic/wool blend provides a less expensive and more durable alternative to 100% wool. An acrylic/cotton blend adds elasticity to an otherwise nonelastic cotton.

Selecting Your Yarn

Always purchase the best quality yarn that you can afford. You will spend many hours working on your knitted garment, and the quality of yarn you choose will make all the difference in its longevity.

When I was much younger, I made the mistake of buying cheap yarn. I ordered it from a mail-order firm and couldn't believe the condition of the yarn when it arrived. I never would have purchased it if I had seen it beforehand. Don't buy yarn just because it's inexpensive.

It's important that you select a yarn suitable for your garment, and vice versa. If you choose the yarn first, then you must select a garment pattern suitable for the yarn. For instance, a textured yarn necessitates simple stitches because fancy stitches won't show up. Plain yarn, on the other hand, works well with a fancy stitch.

Sometimes a yarn will disappoint you. Find the qualities you do want in a yarn and then compromise. Just because a yarn looks attractive doesn't mean it's the right one for you. Accept the fact that some yarns are difficult to knit with, and that a few of the more luxurious yarns are better left to experienced knitters.

> ## Handy Hint
>
> Keep an emery board handy for those snagged fingernails that can make knitting difficult.

The Yarn Wrapper

The paper wrapper found around most balls or skeins of yarn contains valuable information that you'll want to retain. Keep your wrappers until you're finished with your project, and always keep at least one wrapper for future reference.

Keep your yarn wrapper handy by attaching it, and some of the corresponding yarn, to a piece of paper in a notebook with a description of the garment, and any cleaning requirements.

Most yarn wrappers contain the following valuable information:

- **Manufacturer's name:** Reynolds or Schoeller-Esslinger
- **Yarn name:** Lopi or Fortissima
- **Color:** 0058 or 134
- **Dye lot:** 0265 or 337384
- **Gauge:** 3½ stitches and 5 rows = 1 inch on #10 needles
  30 stitches and 40 rows = 10 centimeters on 2.5 to 3 millimeter needles
- **Yardage:** 110 yards (Lopi) or 210 meters (Fortissima)
- **Weight:** 100 grams or 50 grams
- **Yarn ingredients:** 100% wool or 75% virgin wool, 25% nylon
- **Care instructions:** Hand wash or machine washable

Yarn Yardage and Weight

Pay special attention to the yardage on the yarn wrapper. A 50-gram ball of yarn may vary anywhere between 50 and 300 yards, depending on the yarn. Generally, a woman's large, or a man's medium long-sleeved sweater (chest size 40 to 42 inches) requires 1,100 yards of bulky yarn, 1,250 yards of worsted yarn, or 1,600 yards of sport weight yarn (see the list on page 25 for a description of these types of yarn).

The following list describes yarn classifications:

- **Fingering yarn:** A fine yarn with a gauge of 7 to 8 stitches per inch using U.S. size 2 or 3 knitting needles.

- **Sport yarn:** A medium-weight yarn with a gauge of 5.5 to 6.5 stitches per inch. It's normally used with U.S. size 4 to 6 knitting needles.

- **Double-knitting (DK) yarn:** Weighs less than sport yarn but more than worsted yarn. This yarn is usually manufactured in Great Britain.

- **Worsted-weight yarn:** A medium-weight yarn, usually with a gauge of 5 per inch when using U.S. size 7 or 8 knitting needles. Be careful not to confuse worsted with 4-ply yarn, as many people do.

- **Bulky yarn:** A heavy-weight yarn with a gauge of 3 or 4 stitches per inch, or even fewer stitches with U.S. size 10 and larger needles.

Ply

Refers to the number of strands that, when twisted together, make up the yarn. With modern spinning and manufacturing methods, you are just as likely to find a bulky yarn that is only 1-ply, as you are in finding a fingering yarn that is 4-ply (4-ply yarn is composed of four strands that have been twisted together). Ply has nothing to do with the weight of the yarn.

Yarn Colors

Choose your yarn colors sensibly. Before choosing the color of your knitted garment, study different color combinations and determine your own taste. Given all the time you're dedicating to this garment, you must feel strongly about the colors. When making clothes, your color choices should complement your complexion and hair color.

The Rainbow Color Selector, recently introduced by K^1C_2 Innovative Solutions, is a handy tool for distinguishing perfect color combinations. It has see-through windows with seven color values for quick color and value matching. See Resources for K^1C_2 Innovative Solutions' contact information.

Dye Lots

Yarn colors and shades can deceive you. That's why yarn makers stamp dye lot numbers or dye lot letters on the yarn wrappers: to ensure you that the colors in your final project don't vary. Pay special attention to the dye lot. Yarn with the same dye lot number or letter indicates that the dye lots are concurrent. You may not notice a difference in dye lots when looking at the yarn in the store, but you certainly will in a finished garment.

Also, make sure you buy enough yarn from the same dye lot to complete your project. I recommend buying at least one extra ball or skein. Don't think you can purchase additional yarn from the same dye lot later. Often, you may have difficulty finding the same color, or even the same yarn, again.

If you have any doubts about the yarn you're considering, buy a skein or ball of each color and experiment with it at home. You can tell a whole lot about yarn by actually knitting with it. Be sure to check the yarn label for the suggested needle size and gauge. Play around with stitch patterns and knit a 4-inch swatch using all of the colors together. Look at your yarn sample. How does it feel? Is it soft or harsh to the touch? Does it stretch and spring back into shape? After testing your yarn, draw out on paper the dimensions the swatch should be and wash and dry the swatch according to the manufacturer's instructions. Check for signs of color fastness, shrinking, and stretching.

Substituting Yarns

You must substitute yarns when you can't find the yarn your pattern calls for at your local yarn store. Refer to the picture of the yarn

Things to Check for When Buying Yarn

Pay close attention to the following list when buying yarn:

- Check for pilling. Everyone has owned a sweater with those ugly, little, matted balls on the surface. This is called pilling and you can avoid it by purchasing a higher-quality yarn. Poor yarn pills and tears at points of wear. Rub the yarn firmly between your fingers. Don't just pat it. If it pills easily, then you don't want it.

- Does the yarn pull apart when you play with it? Sometimes yarn has a strong ply, but other times the plies are loosely strung together. Unplied yarn will definitely separate during knitting. I don't recommend unplied yarn for a beginner.

- Is the yarn elastic? Does it bounce back when stretched? Wool and most acrylics have elasticity. One-hundred percent cotton won't bounce back, and you will need to adjust for this when knitting. (Don't let that adjustment scare you away from knitting with cotton though.)

- Verify that the yarn is evenly dyed, that it is smooth (unless it is a textured yarn), and that it feels good to the touch.

provided in your pattern and observe its qualities. Is it smooth, or does it look more like a boucle or mohair? To make your finished project as similar to the pattern as possible, the yarn you substitute should resemble the weight and texture of the pattern yarn.

Interchangeable yarns must have comparable gauges. Consider the yardage, as well. A pattern calling for 10 balls of the original yarn doesn't necessarily require 10 balls of the substitute yarn. You may need more or less, depending on the type of yarn. If, for example, your substitute yarn has 100 yards per ball, but the pattern yarn has 150 yards, you will need to make the proper adjustment. Ten balls times 150 yards equals 1,500 yards for the finished sweater. Divide the total (1,500 yards) by the number of yards per ball (100 yards) to get the number of balls you need (15).

Knitting Needles

Created from various materials such as metal, coated metal, plastic, wood, and bamboo, knitting needles are sold as single-pointed, double-pointed, or circular.

Single-Pointed Needles

Single-pointed needles have a tip for knitting on one end and a cap on the other end. They usually come in two lengths: 10 or 14 inches. I recommend that you buy the longer ones. The 10-inch needles are fine, but they only work when you have a relatively small number of stitches. You will need the 14-inch length for knitting adult garments.

Double-Pointed Needles

Double-pointed needles have points on each end. Knitters use them for circular work that is too small for circular needles. I use them for socks, mittens, some neckline edges, and other small items knitted in the round. These needles come in 4-, 8-, 12-inch, and longer lengths. I usually use the 4- and 8-inch lengths of double-pointed needles, because I prefer circular needles for larger work.

Circular Needles

Circular needles come in one piece. Knitters use them to make seamless designs, to knit in the round, and for straight knitting. They are especially convenient when a project is too large for straight needles. The needles are usually made with plastic cords and come with tips ranging from 0000 to 35/36, and lengths from 12 to 60 inches.

Circular needles are superior because they balance the weight of your garment evenly on your lap instead of on your arms. This causes less stress on the arms and wrist joints and alleviates pain from tendinitis or carpal tunnel syndrome.

Circular needles take up little room in your knitting bag and make knitting in tight spots (such as on an airplane) a breeze. The only difference between straight knitting with circular needles and straight needles is that you must turn your work at the end of each row to avoid continuing in the round.

Many professional knitters choose addiTurbo circular needles over any others. Before I began working with these needles, I never enjoyed using circular needles. I couldn't knit fast enough with plastic needles, the stitches slid off metal ones, and the yarn snagged on wooden and bamboo needles. AddiTurbo needles have soft, pliable cables (the material between the pointed tips) and snag-free joints. They are constructed of nickel-plated brass that

> ## Did you know???
>
> Hot tap water will help unravel a new circular needle.

doesn't rust, and they obtain body temperature (warm to the hands) very easily. AddiTurbo needles range in size from 0000 to 36 in U.S. sizes and 1¼ to 20 millimeters in metric sizes. They come in 12-, 16- 20-, 24-, 32-, and 60-inch lengths, so there is a size for just about every project imaginable. Experiment with needles until you find the brand you like best.

Metric–U.S. Needle Equivalents

No uniform standard needle size exists. Needle charts notoriously contradict each other. One chart may compare a metric, 2.5 millimeter with a U.S. size 1, while another compares a metric, 2.25 millimeter with a U.S. 1. Just keep in mind that U.S. needles range in size from a very thin 0000 to a very thick 35/36.

NEEDLES MANUFACTURED IN THE UNITED STATES

METRIC	U.S.	BRITISH
1½ mm	000	16
1¾ mm	00	15
2 mm	0	14
2¼ mm	1	13
2½ mm	none	none
2¾ mm	2	12
3 mm	none	none
3¼ mm	3	10
3½ mm	4	none
3¾ mm	5	9
4 mm	none	8
None	6	none
4½ mm	7	7
5 mm	8	6
5½ mm	9	5
6 mm	10	4
6½ mm	10½	3
7 mm	none	2
7½ mm	none	1
8 mm	11	0
9 mm	13	00
10 mm	15	000

Knitting Tools

Following is a list of basic tools for knitting. Page x in the front of the book lists many of these tools and also provides photos, and many are explained further on pages 32–34.

1. Bobbin
2. Cable needles
3. Markers
4. Stitch holder
5. Crochet hook

addiTurbo NEEDLES

METRIC	U.S.
1.25 mm	0000
1.50 mm	000
1.75 mm	00
2.00 mm	0
2.25 mm	none
2.50 mm	1
3.00 mm	2
3.25 mm	none
3.50 mm	4
3.75 mm	5
4.00 mm	6
4.50 mm	7
5.00 mm	8
5.50 mm	9
6.00 mm	10
7.00 mm	10.5
8.00 mm	11
9.00 mm	13
10.00 mm	15
12.00 mm	17
15.00 mm	19
20.00 mm	36

6. Tapestry needles
7. Row counter
8. Point protector
9. Single-point knitting needle
10. Scissors
12. Stitch gauge
13. Circular knitting needle

Knitting needles and implements

1. Wooden knitting needles

2. 14-inch straight knitting needles

3. Set of five double-pointed needles

4. Needle gauge

5. Knitter's reference cards (two different ones—four sides to show)

    5a. Pocket yarn yardage guide

    5b. Instant yarn calculator

    5c. Knitter's reference card

    5d. Knitter's reference card

- **Bobbins:** Knitters use these plastic devices to store small amounts of yarn while working with intarsia patterns. They come in two sizes: one for regular yarn and the other for bulky yarn.

- **Cable needles:** Knitters use these double-pointed needles while making cables. The needle holds the cable stitches while the other part of the cable is knitted. The "held" stitches are either knitted or purled off the opposite end of the needle. I prefer the cable needle with a hook on it, because it's the best for holding stitches in place.

- **Calculator:** You use this for calculating measurements and yarn yardage.

- **Crochet hook:** You don't have to know about crocheting to knit, but it does help to know some crochet basics if your pattern calls for crochet-edging or finish. Crochet hooks are measured in sizes just like knitting needles. You can also use a crochet hook to pick up dropped stitches (we will discuss stitches in further detail in chapter 4).

- **Fine white crochet thread:** Sometimes you need to mark increases, decreases, or measurements in your knitting. White crochet thread works extremely well. Some knitters use a different color yarn to mark their knitting, but this can leave a slight spot of color that you cannot remove.

- **Knitter's reference cards:** The Patternworks company manufactures and sells these small vinyl "quick reference" cards filled with valuable information. One side of the Pocket Yarn Reference Guide contains a chart that lists the approximate yardage amounts needed for various size garments. The other side contains an instant yarn calculator. The knitters reference card also has a needle comparison chart plus fabric care symbols on one side, and a size chart and yarn equivalents on the other (see Resources).

- **Knitting bag:** These come in many sizes and shapes. I have several bags, all of them full of projects. A knitting bag with small pockets for storing small knitting accessories is best.

- **Magnetic board:** These are similar to counted cross-stitch boards (used for embroidery). They come in handy when knitting a pattern in which the directions are given in charts.

- **Markers:** Knitters use these circular, ring-like devices to separate patterns or mark a place in the work. A ring marker slips from the left needle to the right needle just like a slipped stitch. You can place open-end markers directly into the work and remove them later.

- **Marking tags:** These are white or colored tags used as price tags. You can also write notes to yourself on them and use them as knitting markers or for labeling various swatches. Many knitters refer to these as "idiot tags."

- **Needle gauge:** This measures the device-needle size. Many double-pointed and circular knitting needles do not have the size imprinted on them. Needle gauges measure both metric and U.S. sizes.

- **Needle pouch:** You'll find this very handy for carrying circular needles, double-pointed needles, and crochet hooks.

- **Paper and pen/pencil:** Jot down notes related to your knitting. I prefer to organize my notes by project.

- **Point protectors:** These small rubber caps slip onto the ends of your knitting needles when they are not in use. They are especially good for single-pointed needles because they keep stitches from slipping off needles and prevent the point from hurting someone or damaging your knitting or knitting bag.

- **Ruler/Tape measure:** A good tape measure must be accurate and incapable of stretching out of shape, and it must be a device with both inches *and* centimeters marked because knitting patterns refer to both. You can also use rulers, but they should be at least 12 inches in length.

- **Scissors:** You should always have a pair of scissors handy. Small scissors with a sharp point are best. Place a protective covering over the point to avoid cutting yourself when rummaging through your knitting bag.

- **Small cosmetic bag:** These are perfect for carrying smaller implements such as a tape measure, scissors, a tapestry needle, markers, a cable needle, stitch holders, bobbins, a needle gauge, knitter's reference cards, row counters, index cards or notebook paper, and pens.

- **Stitch gauge:** You can sometimes find these on the needle gauge. They are usually metal with a ruler marked in inches on one side and centimeters on the other.

- **Stitch holder:** A handy little gadget that looks like a safety pin with blunt ends. It's not a good idea to use regular safety pins as a stitch holder because the sharp points may split the yarn. When placing your stitches on a stitch holder, slip them on as if to purl them. This will keep the stitches from twisting.

- **Tapestry needle:** This needle has a large eye, a blunt tip, and is used for "sewing" your knitted pieces together. Make sure the needle eye is large enough for the yarn to fit through. A size 16 or 18 tapestry needle will suffice. The smaller the size, the larger the needle.

Finding Your Knitting Supplies

With the increase of chain and discount stores, more and more local yarn shops have closed. But a large variety of mail-order firms sell yarn and knitting supplies. You will find a comprehensive list of recommended mail-order firms in Resources. A number of knitting Web sites that sell supplies are also listed there.

Keeping Your Knitting Supplies Clean

Keep your supplies clean by storing them in a clean knitting bag. I use a separate knitting bag for each project.

To avoid dirtying a light-colored yarn, keep your yarn and project in a plastic zip storage bag. Pull the yarn from the center of the ball and not from the outside. This helps keep the yarn clean, and it prevents tangling and unnecessary unraveling.

Also, make sure your hands are clean before you start to knit. Hand cream is fine for your chapped hands, but don't apply it before knitting. Unscoured wool, which still has lanolin in it, is great for your hands.

Caring for Your Handknits

Proper cleaning of handknits is essential to the life of the fabric. You must wash many handknits by hand, but some of the newer yarns can be machine-washed or dry-cleaned. It's important to carefully read the recommended care on the yarn label.

The Proper Handknit Treatment

- Be sure your handknits are clean before you put them away.
- Store your handknits flat, not on hangers.
- Closely follow yarn wrapper instructions when you wash and dry your handknits.
- Wash the gauge swatch before you wash the entire garment.
- Use mild soap or baby shampoo—not harsh detergent—to wash your handknitted items.

Washing

When you use more than one color, you must watch out for color fastness before you wash. Some dyes fade under certain conditions such as sunlight, dry-cleaning solutions, and even perspiration. A few years ago, I had a very sad experience with colorfastness: I ruined a beautiful sweater because the yarns bled into the main off-white color. The directions stated that you could wash it by hand, and I followed them explicitly but still ruined the sweater. All I could do was contact the yarn company. The company reimbursed me for the cost of the yarn, but that didn't come close to relieving my frustration. I now test-wash a sample of each yarn before I even start knitting.

Only use a washing machine for handknits when "machine wash" appears on the yarn label. Use the delicate cycle and put your sweater in a loosely closed pillowcase to protect it from snags. Before you do any washing, remove any non-washable trimmings and turn your knitted garments inside out.

Use lukewarm or cool water to hand wash, and dissolve a little soap solution specially made for delicate fabrics. Do not use ordinary laundry detergent as it may contain harsh chemicals. Immerse the item in the water, making sure that there is enough water to completely cover it. Unless the item being washed is very small, wash only one item at a time. Do not agitate, as this can damage the garment. Rinse several times with lukewarm or cool water until the water runs clear. Squeeze out as much water as you can without wringing. Place your knitting flat on a towel, and roll it to remove excess moisture. You may need to repeat this process using more than one towel.

Drying

To keep the proper size and shape, make a guide before you wash your item by drawing an outline on paper or a large piece of interfacing fabric. You will then have an idea of what the finished size should be after you have washed it.

Lay your wet knitting on a towel, shape it to the proper size, and dry it in a warm place away from direct sunlight and heat. Avoid washing on a hot, humid, summer day if you do not have air conditioning. You do not want the item to take too long to dry as it might mildew and develop a musty odor. Do not *hang* knitting to dry because it will lose its shape.

Dry cleaning

Some yarns must be dry-cleaned. If you are not sure how to launder your item, dry cleaning is your safest bet. Check the yarn wrapper or label for any instructions and be sure to tell the dry cleaners not to iron your garment.

Ironing

You should never iron knitting, but you can do a little *steam-shaping*. Do this on the inside part of the item on a well-padded surface. Place a dry cloth over the knitting, set it to the proper heat for the garment's fibers, and gently press it with a steam iron. Alternatively, you can use a dry iron with a wet cloth on the garment. Do not press the ribbing or areas that have elastic, and never let the iron touch the actual knitting. Some yarn labels warn against pressing; follow the directions on the label.

Moth protection

Prevention is the best way to avoid moth problems. First and foremost, it is very important to thoroughly clean your knitted items before storing them. Cleaning kills any eggs, and removes the perspiration odors that can attract moths.

To be effective, a cedar chest or closet must have at least 3/4-inch thickness of heartwood, and must close tightly. The concentration of volatile oil in the heartwood of cedar kills moth larvae, but the smell does not repel them.

Hold On! The Projects Are Just Around the Corner!

We have covered a lot of information in this chapter, and you're probably dying to dive into a knitting project. Once you start learning about all the beautiful things you can make—and that it's not as difficult as you'd imagined—it's easy to get antsy. The knitting projects appear in chapter 5. Until then, the next two chapters will cover a few things you still need to learn before you start knitting. Chapter 3 walks you through the process of setting up a personal workspace, and you will finally get to pick up your needles in chapter 4, in which you will learn some basic stitches.

Setting Up Your Personal Workspace

▼▼▼▼▼▼▼▼▼▼▼▼▼▼▼▼▼▼▼▼▼▼▼▼▼▼▼▼▼▼▼▼▼▼▼▼▼▼

BECAUSE OF ITS CONVENIENCE, knitting doesn't require a special room or workspace. Still, almost every knitter I know has a favorite spot to knit. Janet Johnson Stephens, who I mentioned earlier, loves to knit in her comfortable leather chair with her feet on the footstool, while watching television with her family. "I can't stand to work in a mess, so my spaces are very orderly," Jan says. "I lose my creativity in clutter."

Using Your Computer

Computers can take your knitting to a new level. The personal computer plays a major role in knitting today, making designing much easier and far less time consuming than the old and stale manually designed patterns and knitting styles.

Computers can compile lists of knitting books, supplies, yarn, or anything else you want organized. Today's software simplifies the bookkeeping for your small business and organizes your contact

Beau, the Knitting Poodle

When he wasn't much more than a puppy, our miniature poodle, Beau, decided he wanted to knit. At least, that's the way it appeared when we saw the finished product. I had been working on some lace knitting using a ball of cotton. The dear little devil took my knitting off the table after I had cast on about 200 stitches. He grabbed the ball of cotton in his mouth, and dragged the needle and stitches around the living room, encircling chair legs, and wrapping the knitting around everything in sight, including the circular knitting needle. The result looked like a massive spider web. He looked so innocent, that I couldn't punish him. Oh, how I wish I had taken a picture to preserve his masterpiece! What fun he must have had!

information. The Internet and the World Wide Web offer some marvelous knitting information sources, as well. But a computer requires a computer workspace. If you're lucky, you may even have a spare room to set up shop.

Stashing Your Yarn

Storage is a knitter's biggest challenge. Yarn, books, and knitting supplies eventually pile up and clutter a workspace. "I have a very impressive yarn stash because I can never resist a bargain—ever," says Catherine, a professional knitter. "I'm knitting as fast as I can, but the stash keeps growing at an alarming rate. I also collect books, especially knitting books. The knitting magazines are threatening to take over the house. I need to get organized really quick."

I often receive letters just like this one from knitters whose homes spill yarn from closets, dresser drawers, under beds, in the garage, behind furniture, and even in bathroom linen cabinets. "My closets are full of yarn, and my bookcases are full of knitting books," says my friend Nancy Davenport. As Nancy's children grow up and move out, she fills their empty closets with yarn.

Let's face it, knitters are nuts about their yarn. Almost every knitter I know has a sizeable yarn stash, and if you knit for any length of time you will, too.

Creating a System

What's the best way to organize your beloved yarn? The perfect organizing system should keep your yarn clean and neat, and give you quick access to your yarn.

Imagine yourself six months from now. Your yarn is nicely stored away, and you've purchased a new knitting pattern you can't wait to dive into. That hunter green wool yarn would be perfect for this garment, but how do you find it? Do you pull box after box out of your storage closet until you find the right one? Nope. To create a yarn filing system, you'll need the following items:

- Index cards
- A box to store the index cards (such as a recipe box)
- A–Z dividers for the box
- A brightly colored permanent marker
- Large, square labels
- Boxes large enough to store several skeins of yarn
- A space to store the filled boxes

Handy Hint

Buy multicolored index cards— they may help you when trying to find a specific color or type of yarn

Boxes can vary in size depending on your home and available space. I recommend those large, transparent plastic boxes with lids. They give you quick visual access to the yarn without opening the box, and they keep the contents dust and pest free.

Next, you'll need to sort out your yarn collection. I recommend a two-fold sorting process. First, sort your yarn by color. An extremely large selection of a single color warrants further sorting into lighter and darker shades.

After sorting by color, separate the yarn by fiber. For instance, you might have several different fibers of red yarn such as wool, angora, or acrylic.

Place the individual stacks into boxes. If a stack is too large to fit into one box, separate it into two or more boxes. Be sure to keep the same dye lots together when you're doing this. Store small quantities of different types of yarns together in one box labeled "Mixed."

Now place a label on each box. Your box labels should, at a glance, identify what type of yarn each box contains. For instance, I label my *cotton* yarn boxes with a "C" and the yarn's color: C-red, C-blue, C-cream, and C-green. Label wool yarn boxes with a "W," and so on. For large collections of certain types of yarn, simply add a number to the box label: A-red-1, A-red-2, A-red-3, and so on, for three boxes of red angora yarn.

Now you're ready to fill out your index cards. First, fill out your "key" card. This card acts as a key for your box labels in case you forget what they mean. It reads something like this: A = Angora, C = Cotton, W = Wool, and so on. File this card in the very front of your yarn box.

Next, fill out a card for each type of yarn in your stash. See the following diagram for a sample card.

Fluffy — Burnt Orange   **Box W-Orange-3**

20 Skeins — All from the same dye lot

150 yards per skein — Total of 3000 yards

Gauge — 3 stitches = 1 inch on #10 needles

75% Wool, 25% Nylon

Hand wash only

Manufactured by XYZ Company

*This yarn is a gorgeous, rich color that will complement Grandma's complexion.

Finally, file the cards in your box. You would file the card in the diagram under "O" for "Orange," not "B" for "Burnt Orange." Why? Because using broad color ranges simplifies your filing system. Believe me, you won't be able to find anything if you file Turquoise Blue under "T," Chocolate Brown under "C," or Seafoam Green under "S."

Two Successful Storage Systems

Ellen Keating, a true knitaholic, has a large room with a drop-leaf table and bed on which she lays out large projects. The room's large walk-in closet serves as her personal yarn shop. In addition to storing yarn in clear plastic containers, she also hangs her large skeins of hand-dyed yarn on hangers. She loves the easy access to her yarn: "I can shop in my own home and plan all these wonderful projects!" she says. She simply followed the example of a fantastic yarn shop's storage system.

Poochie Myers has taken the clear storage box idea and expanded it. She owns around 50 of the large, heavy plastic storage

▼▼

Pepper, the Yarn Thief

Pepper, a 20-pound cat, loves the smell of wool. If the door to Ellen's knitting room is open, the cat ultimately finds its way to the yarn. One day Ellen came home and found her wool yarn wrapped all around the jungle plants in the solarium. When this feisty cat gets hold of Ellen's yarn, she often refuses to give it back!

▲▲

boxes. She stores her yarn in these boxes on shelves stacked 16 feet high from floor to ceiling. To reach the top boxes, Poochie uses a tall ladder on wheels, such as those found in bookstores. She stores her needles and other knitting supplies in boxes, as well.

Books, Books, and More Books

Aside from knitting, I have one other passion: books. My bookcases overflow with them. Because I am a general crafter, I also purchase books about sewing, quilting, gardening, cooking, needlepoint, and so on.

The best way to keep books organized is to sort them by craft. When my bookshelves are full, I sometimes pull older books off the shelves and pack them away using that same yarn organizing system. I mark my book boxes Book-1, Book-2, Book-3, and so on, and fill out cards with the title and author information. If one of the books contains a special article or pattern that I might need in the future, I note that on the card. Organize your books according to the following steps:

1. Put all the books you are organizing in one area.
2. Separate bookshelf books from storage books.

3. Pack the storage books into boxes and fill out a card for each box. Fill out the cards thoroughly.

4. Separate the remaining books into categories: knitting, crocheting, small business, holiday decorations, and so on.

5. Separate them again into subcategories: knitting history, knitting and colors, knitting with advanced stitches, knitting afghans, knitting children's clothes, and so on.

6. Choose an area on your shelves for each category, and alphabetize the books either by title or author, whichever is easier for you to remember.

   After you've read a book, take the time to place it in its proper place on the shelf.

Creative
How-To's

▼▼

LET'S START KNITTING! This chapter gives you detailed instructions and helpful information about knitting stitches and techniques.

- **Common knitting terms, symbols, and abbreviations**
- Casting on
- Holding the needles
- Knit stitch
- Purl stitch
- Binding off
- Pattern stitches

    Ribbing

    Slip stitch

    Seed stitch

    Increases

    Decreases

    Yarn overs

    Cables

- Picking up stitches
- Finishing
- Gauge

- Errors
    Knots
    Twisted stitch
- Hints

Note to readers: If you already know how to knit, you may want to skip this chapter, or do a quick review.

A Few Common Knitting Terms

- **Bind off:** To remove stitches from the needle; to permanently finish off.

- **Bobble:** A large knot-type stitch that is made by working several times into the same stitch, then knitting and/or purling several times across these stitches and then decreasing back to one stitch. They are used in many decorative patterns, especially in Aran knitting.

- **Cast on:** Placing the stitches on the needle.

- **Continental method:** Knitting when the yarn is held in the left hand.

- **Cords:** Strands twisted or woven together.

- **Edge:** Border of a piece (side, top, or bottom).

- **Elasticity:** The ability to recover size and shape after being stretched.

- **Elongated stitch:** Stitch made by wrapping yarn around the needle more than once, then dropping the extra wraps on the following row.

- **English (American) method:** Knitting with yarn held in the right hand.

- **Eyelet pattern:** An opening in knitting separated from other openings by more than two strands of yarn. A grouping of lace holes can also be referred to as eyelet knitting.

- **Garter stitch:** The result when every stitch on every row is knitted.

- **I-Cord:** A knitted cord used in trimming.

- **In pattern:** To follow the pattern as written.

- **Knit stitch:** The basic stitch in knitting, made by holding the yarn in the back of the work.

- **Mock cable rib:** Rib stitch that looks like a cable, but is made without using a cable needle.

- **Picot pattern:** A combination of increases and decreases to make a special edge.

- **Popcorn:** A small bobble. A pattern stitch in which a small knot shows on the surface of the work

- **Purl stitch:** The opposite of a knit stitch.

- **Reverse stockinette stitch:** Stockinette stitch in which the purl side is the right side and the knit side is the wrong side.

- **Ribbing:** A pattern stitch often used at the top, bottom, and edges of a garment. Stitching characterized by vertical ridges that have crosswise elasticity.

- **Right side row:** The side of knitting that will be on the outside of the project when finished.

- **Round:** A row in circular knitting; each stitch on a set of four or five double-pointed needles or a circular needle.

- **Row:** A horizontal series of stitches.

- **Row gauge:** The number of rows per inch.

- **Selvage:** The edge of a piece of fabric that has been finished to prevent raveling.

- **Slipped stitch:** A stitch that has been slipped from one needle to the next without being worked.

- **Slip knot:** The first stitch in a cast on row.

- **Stitch gauge:** The number of stitches per inch.

- **Stockinette stitch:** The most common stitch in knitting, made when you knit one row and purl the next row. In knitters' jargon, the "right side" is the knit side and the "wrong side" is the purl side. Patterns that use the purl side as the right side are called *reverse stockinette* stitches.

- **Texture stitch:** A stitch with a surface or textural interest. Texture stitches can be a combination of knit and purl stitches, cables, popcorns, bobbles, twisted stitches, and others.

- **Turn your work around:** When you finish a row, you turn the work around so that the end with the yarn is on the right end of the left needle so you can begin the next row.

- **Twisted rib:** Rib stitch in which the knit stitches are twisted by knitting into the back instead of the front loops.

- **With the yarn in the back:** When the yarn is held in the back, away from the knitter. The yarn is held in the knit position.

- **With the yarn in the front:** When the yarn is held in front, toward the knitter. The yarn is held in the purl position.

- **Work:** Another name for the knitting project that you are currently working on.

- **Working stitch:** The stitch you are presently working on.

- **Working yarn:** The yarn you are using to knit.

- **Wrong side row:** The side of the knitting that will be on the inside when finished.

Knitting Instructions and Symbols

Many of the knitting patterns found in books and magazines use symbol charts and/or directions written in a strange language. The language and symbols consist of special punctuation marks and abbreviations plus other terms that can be very easy to follow once you become familiar with them. Some knitters don't care for the symbol charts, but others find them easy to work with. I prefer symbol charts because it's much easier than reading long knitting directions. On the other hand, sometimes I like to see the directions explained in full, just in case I don't understand what a certain symbol means.

As you study these knitting symbols, you will find that different sets exist. In fact, there are many symbols for the same stitch. For years, designers have tried to make the Japanese symbols standard, and the symbols in this book are Japanese. All of this terminology will be explained in this chapter, so don't fret if you don't understand a term or definition just yet. The following chart (see figure KS-1) defines some of the symbols and abbreviations you will find in knitting instructions:

Figure 1. Knitting Symbols and Abbreviations.

Symbols/ Abbreviations	Meaning
⊡	Knit on the right side row, purl on wrong side row, but seen as a knit from the right side.
⊟	Purl on the right side, knit on the wrong side, but seen as a purl stitch from the right side.
⊙	Yarn over.
⊠	Knit two together.
⊠	ssk.
☐	Knit on the right side. Instead of filling in the space, a blank space is sometimes used, meaning a knit as seen from the right side.
[ ]	Repeat whatever is in the brackets the number of times that is written immediately after the brackets (similar to the way numbers are grouped in algebraic equations). For example, *[p1, k1]* 2 times means *p1, k1, p1, k1*.
C4B	Cable 4 back, right-slanting cable. Slip the next 2 stitches as if to purl on to the short end of the cable needle and hold the needle in the back of the work. Knit the next 2 stitches from the left needle. Bring the cable needle to the front of the work and knit the 2 stitches from the long end of the cable needle, being careful not to twist the stitches.
C4F	Cable 4 front, left-slanting cable. Slip the next two stitches as if to purl onto the short end of the cable needle and hold the needle in the front of the work. Knit the next 2 stitches from the left needle. Knit the two stitches from the long end of the cable needle, being careful not to twist them.
dec	Decrease.
inc	Increase.
k1	Knit 1 stitch.
k1, p1	Knit 1 stitch, purl 1 stitch.
k1 tbl	Knit through the back loop instead of through the front loop. Makes a twisted stitch.
k2	Knit 2 stitches.
k2 tog	Knit 2 stitches together as if they were one stitch.

kfb	Knit into the front and back loops of a stitch.
m1	Make 1 increase.
p1	Purl 1 stitch.
p1, k1	Purl 1 stitch, knit 1 stitch.
p1 tbl	Purl one stitch through the back loop.
p2	Purl 2 stitches.
p2 tog	Purl the next 2 stitches together.
psso	Pass the slipped stitch over.
repeat from*	Repeat the stitch the number of times written after the *. For example, *k8, p5; repeat from *5 more times* tells you to work *k8, p5* six times (counting the first time). If the * wasn't used, the direction would read: *k8, p5, k8, p5, k8, p5, k8, p5, k8, p5, k8, p5.*
sl	Slip.
sl st	Slip stitch.
sl1, k1, psso	Slip 1 stitch, knit the following stitch, pass the slipped stitch over the knit stitch and off the needle.
ssk	Slip, slip, knit 2 together. Slip the next two stitches from the left needle to the right needle, slipping them one at a time as if to knit. Insert the tip of the left needle from the left into the front of these two stitches and knit them together.
st	Stitch.
st st	Stockinette stitch. Knit the right side row, purl the wrong side row.
tbl	Through back loop.
tog	Together.
X	Times. For example, 2x means 2 times.
yfon	Yarn forward and over the needle.
yfrn	Yarn forward and around the needle.
yo	Yarn over. Bring the yarn forward between the needle points and knit with the yarn in the purl position.
yon	Yarn over the needle.
yrn	Yarn around the needle.

See Glossary for a complete list of terms and abbreviations.

Casting On

The first step in knitting begins with placing the stitches on the needles. This step is called *casting on,* which means simply placing the first row of stitches onto the knitting needles. These stitches serve as a foundation for the rest of the knitting project. You must begin with one stitch on the needle before casting on the rest of the stitches. See the next section, Making a Slip Knot, for more information.

Making a Slip Knot

The first stitch you make should be a slip knot. Many of you may be familiar with the basic slip knot:

1. Wind the yarn twice around two fingers of your left hand, crossing the second strand over the first. Place a knitting needle under the bottom strand and over the top strand (see step SK-1).
2. Using the needle, pull the bottom strand through the top strand and form a loop (see step SK-2).
3. Pull the needle up, tightening the knot. This gives you a slip knot on the needle, which serves as your first "stitch" (see step SK-3).

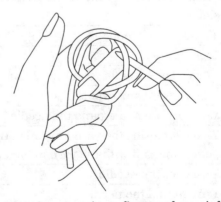

Step SK-1. Wind the yarn twice around two fingers of your left hand, crossing the second strand over the first. Place a knitting needle under the bottom strand and over the top strand.

Step SK-2. Using the needle, pull the bottom strand through the top strand and form a loop.

Step SK-3: Pull the needle up, tightening the knot. This gives you a slip knot on the needle, which serves as your first "stitch."

Examples of Cast On Stitches

There are many methods of casting on, but I've chosen to discuss the two most common, explained below.

Cast On Method #1: Double-Strand Cast On

The cast on method I prefer has several names: slingshot, half hitch, double-strand, two-strand, one needle, and double cast on. I prefer "double-strand cast on." This method produces an elastic, strong, and versatile edge of stitches.

As you cast on, you will begin creating your first row of knitting. The next row worked will be a wrong side row. Begin with one knitting needle (whatever size the pattern calls for) and your yarn. Pull out enough yarn to complete your cast on stitches: the rule of thumb is 1 inch of yarn per cast on stitch, followed by an additional 6 inches. So, if your directions tell you to "cast on 60 stitches," then you will need 66 inches of yarn.

1. Begin with the slip knot, which is your first cast on stitch. For this practice cast on, you will use 20 stitches, so pull out 26 inches of yarn. If possible, pull yarn from the center of the ball (where the yarn is wrapped) rather than the loose end on the outer edge.

2. Hold the needle with the slip knot (first stitch) in your right hand and place the tail end of yarn over your left thumb. Bring the working yarn (yarn from the ball) over your left index finger, and hold both ends of yarn with your three other fingers (see step CO-1).

3. Move your left hand slightly forward while pivoting your left thumb. Insert the needle held in the right hand, from the bottom, under the loop formed by the thumb (see step CO-2). Move the needle up and around the strand on your index finger, and then come back under this strand with the tip of the needle. Next, with the tip of the needle, come back under the thumb strand, drawing the stitch just made through this loop (see step CO-3).

4. Slide your thumb out of the loop and slightly tighten your new stitch (see step CO-4).

5. Again, insert your thumb and index finger between the two strands and you're ready for the next stitch.

Only practice makes you an expert at this cast on method. Figure 2 and figure 3 show the finished results of the right side cast on edge, double-strand method and the wrong side cast on edge, double-strand method.

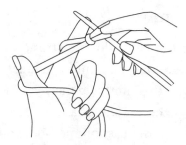

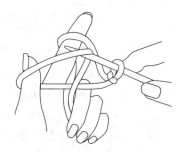

Step CO-1. Hold the needle with the slip knot (first stitch) in your right hand and place the tail end of yarn over your left thumb. Bring the working yarn (yarn from the ball) over your left index finger, and hold both ends of yarn with your three other fingers.

Step CO-2. Move your left hand slightly forward while pivoting your left thumb. Insert the needle held in the right hand, from the bottom, under the loop formed by the thumb.

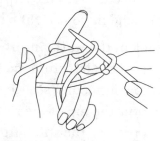

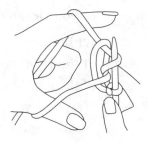

Step CO-3. Move the needle up and around the strand on your index finger, and then come back under this strand with the tip of the needle. Next, with the tip of the needle, come back under the thumb strand, drawing the stitch just made through this loop.

Step CO-4. Slide your thumb out of the loop and slightly tighten your new stitch.

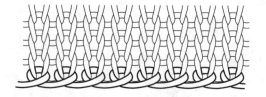

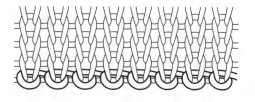

Figure 2. The right side of a cast on edge, double-strand method.

Figure 3. The wrong side of a cast on edge, double-strand method.

Cast On Method #2: Knit Cast On

Knit cast on tends to be slower than the double-strand cast on method. It also pulls out of shape more easily, and produces a less attractive edge. It is helpful to know this method when you need to cast on stitches at the beginning or the middle of a row. If you find this method easier than the double-strand cast on method, you may also use it for your cast on row as long as you realize the "pitfalls" I discussed above. The knit cast on method will be easier to understand after you have learned the knit stitch, which is discussed later in this chapter.

1. Form a slip knot about 12 inches from the tail end of the yarn for your first stitch. Hold the needle with the slip knot in your left hand and the other needle in your right hand.

2. While holding the yarn in the back of the work, insert the tip of the right needle as if to knit (from the left) into the front of the first stitch (slip knot) on the left needle (see step C2-1). Wrap the yarn from left to right, over the top of the right needle, and knit one stitch. Don't remove the stitch from the needle (see step C2-2).

3. Transfer the one stitch to the left needle by placing the tip of the left needle (from the left) into the new stitch. Slide the stitch to the left needle (see step C2-3).

4. Insert the right needle again into the stitch as if to knit and repeat steps 2 and 3 for the desired number of stitches.

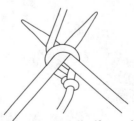

Step C2-1. Insert the tip of the right needle (from the left) into the front of the first stitch on the left needle.

Step C2-2. Wrap the yarn from left to right, over the top of the right needle, and knit one stitch.

Step C2-3. Transfer the new stitch to the left needle.

Holding Your Needles

Before you begin knitting, you must learn how to hold the knitting needles and yarn. Hold the left needle between your left thumb and index finger, and hold the right needle as you would hold a pencil (see step ND-1).

Wrap the yarn coming from the ball (from right to left) around your right index finger and regulate its flow from the ball or skein with the three other fingers of your right hand (see step ND-2).

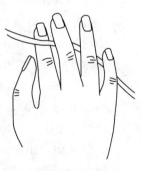

Step ND-1. Hold the right needle as you would hold a pencil.

Step ND-2. Wrap the yarn coming from the ball (from right to left) around your right index finger and regulate its flow from the ball or skein with the three other fingers of your right hand.

Types of Stitches

Knit and purl form the basis of knitting. Other stitches you will learn are really forms of knit and purl or are methods by which the yarn is wrapped around the needle. The first stitch you will learn is the knit stitch.

The Knit (*k*) Stitch

The knit stitch is the first stitch learned in knitting, and is the opposite of a purl stitch. This is the basic stitch and the stitch that you usually see if you look at a store-bought sweater. On the right side, the knit stitch appears as a "V," but if you look at an individual stitch on the knitting needle, it looks like an upside-down "U."

Essentially, the hand with which you hold the working yarn defines your knitting method. Holding the yarn in the right hand is called the *English,* or *American,* method; holding the yarn in the left hand is called the *continental* method.

Many knitters prefer the continental method because they believe it is faster, but I knit faster with the English method. You'll need to know both methods for *two-color* or *stranded* knitting. I suggest you try both methods to see which method works best for you. As long as you wrap the yarn the right way around the needle, the finished result is the same. The method you choose is really a matter of personal preference and knitting comfort.

Even if you're left-handed, you should try learning to knit with your right hand to avoid confusing yourself when reading patterns, which are predominantly written for right handers. Of the thousands of knitters I know, only two left-handed knitters couldn't learn to knit right-handed.

English (American) Method

1. Hold the needle with the cast on stitches in your left hand (with the point of the needle facing toward the right) and the

empty needle and yarn in your right hand. While holding the yarn in the back of the needle, insert the tip of the right needle from the left into the front of the first stitch on the left needle. The two needles should be crossed at this point, with the right needle under the left needle (see step EMK-1).

2. Bring the yarn under the right needle and wrap it over the top of the right needle from left to right (see step EMK-2).

3. Pull the needle with the yarn through the stitch, forming a new stitch on the right needle (see step EMK-3).

4. Slip the stitch off the left needle, keeping the new stitch on the right needle.

5. Repeat steps 1 through 4 until you have knitted all the stitches in the row.

6. To start a new row, turn your work around and repeat the process.

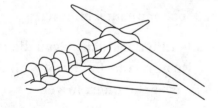

Step EMK-1. Hold the needle with the cast on stitches in your left hand (with the point of the needle facing toward the right) and the empty needle and yarn in your right hand. While holding the yarn in the back of the needle, insert the tip of the right needle from the left into the front of the first stitch on the left needle. The two needles should be crossed at this point, with the right needle under the left needle.

Step EMK-2. Bring the yarn under the right needle and wrap it over the top of the right needle (from left to right).

Step EMK-3. Pull the needle with the yarn
through the stitch, forming a new stitch on
the right needle.

Practice what you've just learned with the knit stitch by knitting several rows onto the 20 stitches you previously cast on. When every row is knitted, the pattern is called *garter stitch*. When you feel comfortable with the knit stitch worked this way, you can try the continental method below.

Continental Method

If you ever do two-color stranded knitting such as Fair Isle or Icelandic designs, you will want to know this method. You must hold the working yarn in your left hand for continental knitting.

1. Insert the tip of the right needle into the stitch as you did for the English method. Hold the yarn in your left hand with the yarn draped (from right to left) over the index finger.

2. While holding the yarn and the needle with the work in your left hand, take the yarn over the right needle from the left to the right and finish the stitch, just like you did while working the English method. Continue across the row in the same manner.

Purl (*p*) Stitch

The purl stitch, which looks like a horizontal bump, is the opposite of the knit stitch. You will learn that when knitting, you hold the yarn in the back of the work, and when purling, you hold the yarn in the front of the work. After you work a purl stitch, turn the work over and you will see a knit stitch on the opposite side.

English (American) Method

1. Hold the needle with the stitches in your left hand and the spare needle in your right hand. While holding the yarn in front of the work, insert the tip of the right needle (from the right) into the front of the first stitch on the left needle (see step EMP-1).

2. Wrap the yarn over the top of the right needle (from right to left) (see EMP-2).

3. Bring the needle with the yarn through the stitch, forming a new stitch on the right needle (see step EMP-3).

4. Slip the original stitch off the left needle, making sure to keep the new stitch on the right needle (see step EMP-4).

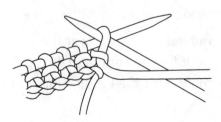

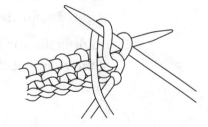

Step EMP-1. While holding the yarn in front of the work, insert the tip of the right needle (from the right) into the front of the first stitch on the left needle.

Step EMP-2. Wrap the yarn over the top of the right needle (from right to left).

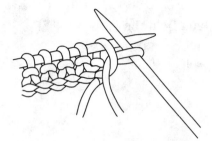

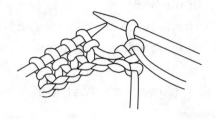

Step EMP-3. Bring the needle with the yarn through the stitch, forming a new stitch on the right needle.

Step EMP-4. Slip the original stitch off the left needle, making sure to keep the new stitch on the right needle.

Now that you have learned how to purl, you should practice what is called *stockinette* stitch, which consists of knitting one row and purling the following row, then repeating these two rows for as long as necessary. After you have worked a few inches on your practice swatch (you can start working stockinette on top of the garter stitch practice swatch that you should have already made), take a look at your knitting. The knit side (right side or outside) will look like "V"s, and the purl side (wrong side or inside) will have horizontal bumps.

Continental Method

1. Insert the right needle into the stitch on the left needle just as you did for the English method.

2. Holding the yarn in the left hand, take the yarn over the top of the right needle (from right to left) and complete the purl stitch in the same manner as you did for the English method.

Binding Off

Binding off simply means removing your stitches from the needle. Unless your directions tell you otherwise, always bind off in pattern: that is, bind off in knitting during a knit row and in purl during

▼▼

Bind Off Hints

To avoid stair-steps (or ragged edges), always slip the first stitch of bind-off rows. Slipping this first stitch, instead of knitting or purling, will make your edges more even.

Knitting directions ask you to bind off stitches at the beginning of the next row to remind you that you can only bind off at the beginning or middle of a row, never at the end of a row. Binding off at the end of a row creates an extra stitch to contend with, and your working yarn will be at the wrong side of your work.

You need two stitches to bind off one stitch. To be sure you have the correct number of bound-off stitches, count each stitch as it is bound off, not as it is worked in the row.

Bind off stitches loosely. Since bind off often occurs after ribbing, to make a finished size that is appropriate, the finished edge must be able to stretch.

Make sure you bind off neckbands loosely. Neck stitching must be loose enough to pull over someone's head.

▲▲

a purl row, and so on. Knitters bind off when they're finishing a section or an entire piece of knitting. There are several ways to bind off a piece of knitting, but following is the most popular way.

Simple Bind Off

The simple bind is the most popular method. Here's how you do it.

1. Knit or purl two stitches in pattern.
2. Insert the tip of the left needle (from the left) into the first stitch (see step BO-1), and pull it over the second stitch and off the needle (see step BO-2).
3. As you work across the row, continue binding off as many stitches as indicated in the pattern.
4. If all the stitches have been bound off, take the end of the yarn through the last stitch to anchor.

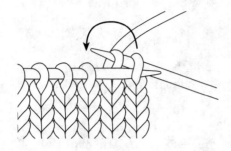

Step BO-1. Insert the tip of the left needle (from the left) into the first stitch.

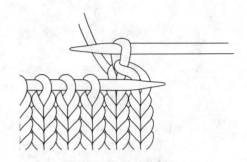

Step BO-2. Pull the first stitch over the second and off the needle.

Pattern Stitches

Following are some of the most popular stitches you will come across when using patterns.

Ribbing

Vertical ridges and elasticity characterize rib stitches. Knitters use rib stitches for the bottoms of garments and for necklines and cuffs. Hundreds of rib patterns exist. The following examples contain some of the most common:

Ribbing Example #1 (*k1, p1*)

Knit 1, Purl 1 (k1, p1), also called a *1 × 1 rib*, means that on your first row of ribbing you work **k1, p1; repeat from * across row.*

When you have rows with an even number of stitches, you will work every row the same. **Row 1 and all rows:** **k1, p1; repeat from * across the row.*

When you have rows with an odd number of stitches, you will need to compensate for the extra stitch. **Row 1:** **k1, p1; repeat from * across row until 1 stitch remains, k1.* **Row 2:** **p1, k1; repeat from * across row until 1 stitch remains, p1.* Repeat rows 1 and 2 for pattern.

In most instances, I find it better to work ribbing on an even number of stitches because, when sewing the sides of a garment together, you usually take in one stitch on each side (see finishing). However, if the item is bulky, or if you want a thin seam (as in socks), you may want an odd number of stitches for matching seams.

Ribbing Example #2 (*k2, p2*)

Knit 2, Purl 2 (k2, p2), also called 2 × 2 rib

This pattern often appears in multiples of 4 plus 2 stitches so that the stitches will match when it is sewn together.

Row 1: *k2, p2; repeat from * across row until 2 stitches remain, k2*
Row 2: *p2, k2; repeat from * across row until 2 stitches remain, p2*

Ribbing Example # 3 (Twisted Rib)

Because twisted ribs make tighter ribs, they're often used for fisherman knits or with cotton yarn. Cotton yarn is nonelastic, so this extra tightness helps make a rib that will not stretch out as much. They are also common as part of Aran (fisherman knitting) patterns. Four different examples of twisted ribs are given here.

Problems You May Encounter With Ribs

You must move yarn *between* the needle points, not *over* the needle points when changing from knit to purl or from purl to knit stitches. If you're not sure which stitch is next, look at the working stitch and see if it looks like a chain (knit) or a bump (purl).

Although the needle size is smaller, knit stitches look larger when working *k1, p1 rib*. To help prevent this problem, pull the yarn tighter when changing from the knit to the purl stitch. The same thing happens when working the second knit stitch, *k2, p2 rib*. Again, give an extra tug when you bring the yarn to the front to purl. You will notice that it's easier to give an extra tug to the yarn when taking the yarn to the back after a purl, than it is when bringing the yarn to the front to knit.

- Example A: Knit all knit stitches on right side rows through the back loops instead of through the front loops. (Worked on an even number of stitches.)

  Row 1: *k1 tbl, p1; repeat from * across row*
  Row 2: *k1, p1; repeat from * across row*

- Example B: The same stitch gets twisted on every row. (Worked on an even number of stitches.)

  Row 1: *k1 tbl, p1; repeat from * across row*
  Row 2: *k1, p1 tbl; repeat from * across row*

- Example C: Knit stitches are twisted on every row. (Worked on an even number of stitches.)

  Row 1: *k1 tbl, p1; repeat from * across row*
  Row 2: *Repeat row 1*

- Example D: Mock cable rib. (Worked on a multiple of 4 plus 2 stitches.) This stitch looks like a small cable, but is made without using a cable needle. This is a fast way to make a "mini" cable.

  Tw2: Mock cable that slants toward the right. *k2 tog,* but do not remove from the needle; go back and knit the first stitch again, remove both stitches from the needle.

  Row 1: *p2, Tw2; repeat from * until 2 stitches remain; p2*

  Row 2: *k2, p2; repeat from * until 2 stitches remain, k2*

  Row 3: *p2, *k2, p2; repeat from * across row*

  Row 4: *Repeat row 2*

Slip Stitch

A slip stitch is one that is "slipped" from one needle to another without knitting or purling it. Unless the directions tell you otherwise, a

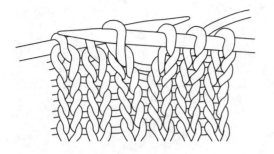

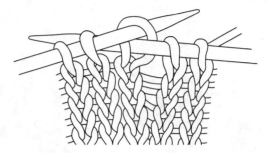

Figure 4. Slipping a stitch as if to purl.   **Figure 5.** Slipping a stitch as if to knit.

stitch is normally slipped as if to purl (see figure 4), unless it is part of a decrease (which you will read about later in this chapter), when it is slipped as if to knit so it will not be twisted (see figure 5). Slip stitches are popular, useful stitches used in *left-slanting* decreases and in numerous *texture pattern* stitches.

Seed Stitch

Seed stitch—a pattern stitch alternating knit and purl stitches—lies flat with no obvious curling of the edges. They're great stitches for borders. Across the first row, you work *k1, p1;* on the following row, you knit the purl stitches as they face you, and purl the knit stitches as they face you.

Understanding Increases

Increases *(inc)* allow you to add one or more stitches to a pattern. There are four basic types of increases: *bar* increases, *make 1* increases, *lifted* increases, and *yarn-over* increases. Various knitting authors and teachers refer to increases by different names. I use the most common names in this book.

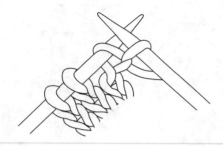

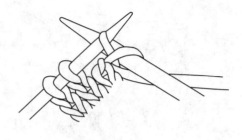

Step BI-1. Knit into the next stitch on the left needle as usual (like you usually knit), but do not remove the stitch from the needle.

Step BI-2. Take the tip of the right needle to the back and knit into the back loop.

Bar Increase

Knitting into the front and back of a stitch is called a bar increase. The name comes from the little bar that is left after the increase is made. Follow these steps to use a bar increase when the instructions call for it:

1. Knit into the next stitch on the left needle as usual (like you usually knit), but do not remove the stitch from the needle (see step BI-1).

2. Take the tip of the right needle to the back of the stitch on the left needle, and knit into the back loop (see BI-2).

3. Remove both stitches from the left needle.

The bar always follows the stitch that made the increase. For example, if you're making a bar increase at each end of a row, you will make the first increase in the first stitch and the final increase in the *next-to-last* stitch to avoid placing the bar on the outside edge. The bar should lie between the first and second stitches and the next-to-last and last stitches.

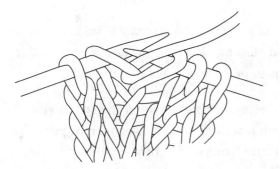

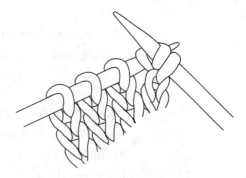

Step MI-1. Knit into the stitch as usual, but don't remove it from the needle.

Step MI-2. Bring the yarn to the front as if to purl and insert the tip of the right needle (from the right) into the stitch. Purl into the front loop.

Variations on Bar Increases

Following is a variation of the bar increase. The finished result is very similar.

Moss Increase Knitters make moss increases by knitting and purling into the *same* stitch, rather than knitting into the front and back of a stitch, as you do with a bar increase. Follow these steps to perform a moss increase:

1. Knit into the stitch as usual, but don't remove it from the needle (see MI-1).

2. Bring the yarn to the front as if to purl and insert the tip of the right needle (from the right) into the stitch. Purl into the front loop (see step MI-2).

3. Remove both stitches from the left needle.

Make One Increase

An almost invisible increase, make one increases *(m1)* are sometimes referred to as *blind stockinette stitch* increases or *raised* increases. Follow these steps to perform a make one increase:

1. Pick up the horizontal strand lying between the stitch you just worked and the stitch that follows it, by inserting the tip of the left needle from the front under this strand and placing it on the left needle (see step MO-1).

2. Knit or purl into the back loop (see step MO-2). (If you work into the front loop instead of the back loop an unwanted hole will appear.)

3. To work a reverse make one increase, insert the tip of the left needle from the back into the strand lying between the stitch you just worked and the stitch that follows it (see step MO-3). Knit this strand through the front loop.

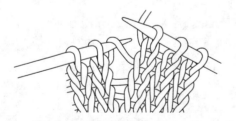

Step MO-1. Pick up the horizontal strand lying between the stitch you just worked and the stitch that follows it, by inserting the tip of the left needle from the front under this strand and placing it on the left needle.

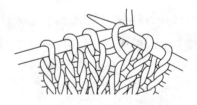

Step MO-2. Knit or purl into the back loop.

Step MO-3. To work a reverse make one increase, insert the tip of the left needle from the back into the strand lying between the stitch you just worked and the stitch that follows it. Knit this strand through the front loop.

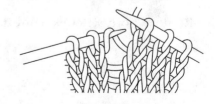

If you're working a raglan sweater, for example, you should consistently make a regular make one increase on one side of the seam (center) stitch, and a reverse make one on the other side. If you're increasing for sleeves, you should consistently make a regular make one on one edge, and a reverse make one on the other to balance the increases.

Lifted Increase

Like make one increases, lifted increases are almost invisible. There are two different types of lifted increases, which you can match on either side of a center stitch or sleeve when you make increases. You can use lifted increases, for example, to reinforce the thumb of a mitten. You should not use lifted increases more often than every other row, preferably every fourth row.

■ **Lifted Increase Right:** Insert the tip of the right needle from the front into the right side of the stitch below the next stitch on the left needle. Knit this loop through the front, and then knit the stitch on the left needle (see step LR-1).

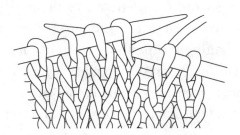

Step LR-1. Insert the tip of the right needle from the front into the right side of the stitch below the next stitch on the left needle. Knit this loop through the front, and then knit the stitch on the left needle.

■ **Lifted Increase Left:** Knit the next stitch and insert the tip of the left needle from the back into the left side of the stitch, two rows below the last worked stitch on the right needle. Pull this loop out and knit it through the back loop (see step LL-1).

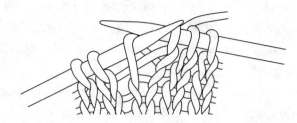

Step LL-1. Insert the tip of the left needle from the back into the left side of the stitch, two rows below the last worked stitch on the right needle. Pull this loop out and knit it through the back loop.

Yarn-Over Increases

You will use a yarn-over stitch for any type of increase in which a hole is desired or called for in a pattern. You make yarn-over stitches by wrapping the yarn an extra time around the right needle. A yarn-over stitch should lie in the same direction as the other stitches on the needle, unless the directions specify otherwise, meaning that the right side of the stitch is on the front of the needle. You don't actually complete a yarn-over stitch until you work the next row, when you will knit, purl, slip, or drop it.

Although a yarn over is easier than a knit or purl stitch, as a beginner you must first learn to knit and purl before attempting yarn overs. Many beginning knitters inadvertently make a yarn over when they are learning to make ribbing. They accidentally take the yarn *over* the needle instead of bringing the yarn *between* the points of the needle during the change from a purl to a knit stitch.

Understanding Decreases

Decreases are ways of working two or more stitches together as a means of eliminating stitches. Decreases can slant toward the left, right, and occasionally toward the center.

Right-Slanting Decreases

- **Knit two together** *(k2 tog)***:** Knit the next two stitches together by taking the right needle into the front of the second stitch on the left needle. At the same time, take the right needle into the front of the first stitch on the left needle, and knit the two stitches together as if they were one stitch. This decrease slants toward the right (see step RD-1). This is the most common decrease and the fastest to make.

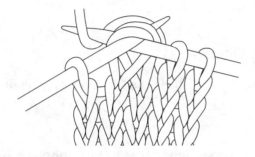

Step RD-1. Knit the next two stitches together by taking the right needle into the front of the second stitch on the left needle. At the same time, take the right needle into the front of the first stitch on the left needle, and knit the two stitches together as if they were one stitch.

- **Knit three together** *(k3 tog)***:** Knit the next three stitches in the same manner as a knit two together, except start by taking the right needle first into the third stitch on the left needle, and then go into the second and first stitches, in that order. Knit all three stitches together as if they were one. This is a double decrease that slants toward the right.

- **Purl two together** *(p2 tog)***:** Purl two stitches together by taking the right needle from the right into the front of the first stitch on the left needle. At the same time, continue taking the right needle through the second stitch and purl these two stitches together as if they were one stitch (see step RD-2).

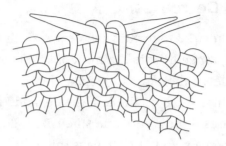

Step RD-2. Purl two stitches together by taking the right needle from the right into the front of the first stitch on the left needle. At the same time, continue taking the right needle through the second stitch and purl these two stitches together as if they were one stitch.

Left-Slanting Decreases

■ **Slip, slip, knit** *(ssk)*: This is the best left-slanting decrease and the desired one when you need a decrease that will match the right slanting decrease.

1. Slip the next two stitches as if to knit, one at a time from the left to the right needle (see step LD-1). (The left side of these two stitches will be on the front of the needle instead of the right side, which is normal.)

2. Insert the tip of the left needle (from the left) into the front of these two stitches and knit them together (see step LD-2).

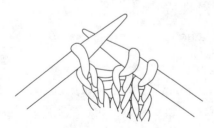

Step LD-1. Slip the next two stitches as if to knit, one at a time from the left to the right needle.

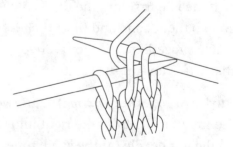

Step LD-2. Insert the tip of the left needle (from the left) into the front of these two stitches and knit them together.

- **Slip, slip, purl *(ssp)*:** *Ssp,* which is usually worked on the purl row, appears to be identical to the *ssk* from the right side. Slip the next two stitches from the left needle to the right needle as if to knit, one at a time, and then slip the stitches back to the left needle also one at a time. The stitches should be on the needle facing the opposite direction from the other stitches on the needle, with the left side on the front of the needle. Take the tip of the right needle to the back and insert it from the left into the back of the second stitch, then into the back of the first stitch. Purl them together.

- **Slip one, knit one, *psso* (skp or *sl 1, k1, psso*):** The abbreviation "psso" translates as *pass the slipped stitch over.* It resembles the *ssk,* which is the preferable stitch since the *ssk* gives a smoother finished appearance. Directions for *skp* or *sl 1, k1, psso* often appear in knitting pattern directions. When you see directions for *sl 1, k1, psso,* you may substitute *ssk.* Follow these directions to use this stitch:

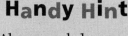

Handy Hint

Always work decreases at least one stitch in from the outside edge to avoid interfering with the seam.

1. Slip the next stitch on the left needle to the right needle as if to knit (see step PSSO-1).

2. Knit the next stitch on the left needle (see step PSSO-2).

3. Insert the left needle (from the left) into the front of the slipped stitch. Pass the slipped stitch over the knit stitch and off the needle (see step PSSO-3).

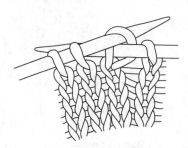

Step PSSO-1. Slip the next stitch on the left needle to the right needle as if to knit.

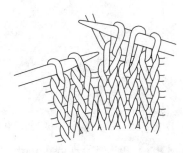

Step PSSO-2. Knit the next stitch on the left needle.

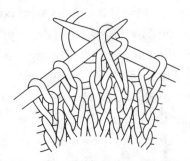

Step PSSO-3. Insert the left needle (from the left) into the front of the slipped stitch. Pass the slipped stitch over the knit stitch and off the needle.

Sometimes directions say to decrease at each end of the row, but do not tell which kind of decrease to make where. To ensure that your decreases match at each end of the row, you must make paired decreases (see step PD-1 for a sample showing *ssk* at the beginning of the row and *k2 tog* at the end of the row). To make this sample, each right side decrease row would be made as follows: *k1, ssk, work in pattern across the row until 3 stitches remain, k2 tog, k1.* (See step PD-2 for a sample with *k2 tog* at the beginning of the row and *ssk* at the end of the row.) To make this sample each right side decrease row would be made as follows: *k1, k2 tog, work in pattern across the row until 3 stitches remain, ssk, k1.*

Step PD-1. Paired decreases with *ssk* at the beginning of the row and *k2 tog* at the end of the row.

Step PD-2. Paired decreases with *k2 tog* at the beginning of the row and *ssk* at the end of the row.

■ **Slip 1, knit two together, psso** *(sl1, k2 tog, psso)***:** Slip the
next stitch as if to knit from the left needle to the right needle.
Knit the next two stitches together and pass the slipped stitch
over the knit two together. This double decrease, which slants
toward the left, matches the double decrease *k3 together.*

Lace Knitting and Yarn Overs

The yarn-over stitch *(yo or yf)* is one of the simplest stitches, but it
becomes more complex in intricate lace patterns. You cannot exe-
cute exquisite lace and eyelet patterns without the yarn-over stitch.
The versatile yarn-over stitch is often used during increasing and in
many texture patterns. Sometimes you may not even recognize the
yarn-over stitch in a pattern. Some of the more popular uses of yarn
overs are increasing, ribbing, beading, creating holes for ribbons
and cords, bobbles, popcorns, texture patterns, elongated stitches,
lace, eyelet stitches, and picot edges.

In lace knitting, yarn overs normally accompany decreases, on
either the same or a different row. Ensuring a correct yarn over depends on how you worked the stitches before and after the yarn over.

Yarn-Over Stitches

The way the yarn is wrapped over or around the needle in making a
yarn over depends on what stitch (knit or purl) comes both before
and after the yarn over. Often the directions will only say *yo* and
other times they will write out one or more of the abbreviations discussed below.

■ **Yarn over between two knit stitches** *(yfon or wfon)***:** yarn
forward and over the needle. Bring the yarn forward between
the needle points to the front of the work, and then take it back
over the top of the needle and knit. This stitch is comparable

to working a knit stitch with the yarn held in the purl position (see step YO-1).

- **Yarn over after a knit stitch and before a purl stitch** *(yfrn or wfrn)*: yarn forward and around needle. Bring the yarn forward between the needle points, then take it back over the top of the right needle, then forward between the needles again and purl the next stitch (see step YO-2).

- **Yarn over after a purl and before a knit stitch** *(yon or won)*: Yarn over needle. Take the yarn from the front to the back by taking it over the top of the right needle to the back (see step YO-3). This yarn-over uses very little yarn. To standardize your hole size, hold the yarn a little loosely when taking it over the top of the needle to knit.

- **Yarn over between two purl stitches** *(yrn or wrn)*: Yarn around the needle. Take the yarn from the front to the back over the top of the right needle and bring it back again to the front by bringing it under the needle. Purl the next stitch (see step YO-4).

- **Yarn two times over the needle** *(y2on)*: Work the first yarn over as you normally would (depending on the stitch before and after it), then wrap it around the right needle another time and proceed to knit or purl (see step YO-5).

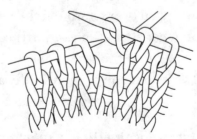

Step YO-1. *yfon: yarn forward and over the needle.* Bring the yarn forward between the needle points to the front of the work, and then take it back over the top of the needle and knit. This stitch is comparable to working a knit stitch with the yarn held in the purl position.

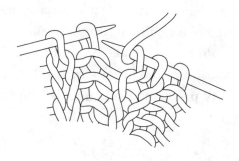

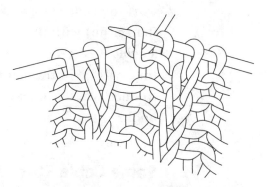

Step YO-2. *yfrn: yarn forward and around needle.* Bring the yarn forward between the needle points, then take it back over the top of the right needle, then forward between the needles again and purl the next stitch.

Step YO-3. *yon: yarn over needle.* Take the yarn from the front to the back by taking it over the top of the right needle to the back.

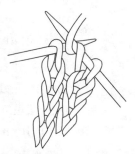

Step YO-4. *yrn: yarn around needle.* Take the yarn from the front to the back over the top of the right needle and bring it back again to the front by bringing it under the needle. Purl the next stitch.

Step YO-5. *y2on: yarn two times over the needle.* Work the first yarn over as you normally would (depending on the stitch before and after it), then wrap it around the right needle another time and proceed to knit or purl.

Cables (c)

Cables are selected stitches that have been twisted around each other to make a rope-like design. Sometimes referred to as slants, crosses, and twists, cables are created by changing the working order of a small number of stitches (not usually more than nine) with the assistance of a double-pointed needle called a *cable needle*. Slip stitches onto the cable needle as if to purl, so they will lie in the same direction as the other stitches. I will introduce you to cables using my preferred cable needle: the cable hook.

Some Cable Stitches

- **Cable 4 back (*C4B*):** Slip the next two stitches on the left-hand needle one at a time as if to purl onto the short end of the cable needle. Hold the cable needle to the back of the work and knit the next two stitches from the left needle. Bring the cable needle to the front of the work and knit the two stitches off the long end of the cable needle (opposite end). This type of cable slants toward the right (see figure 6). Be sure not to twist your stitches as you work them off the cable needle.

- **Cable 4 front (*C4F*):** Slip the next two stitches on the left-hand needle one at a time as if to purl onto the short end of the cable needle and hold the needle in the front of the work. Knit the next two stitches from the left needle. Then knit the two stitches off the long end of the cable needle (opposite end). This is a left-slanting cable (see figure 7).

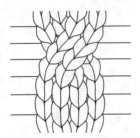

Figure 6. Back or right cable.

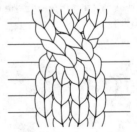

Figure 7. Front or left cable.

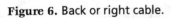

Cable Knitting Hints

To avoid confusion when you start to work cables, follow these simple hints:

- Always slip stitches onto the cable needle as if to purl.
- When working the stitches off the cable needle, make sure you do so at the opposite end from which you started.
- Make sure you don't twist the stitches as you take them off the cable needle.
- Front cables slant toward the left; back cables slant toward the right.
- The number in the cable directions refers to the total number of stitches being worked, not just the number being placed onto the cable needle.
- Always read through all your directions before you begin.
- Gauge is apt to be tighter when working cables.

Picking Up Stitches

You normally pick up stitches to work a border or complete an unfinished edge, or from a finished section so you can knit in a different direction. You should pick up stitches evenly from the right side, and you actually make a knitted stitch each time you pick up a new stitch. I prefer using a knitting needle to pick up stitches. Some like using a crochet hook, but I find this awkward and time consuming.

1. Insert the knitting needle from the front to the back, under the two strands from the bind-off edge, or between the edge stitch and the next stitch.
2. Wrap the yarn around the needle as if to knit and actually knit a stitch.
3. Continue picking up as many stitches as required, working from right to left.

See figures 8 and 9 for examples of picking up from vertical and horizontal edges.

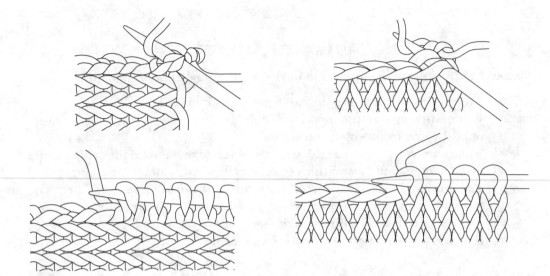

Figure 8. Picking up stitches from vertical edges.

Figure 9. Picking up stitches from horizontal edges.

Usually, knitting directions ask you to "Pick up and knit" a certain number of stitches. If the instructions neglect to mention the number of stitches to pick up, then you must measure the edge along which the stitches will be picked up, and estimate the number of stitches you will need. If you're picking up a large number of stitches, you may want to place markers along the edge to evenly divide your stitches. (These markers can be a piece of white yarn tied at even intervals along the edge.) An even, neat edge means that you picked up the correct number of stitches; however, if you pick up too many stitches, the finished edge will flare out. If you pick up too few stitches, the edge will pull in.

Finishing

Want to avoid that "homemade" look? Then you must learn to finish your knitting properly. Some knitters dislike finishing a project;

therefore, it's not uncommon for knitters to avoid the seamstress's finishing touch.

Proper seams require a good tapestry needle, which is a blunt-pointed needle with a large eye. Don't use a sharp pointed needle because it can split your yarn. You can use the tail end of yarn left over from your knitting to sew the pieces together, but it's best not to use a length of yarn longer than 18 inches because a long piece can stretch and fray from finishing. If your sewing yarn becomes too thin you'll need to cut it and start with a new piece.

Probably almost as many seam possibilities as knitting stitch combinations exist. Some seams work better with stockinette stitches, others with garter stitches, and still others with ribbing. There are also seams made especially for shoulders and for matching

Hints for Seams

1. You should sew seams by hand rather than with a sewing machine, as a machine cannot sew stitch by stitch into each knitted stitch.

2. Whenever possible, use the same yarn for seams that you used for your garment. The only exception is if the garment yarn has a nubby texture and will not fit through your tapestry needle. In this case, substitute with a plain yarn of the same color.

3. If you created your garment with stripes or different colors, you must seam each color with matching yarn.

4. Do not use common sewing thread for any of your knitting seams, as sewing thread is way too thin.

5. Work in from the edge the same number of stitches on each side. If you work in one stitch on one side, you must also work in one stitch on the other side.

6. Learn to recognize a knit stitch from the bottom up (as you knit) and upside down (see figures 10 and 11). Turning figure 11 upside down reveals what looks like the center of a knit stitch. Also learn to recognize the space between two stitches.

vertical and horizontal edges with each other. Authors and designers use many different names for seaming: grafting, weaving, ladder stitch, vertical grafting, mattress, backstitch, Kitchener stitch, slip-stitch crochet, edge to edge, invisible, and so on.

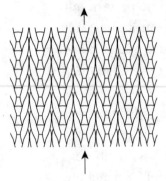 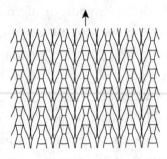

Figure 10. Arrows following the center of a knit stitch from bottom to top.

Figure 11. Stockinette stitch as it looks upside down, with arrow now showing between the knit stitches. Turn the page upside-down and reveal what looks like the center of a knit stitch.

Ladder Stitch Seams

In addition to the name "Ladder Stitch," this seam is also referred to as *invisible* or *vertical grafting*. I like the name ladder stitch as the seaming process actually resembles a ladder. Ladder stitch combines two vertical edges. You usually work it in one stitch from each edge, but sometimes it is worked in only one-half stitch to lessen the bulk of the yarn, or when knitting a sock when you don't want to feel the seam on your foot. Ultimately, when finished, seams should look like a continuous knit stitch. If properly made, the only way to locate the seam is to feel the slight bump along the seam line.

To work a ladder stitch, lay the two pieces to be seamed right side up on a flat surface. The cast on and bind-off edges should match and the corresponding stitches should align. I prefer to sew seams from the bottom up by laying the pieces with the cast on edges at the bottom, and working up from this point just as the pieces were knit.

1. Thread the tapestry needle with the tail end of yarn left from the knitting (if it is long enough). I usually use a size 18 or 16 tapestry needle, depending on the thickness of the yarn. You should have enough yarn left for the seam, but if you don't, use a spare piece of yarn and work the tail end in later. If you have to start with a new piece of yarn, hold the tail (allowing at least 4 inches to be worked in later) with your left hand until it is anchored so it will not pull through.

2. You first need to secure the bottom edges. To do this, bring the needle up from the bottom through the first cast on stitch on the edge of one side, and then bring it over to the other side and go through the bottom edge stitch on that side to the back of the work.

3. Look at your knit stitches on each side edge where you are working. Pull the knitting slightly so you can see the horizontal thread that lies between the edge stitch and the second stitch on the first row (bottom row).

4. Bring the needle up under this strand to the top. Go across to the other side and take the point of the needle under the horizontal strand between the edge stitch and the second stitch on the first row on that side. Pull the yarn through to the top. Go back to the other side and repeat the process.

5. Continue, back and forth from side to side, taking the needle under the strand between the edge stitch and the next stitch each time (see step LS-1). Go under only one horizontal strand each time you work.

If you have the same number of rows on each side, everything will come out fine. Some directions may tell you to go under two strands each time, but this makes too loose a seam unless you're using very fine fingering yarn. This type of seam sounds more difficult than it actually is. Refer to the steps for help. You do not have to pull the yarn tight after each stitch; just pull it snug after every inch or so.

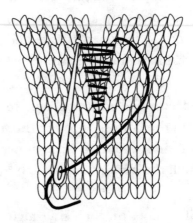

Step LS-1. Continue, back and forth from side to side, taking the needle under the strand between the edge stitch and the next stitch each time. Go under only one horizontal strand each time you work.

Garter Stitch Seams

To work a seam with garter stitch, secure the bottom edges as done for ladder stitch; then bring your threaded needle (from right to left) on the right-side piece through the lower vertical left edge part of the stitch. Go across to the left piece. From bottom to top, go under the upper edge part of the horizontal bump (see step GS-1). This may sound a little strange but looking at the illustration should help you.

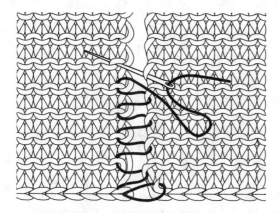

Step GS-1. Bring your threaded needle (from right to left) on the right-side piece through the lower vertical left edge part of the stitch. Go across to the left piece. From bottom to top, go under the upper edge part of the horizontal bump.

Kitchener Stitch Seam

Kitchener stitch is another name for grafting stitches from knitting needles. It's a way to join two pieces horizontally and finish with a smooth elastic edge. You weave the stitches together directly from the knitting needles, and the final appearance, when worked in stockinette stitch, is of a continuous knit stitch. Even with close inspection, you shouldn't be able to find the seam.

Kitchener stitch is the best way to finish the toe of a sock. It's also good for working underarm seams. In order to work Kitchener stitch, you must have the same number of stitches on each of the two needles. The points of the needles must both be on the right end of your work. Hold the two pieces together with the wrong sides facing each other and the right sides on the outside, using a blunt-pointed tapestry needle. Make sure you have enough yarn left from your knitting, at least an inch per stitch. Thread the needle with the tail end and sew from right to left.

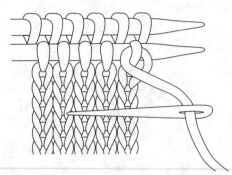

Step KS-1. Insert the tapestry needle all the way through the first stitch on the top needle as if to purl to work the preliminary stitch.

Work the preliminary step by passing the needle all the way through the first stitch on the right end of the front needle as if to purl (see step KS-1). Leave the stitch on the needle and take the needle to the back of your work, passing it all the way through the first stitch on the back needle as if to knit. Leave the stitch on the needle. Now you're ready to work the main part of a Kitchener stitch.

1. Insert the tapestry needle all the way through the first stitch on the top needle as if to knit. Remove the stitch from the needle and insert the tapestry needle through the second stitch on the top needle as if to purl. Leave this stitch on the needle.

2. Insert the tapestry needle all the way through the first stitch on the back needle as if to purl. Remove the stitch from the needle and pass the tapestry needle as if to knit all the way through the second stitch on the bottom needle. Leave the stitch on the needle.

3. Repeat steps 1 and 2 until all the stitches have been worked off the needles. Take the yarn tail through to the wrong side. Weave into the fabric on the wrong side to secure.

Gauge/Tension

Gauge (also referred to as tension) is the number of stitches and/or rows required per inch. You will often see the following text in knitting instructions: "It is always necessary to check gauge in order to obtain a proper fit." The word *gauge* usually appears in capital letters in your pattern instructions.

To obtain the correct gauge, it's often necessary to use a different needle size (one or two sizes larger or smaller) than the recommended size. Obtaining the proper gauge in knitting can make all the difference between a wonderful garment and a complete disaster. After all, we all knit differently, as I learned several years ago when I taught a knitting correspondence course. Three of my students, all using the same size needles, yarn, and pattern, sent in samples that differed dramatically, ranging in size from 7 to 12 square inches. The vast difference in individual knitting tension showed me how important it is to check the gauge.

When checking your gauge, always use the needles, yarn, and pattern stitch that you will be using for the final project. Just because you've used the same type of yarn before doesn't mean you can skip creating a test swatch. Don't rely on someone else's swatch either. You must make your own swatch.

Many factors can affect the gauge. Humidity can affect your knitting by causing the stitches to stick to the needles. If I'm tense or upset, my knitting is apt to be tighter, whereas if I'm relaxed the knitting is looser than normal.

Some knitters dread making a gauge swatch. But I'm sure they would all rather spend a short amount of time knitting a 4-inch swatch, instead of making an entire garment that doesn't fit. Yes, you have all that lovely yarn and you're just itching to get started on that beautiful sweater, but please spend those extra minutes on the gauge sample. It's time well spent.

Don't Get Discouraged

Dorothy Kleinendorst began knitting at age 18 because she wanted a pair of argyle socks. "Luckily, I didn't know what a hard project it really was," says Dorothy. A true knitaholic, Dorothy always travels with her knitting; she even knitted lying flat on her back while recovering from back surgery. "If I'm not knitting, my husband is convinced I'm sick," she says.

Over the years, Dorothy has won an amazing 148 ribbons at county fairs. In her final year of participation, Dorothy entered seven items into three separate fairs and won ribbons for each and every entry! Dorothy has pictures of all her entries and the rest of her work in two bulging photo albums. She sells many of her items, including Barbie doll clothes, baby sweater sets, mittens, hats, booties, slippers, and knitted Christmas ornaments such as bells, wreaths, and small Santa and Mrs. Santa dolls at local craft bazaars.

Making a Gauge (Sample) Swatch

Knitting patterns usually suggest making at least a 4 × 4-inch square gauge swatch. Cast on the appropriate number of stitches for 4 inches, plus an additional 4 stitches. Knit three rows in garter stitch for a border, and then knit, using the requested stitch pattern, always knitting the first and last stitches of every row for a selvage. Knit 4 inches and measure how many stitches you have per inch. Too many stitches per inch means that you must switch to larger needles. Too few stitches per inch means that you must switch to smaller needles. Of course, a change in needle size requires a whole new swatch.

After you have knitted 4 inches, knit three rows of garter stitch. Bind off and wash and dry the swatch according to the yarn label. Check for color fastness, shrinkage, and growth.

Sometimes obtaining the correct stitch gauge is easier than obtaining the correct row gauge (row gauge being the lengthwise measurement and stitch gauge being the width measurement). An accurate stitch gauge is extremely important except in a horizontal garment, where the row gauge takes precedence. Of course, both gauges should match the pattern suggestions, if possible.

Check Your Gauge Regularly

To avoid possible problems, you should check your gauge every few inches. When I owned a retail yarn shop, one of my customers made a raglan sweater with bulky yarn that was knitted from the top down. She checked her gauge swatch and found 4 inches to an inch, which was exactly what the pattern suggested. After the sweater was completed down to the ribbing, she brought it in to the shop, but something didn't look right. The bottom part was about 3 inches wider on both front and back than the top part. Her gauge had changed to 3½ stitches an inch instead of 4 stitches per inch. What was supposed to be 44 inches was now 50 inches. I felt so bad

Watch Out For Those Knots!

Be wary of knots in your yarn. Even good yarn will have knots in it. Never leave a knot in your work; they can create weak spots that leave ugly holes. Develop the habit of pulling enough yarn from the skein to finish the row you're working on. (This equates to three times the length of the row.)

When you do find a knot, cut it out and start a new row. When starting with new yarn, leave at least 4 inches that you can use for your seam. Start using the new yarn for the first stitch of a new row by wrapping it around the needle (leaving at least a 4- to 6-inch tail) and using it to knit or purl your first stitch.

I have seen two disasters caused by knots left in knitting. I was judging a knitting competition at a county fair where a beautiful, lacy sweater had been entered. Unfortunately, a knot had pulled apart and left a hole that grew as the knitting unraveled.

Another time, a customer came into my yarn shop with a famous designer sweater that had a large knot at the bottom front edge. All I could do was try to tuck in the knot and ends as much as possible.

because she had to rip out practically the entire sweater. She could have avoided this error if she had checked her gauge regularly.

Common Knitting Errors

Some of the more common knitting mistakes occur when inadvertently twisting a stitch or when working ribbing stitches. Don't let errors bother you, because they happen to everyone, including me.

I taught a knitting class in which a student asked me how to assemble shoulder seams. I began by taking two shoulders, matching them, and then grafting them together, but I didn't realize that I had sewn the wrong shoulder seams together until I had finished.

Twisted Stitches

Learn to recognize twisted stitches (see figure 12). A twisted stitch can occur when the yarn has been wrapped the wrong way around the needle. Always keep your stitches on the knitting needle with the right side of the stitch on the front of the needle. When you are picking up dropped stitches or stitches that you have ripped out by taking them off the needle, these stitches often become obstinate and want to go back on the needle in the wrong direction. Unless you are working on some special pattern stitches, the right side of the stitch, whether it is a knit or a purl, should always be on the front of the needle (see figure 13). That way, when you knit and purl the resulting stitch won't be twisted (see figure 14).

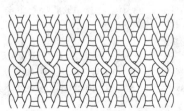

Figure 12. Twisted stitches.

Figure 13. The correct way to place the stitch on a needle.

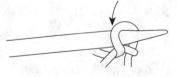

Figure 14. The wrong way to place the stitch on the needle.

Tips Grandma Never Taught You

1. Sometimes you will see the letters *yf*, which mean *yarn to the front*, and *yb*, which mean *yarn to the back*. You may also see the terms *knitwise* which means *as if to knit*, and *purlwise*, which means *as if to purl*. The term *wyif* means *with the yarn to the front* (toward you, the knitter), and *wyib* means *with yarn in back*, or away from you.

2. Whenever possible, start a new yarn at the beginning of a row to avoid loose ends in the body of your work. Start the row by using the new yarn to work the first stitch and continue across the row. Simply wrap the yarn around the needle and knit or purl with it. Be sure to leave enough of a tail so you have something to use later for a seam. Even if you don't want the yarn for a seam, you should leave at least a few inches to work with later.

3. Learn how to spot errors and check your work every inch or so. Frequent checks prevent disasters.

4. Check your gauge for changes every few inches, because it can change without you realizing it. Many environmental factors can affect the gauge. Count your stitches every inch or so. Sometimes you may have added or dropped a stitch without knowing it.

5. *Unknitting* means to take out your knitting stitch by stitch. This is usually done when you spot an error no more than two or three rows down in your work. Unknitting is an easy means of taking out your knitting, even if it is stitch by stitch. It usually takes less time to unknit a few rows than it does to rip out and then have to place all those stitches back on the needles, going in the right direction.

   To unknit, hold the work as you would to knit or purl. From left to right, insert the tip of the left needle (from the front) into the stitch below the stitch on the needle. Pull a little, and the stitch will come off the right needle. Work from left to right across the row as far as necessary. If necessary, turn and start the next (preceding) row in the opposite direction, as when knitting or purling. The same method follows for either knit or purl stitches.

6. To pick up ripped out stitches (stitches that are pulled off the needle and actually ripped), you use a needle a few sizes smaller than the working needle, immediately changing back to the proper size when finished. As you pick up the ripped out stitches, make sure each stitch lies on the needle with the right side of each stitch on the front of the needle.

7. When you're working in a pattern, and your count doesn't come out as it should at the end of the row, start counting stitch by stitch from the beginning of the row, following your directions until you find where the error occurred. Then unknit, stitch by stitch, until you reach the spot where you made the error. This saves ripping out large amounts of your work.

8. To pick up the inevitable dropped stitch, I prefer to use a knitting needle. Some books suggest a crochet hook, but I work faster with a spare knitting needle. Locate the dropped stitch. Insert the needle into the loop and into the horizontal strand in front of or behind it. Pull the strand through this loop. To correct an error or dropped stitch several rows down in your work, it may be necessary to rip out stitches. Unravel to the problem spot and pick up the stitching, inserting needle (from the back) into each stitch from the right side of the work. Again be sure the stitches lie on the needle with the right side on the front of the needle.

9. Don't be afraid of stockinette stitch rolls (when the edges roll up) because your seam will usually get rid of the roll.

10. Stitches are wider than they are tall so there are more rows than stitches per inch.

11. Cast on and bind-off edges should be as elastic as the knitting.

12. Allow 1 inch of yarn per stitch for casting on or working across a row. It helps to pull out enough yarn so you can check for knots or flaws.

    Always join a new ball of yarn at the beginning of a row whenever possible. Leave a tail of at least 6 inches, which you can use later in the seam. Don't leave knots in the yarn.

13. Always read and understand the directions thoroughly before knitting. Underline or circle all the directions that pertain to the size of the garment that you're making.

14. "Every other row" or "alternate rows" refer to every right side row: 1, 3, 5, 7, 9 or 2, 4, 6, 8, 10, etc., "every fourth row" refers to rows 4, 8, 12, etc., and alternate knit rows are every fourth row in stockinette stitch.

15. When the directions tell you to increase at the end of each row, remember to avoid increasing on the very last stitch to prevent the increase from jutting out into the seam.

    When working a bar increase at each end of the row, increase in the first stitch and the next to last stitch. In this way, each increase would be one stitch in from each outside edge.

16. It's easier to increase on right side rows, but sometimes directions will tell you to increase on each row, which means you must also increase on the wrong side row.

17. For matching decreases at each end of the row, you must make paired decreases: *ssk* at the beginning of the row and *k2 tog* at the end of the row, or *k2 tog* at the beginning and ssk at the end of the row.

18. If a stitch falls off the needle, pick it up and place it back on going in the same direction as the other stitches with the right side on the front of the needle.

19. The last stitch of the row will be the first stitch of the following row.

20. Needles for rib stitches are usually at least two sizes smaller than those you will use for the body of the item you're knitting.

21. Different stitch patterns will give different gauges even though there are the same number of stitches on the needle. Cable stitches will usually tighten your work, whereas lace stitches will loosen it.

22. Always use scissors to cut yarn; never tear it.

23. Sometimes you may inadvertently work an extra stitch at the beginning of a row, especially in garter stitch. Be careful to knit the stitch on the needle and not the loop before the stitch.

24. Become familiar with the knit stitch. It makes counting rows or stitches and checking for errors much easier.

25. When measuring your knitting, don't include the needle. Place your ruler just under the knitting needle.

26. Whenever possible, knit both sides of a cardigan and/or both sleeves at the same time, using a separate ball of yarn for each piece. In this way, each piece will be the same length.

27. Purchase the same weight of yarn as specified in the directions.

28. Always wash your hands before you begin to knit.

29. Needles stuck through a ball of yarn can split the yarn.

30. Always work your gauge swatch with the yarn, needles, and pattern that you will use for the final project.

Creating Your Knitting Projects

▼▼▼

LET'S BEGIN WORKING ON some knitting projects. This chapter introduces you to a variety of knitting techniques, including some easy knit and purl combinations, an Aran (cable) pattern, a sampling of intarsia, and some lace knitting. See the color insert in the center of the book for these finished projects

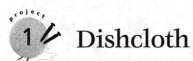 Dishcloth

This 8-inch square dishcloth made from 100% cotton and done in a knit/purl basketweave pattern is a great introduction to knitting. You can also make scarves with this pattern. Simply cast on the same amount of stitches, and then knit it to the desired length. *Warning:* if you choose acrylic yarn, don't use the dishcloth as a potholder because it could melt from the heat.

Materials

1 skein of worsted weight cotton, 100 grams. I recommend using a cotton yarn with a nubby texture to make the pattern more attractive.

1 circular or straight knitting needle, size 8.

Instructions

Gauge: 5 stitches = 1 inch. The exact gauge is not critical in this
   piece since it doesn't need to be a specific size.

To begin, cast on 40 stitches and study the chart, which is shown in
4 row pattern repeats. The first row is actually a wrong side row. Remember, the chart shows the work as seen from the right side of the
work, thus you must read the chart from left to right for wrong side
rows, and right to left for right side rows.

Row 1 first appears as a knit from the right side, but you actually begin from the wrong side with a purl stitch. This may seem
confusing at first, which is why you have both the written directions
and symbol chart to follow. Have patience! In time, you will have no
trouble reading charts (see figure 15). Please refer back to chapter 4
for any information you need as you go along.

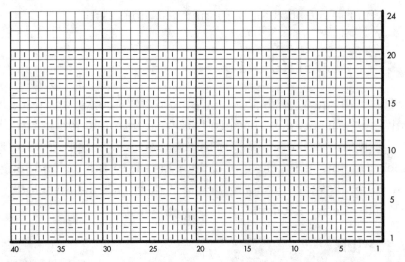

Figure 15. The basketweave pattern for a dishcloth.

Rows 1 to 4: *p4, k4, continue from * across row (Remember: *
means repeat from *.)

Rows 5 to 8: *k4, p4, continue from * across row*

Repeat rows 1 to 8 until you reach the desired length but make sure you finish after row 4 or 8. Bind off in pattern.

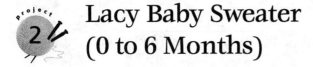

Lacy Baby Sweater (0 to 6 Months)

This lacy baby sweater, a more advanced project, is knitted with the traditional feather and fan stitch (see figure 16). I have modified this pattern slightly: The bottom edge is scalloped and created by the pattern. This design will teach you the basics of yarn overs and lace knitting, and you will have a lovely baby sweater to give as a gift or sell, if you wish.

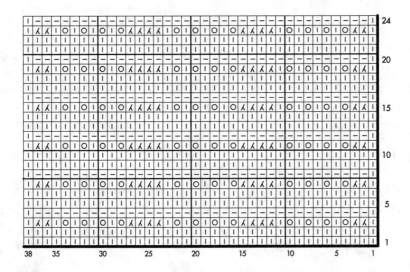

Figure 16. A modified feather and fan pattern.

Materials

2 balls of fingering weight yarn, 40 or 50 grams
1 circular knitting needle, 3.5 mm or U.S. size 4
3 Stitch holders

1 tapestry needle

1 yard 1/4 inch wide ribbon to match the yarn

Instructions

Gauge: 7 stitches = 1 inch. To save time, remember to check the gauge.

Back

Cast on 74 stitches. First, work 3 rows of garter stitch (knitting every row). Begin the pattern with row 1, right side.

Row 1: *Knit*

Row 2: *Purl*

Row 3: (right side) *k1, *[k2 tog] 2 X, [yo, k1] 4 X, [k2 tog] 2 X; repeat from * 5 times, k1*

Row 4: *Knit*

Repeat rows 1 to 4 until the piece measures 6 inches, ending after working row 4. Place the stitches on a stitch holder.

Left Front

Cast on 40 stitches. Work 3 rows in garter stitch. Commence pattern, starting with the right side. It helps if you work both the left and right fronts at the same time using two separate balls of yarn.

Row 1: *Knit,* (right side)

Row 2: *k3, purl across row*

Row 3: *k1, *[k2 tog] 2 X, [yo, k1] 4 X, [k2 tog] 2 X; repeat from * 2 X, k3*

Row 4: *Knit*

Repeat rows 1 to 4 until the piece is the same length as the back and has the same number of pattern repeats, ending after row 4. Place the stitches on a stitch holder.

Right Front

Cast on 40 stitches. Work 3 rows of garter stitch.

    Row 1: *Knit* (right side)

    Row 2: *Purl across row until 3 stitches remain, k3*

    Row 3: *k3, *[k2 tog] 2 X, [yo, k1] 4 X, [k2 tog] 2 X; repeat from * 2 X, k1*

    Row 4: *Knit*

    Repeat rows 1 to 4 until the piece is the same length as the back. Place the stitches on a stitch holder.

Sleeves (make 2)

Cast on 38 stitches. Work 3 rows of garter stitch. To be sure that they turn out the same length, it helps to work both sleeves at the same time.

    Row 1: *Knit* (right side)

    Row 2: *Purl*

    Row 3: *k1, [k2 tog] 2 X, [yo, k1] 4 X, [k2 tog] 2 X; repeat from * 2 X, k1*

    Row 4: *Knit*

    Repeat rows 1 to 4 until the sleeves measure 5 inches, ending after row 4.

Yoke

Row 1: *With the right side facing, starting with the 40 stitches of the right front, k3, *[k2 tog, k2] repeat from * across row until 1 stitch remains, (31 stitches remain). Next, pick up the right sleeve, right side facing, k1, *[k2 tog, k2], repeat from * until 1 stitch remains, k1, (29 sleeve stitches). With right side facing, take stitches from the back, k1, *[k2 tog, k2], repeat from * across row until 1 stitch remains, k1, (56 back stitches). Take left sleeve, right side facing, k1, *[k2 tog, k2], repeat from * until 1 stitch remains, (29 sleeve stitches), and lastly, take* *stitches from left front, right side facing, k1, *[k2 tog, k2], repeat from * across row until 3 stitches remain, k3. 176 stitches on the needle.*

Rows 2 through 8: *Knit*

Row 9: *k4, *[k2, k2 tog], repeat from * across row until 4 stitches remain, k4. 134 stitches on the needle.*

Rows 10 through 16: *Knit*

Row 17: *k3, *[k2 tog, k2], repeat from * across row until 3 stitches remain, k3. 102 stitches on the needle.*

Row 18 through row 24: *Knit*

Row 25: *k3, *[k2, k2 tog], repeat from * across row until 3 stitches remain, k3. 78 stitches on the needle.*

Row 26 through 32: *Knit*

Row 33: *Eyelet row: k2, *[yo, k2 tog] repeat from * until 2 stitches remain, yo, k2*

Rows 34 and 35: *Knit*

1. Bind off using the knit stitch.
2. Sew side seams and side sleeve seams.
3. Starting with the right side, thread 1/4-inch ribbon through the eyelet holes at neckline.

Use a ribbon tie neckline instead of buttons because babies put everything into their mouths, thus ribbons are much safer.

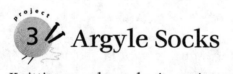

3 Argyle Socks

Knitting argyle socks is an intermediate-level project in which you'll learn the intarsia technique. Sock knitting's popularity can be attributed to the many patterns, colors, and textures of yarn available. Intarsia knitting is a multiple-color technique in which you work blocks of color using separate balls or bobbins of yarn. You don't carry the yarn across the back between the color changes. Used primarily with a stockinette stitch, intarsia knitting is easier with charts rather than row-by-row instructions.

Materials

Size medium needles: If you want a larger size, change to size 2 knitting needles.

Fingering weight yarn 40 or 50 gram balls: Use a yarn with nylon such as Skacel's Schoeller-Esslinger Fortissima, 75% virgin wool and 25% nylon. Nylon gives strength to yarn, which helps prevent holes at points of wear.

Main color (the most predominant color in the sock): 2 skeins

Color A: 60 yards (on the chart in figure 18, this is the color shown in the bottom center of the chart, alone for the top of the foot, and on the sides and in the middle of the chart)

Color B: 45 yards

Color C: 30 yards (these are the diamond cross colors)

1 pair of straight or circular knitting needles, size 1

1 pair of double-pointed knitting needles, size 1

10 bobbins: You will need to wind 2 bobbins each of Main Color, Color A, and Color B, and 4 bobbins of Color C (see the Knitting Tools section on page 30)

1 tapestry needle

2 small stitch holders

1 magnetic board to hold the chart (optional)

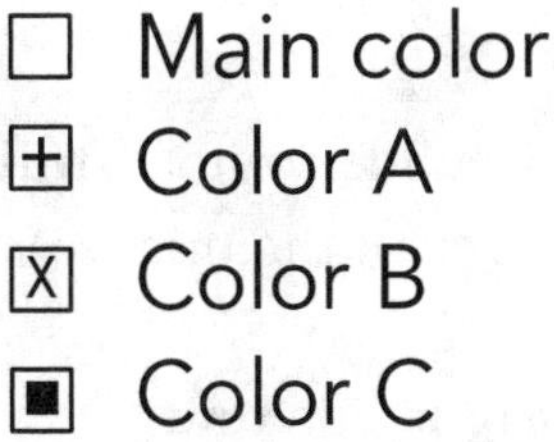

☐ Main color
⊞ Color A
☒ Color B
◼ Color C

Figure 17. Argyle sock symbols.

Instructions

Gauge: 9 stitches = 1 inch

Cuff

Using straight or circular knitting needles, cast on 75 stitches. Work the ribbing for 2 1/2 inches, evenly increasing 5 stitches across the last row of rib (you will have 80 stitches on the needle).

> **Row 1:** (wrong side) *p1, *k1, p1; repeat from * across row*
> **Row 2:** (right side) *k1, *p1, k1; repeat from * across row*

Leg

Start pattern with a side row by following the chart in figure 18.

1. Follow the chart until you make 2 complete diamond patterns, ending after working a purl (wrong side) row.
2. Slip the first 20 stitches onto a stitch holder and work the next 40 stitches by following the chart (the smaller area). Then place the last 20 stitches on another stitch holder.
3. Work one more complete diamond on the center 40 stitches, ending with a purl row.
4. Cut the yarn. You may leave these stitches on the needle or place the stitches on an extra stitch holder.

Heel

1. Place the 20 stitches from each stitch holder onto a straight needle for the heel (with the back edges in the middle). You will have 40 stitches on the needle.
2. Attach yarn to the right edge of the right side row.

> **Row 1:** **sl 1 (as if to purl), k1; repeat from * across row*
> **Row 2:** *sl 1 (as if to purl), purl across remainder of row*

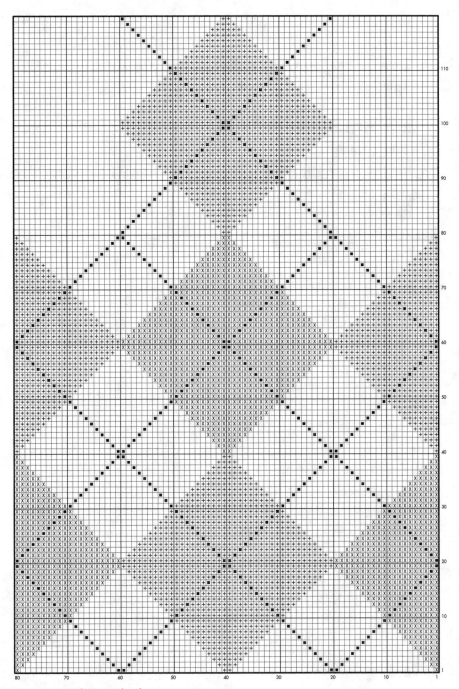

Figure 18. The argyle chart.

Repeat rows 1 and 2 until the heel is 2 1/2 inches, ending after working row 1.

Turn the heel, working straight in short rows using two needles.

Row 1: (wrong side) *sl 1 (as if to purl), p22, p2 tog, p1, turn work without finishing row, leaving 14 stitches on the needle*

Row 2: (right side) *sl 1 (as if to knit), k7, ssk, k1, turn (14 stitches left on the needle)*

Row 3: *sl 1 (as if to purl), p8, p2 tog, p1, turn (12 stitches left on the needle)*

Row 4: *sl 1 (as if to knit), k9, ssk, k1, turn (12 stitches left on the needle)*

Continue adding one more stitch in the center of the row each time, until all the stitches have been worked and there are 24 stitches on the needle. (The stitches worked together in either *p2 tog* or *ssk* involve one stitch before the "hole" and one stitch after the "hole".) End after working a knit row. Cut the yarn.

Heel Gusset

The gusset is the triangular shaped insert between the heel and foot.

1. Using a double-pointed needle and main color, starting at the right edge of the heel, pick up and knit 22 stitches along the heel flap.
2. Knit 12 stitches from the heel and change to another double-pointed needle.
3. Knit the other 12 stitches from the heel and pick up 22 more stitches along the left heel flap. You will have 34 stitches on each needle.

Row 1: (wrong side) *Using a third double-pointed needle, purl across the stitches on the first needle; take the now free needle and purl across the other needle*

Row 2: (right side) *k1, ssk, knit across the remainder of the stitches on the first needle, change needles and work across until there are three stitches left on the second needle, k2 tog, k1*

Continue rows 1 and 2, decreasing on each right side row as in row 2, until there are 20 stitches left on each needle. Then work until the gusset is the same length as the argyle instep, ending after working a right side row.

Foot

Begin working with 4 needles in the round (see figure 19).

1. Using another double-pointed needle, knit across the 40 argyle instep stitches, making sure to pull yarn tightly across the open space.
2. Knit across each needle of heel stitches with 20 stitches on each needle. You will have a total of 80 stitches on the 3 needles. Use the spare needle each time to knit. You will have 40 stitches on the instep needle, and 20 on each of the other 2 needles.
3. Work in rounds until the foot measures 2 inches less than the desired length for the sock (the 2-inch space will let you know when to decrease for the toe).

Toe

Decrease for the toe.

Round 1: *On needle 1: (the needle with the 20 stitches before the argyle instep) knit until 3 stitches remain, k2 tog, k1; on needle 2: (needle with 40 stitches) k1, ssk, knit across until 3 stitches remain, k2 tog, k1; on needle 3: k1, ssk, knit across the rest of the stitches on the needle*

Round 2: *Knit around*

Repeat round 1 and 2 until there are 6 stitches on needles 1 and 3 and 12 stitches on needle 2. Combine stitches from needles 1 and 3 by knitting across. Your stitches will now be on 2 needles with 12 on each needle.

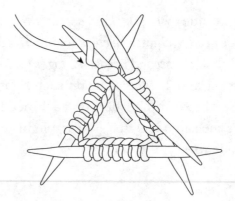

Figure 19. Knitting on four needles.

Finishing

Complete the toe with Kitchener stitch (see chapter 4, page 89).

1. Using matching yarn, starting with the rib at the top of the sock, sew the back seam working in only half a stitch on each side.
2. Sew the side (instep) seams, also working in only one half stitch on each side.

Hints for Working Intarsia

1. Always keep the bobbins on the wrong side of the work.
2. Unwind just enough yarn from the bobbin for the row you are working on. Too much yarn will tangle and you will have a mess.
3. Use as many bobbins as necessary to avoid carrying your yarn across the work.
4. Always pick up new yarn from under the yarn just used to avoid holes.

5. Read the chart from right to left on the right side (knit) rows and from left to right on the wrong side (purl) rows. Start at the bottom right corner of the chart for row 1.

6. Only work into the same color (that is blue into blue, and so on). Be sure to leave at least 6 inches of "tail" yarn on the sides to use for seams.

Fisherman's Hat

This adult hat, knitted with cable stitches and twisted ribbing, will provide some good experience with working cables and introduces you to *Aran* knitting. Aran knitting, otherwise known as "fisherman knitting," has an infinite combination of patterns composed of knit and purl stitches, plus an endless variety of cable stitches.

Materials

2 (100) gram balls of fisherman yarn with a gauge of 4 or 4.5
    stitches per inch
Knitting needles, straight or circular sizes U.S. 8 (5 millimeters)
    and U.S. 10 (6 millimeters)
1 cable needle
1 tapestry needle

Instructions

Gauge: 4.5 stitches = 1 inch, in pattern with larger size needles
    (this gauge is tighter/smaller due to the cable pattern)

Using the smaller knitting needles (U.S. 8; 5 millimeters), cast on 80 stitches. Because this hat has an upturned brim, the cast-on edge, which is really the right side, will be the wrong side. Work in twisted rib pattern (*k1 tbl, p1, repeat from * across each row for 5 to 5 1/2 inches, evenly increasing 13 stitches on the last row (wrong side row). You will now have 93 stitches on the needle. Change to the larger needles and begin the cable pattern.

Pattern Stitches

■ **Twisted rib:** This twisted rib is a common rib in fisherman (Aran) knit patterns.

Row 1 and every row: *knit 1 tbl, p1, repeat from * across row

■ **Cable and rice pattern**

Rice is the part that is not cable (the *p* on odd rows and the *k1, p1* on even rows).

Row 1: p4, *k8, p5; repeat from * 5 more times, k8, p3

Row 2: k1, p1, k1, *p8, k1, [p1, k1] 2 times; repeat from * 5 more times, p8, [k1, p1] 2 times

Row 3: p4, *C4B, C4F, p5; repeat from * 5 more times, C4B, C4F, p3

Row 4: Repeat row 2

Row 5: Repeat row 1

Row 6: Repeat row 2

Row 7: p4, *C4F, C4B, p5; repeat from * 5 more times, C4F, C4B, p3

Row 8: Repeat row 2

Repeat these 8 rows 3 more times.

■ **Decrease rows:**

Row 1: *k2tog, k2 across row, ending k3 instead of k2, 70 stitches

Row 2 and all even rows: Purl

Row 3: *k8, k2 tog, repeat from *across row, 63 stitches

Row 5: *k7, k2 tog, repeat from * across row, 56 stitches

Row 7: *k6, k2 tog, repeat from * across row, 49 stitches

Row 9: *k5, k2 tog, repeat from * across row, 42 stitches

Row 11: *k4, k2 tog, repeat from * across row, 35 stitches*
Row 13: *k3, k2 tog, repeat from * across row, 28 stitches*
Row 15: *k2, k2 tog, repeat from * across row, 21 stitches*
Row 17: *k1, k2 tog, repeat from * across row, 14 stitches*

Fourteen stitches will remain on the needle. Cut the yarn, leaving an 8-inch tail. Thread the end of the yarn into the tapestry needle, pull it through the stitches on the needle. Fasten off the yarn.

Thread the cast-on tail into the tapestry needle and sew up beginning at the bottom edge. Remember that the wrong side will be the right side when the brim is turned up. Start sewing with the wrong (under) side of the hat as the right side (the side on display when the hat is finished). After you have sewn 4 inches, sew with the outside edge as the real right side.

First Knitting Memories

These "beginner" stories, recently shared by several online knitters, will put a smile on your face.

■ Vanessa VanOrman learned the value of dye lots early: "My first project was a blue scarf," she says. "I knitted the first half with a friend's yarn one weekend, but when I bought some additional yarn (same brand and color) to finish the other half, it was from a different dye lot that didn't match. I still have the scarf and wear it every once in a while."

■ "My first project was a scarf that was supposed to be a gift for Dad," remembers Sue Ordiway-Perri. "Mom got me started and I knitted away. It looked great, with no dropped stitches or anything. The only problem was, I knitted it so tightly that it was only about 4 inches wide! I finished it early, and it became a wonderful coaster for Dad's coffee at the office."

■ Annmarie Freeman-Signey had a similar experience with the scarf she knitted for her father: "My mother taught me to knit when I was about nine," she says. "I knitted a simple, rectangular scarf for my dad, but because I only had one small ball of yarn, the scarf wouldn't go around his neck!"

■ "I made a pretty mohair-like sweater with cables," says Deborah Meyer. Unfortunately, Deborah learned a valuable lesson about measuring and gauge, because when she tried the sweater on, she couldn't get it over her head.

■ Lisa G. Bennett learned to knit when she was child, but her interest in knitting didn't peak until she met Joan, her friend's mother: "The day I met Joan she was knitting a space-dyed 100% silk sweater for her daughter," remembers Lisa. "I had never seen any handmade thing so beautiful in my life. I immediately asked Joan if she'd teach me how to knit, and visited her once a week until she proclaimed me an expert knitter. I was so proud!"

■ "My first project (after many warnings from Mom to start with something smaller) was a long summer dress out of *Vogue* magazine," says Kimberley Derowin. "I finished it, tried it on, and it looked awful! The dress sagged in the front, like it was a maternity dress, because my knitting tension got tighter the longer I knitted. Mom asked for the dress years later, took the yarn, and made many slippers with it!"

■ "My Grandma knew how to quilt, but not how to knit," recalls Shirley Bailey Bowers. "We were going to knit a scarf with gold yarn, but none of us were sure what we were doing. The scarf just kept getting longer and longer until we needed to cast it off. No one knew how, so Mom sewed it off with a needle and thread. I don't know what happened to it, but it was so very, very awful. Maybe they took it out into the backyard and gave it a decent burial."

Your Crafts Vision

▼▼

NOW THAT YOU KNOW HOW to knit, will you become a true knitaholic? If you're anxiously looking forward to your next project, or already thinking about selling some of your knitting, then you may be hooked. This chapter will help you decide your next step.

Business Considerations

A knitting business can create many new avenues of opportunity for you, including teaching, writing, designing, and the creation of one-of-a-kind garments. What are you most interested in? You may not know yet, but once you really start exploring your options, you'll find some very exciting possibilities. Take your time with your research, and you'll soon discover the direction you want to take.

Owning a business is a major commitment, and if you're not honest with yourself from the very beginning, your chances of success may be slim. On the other hand, if you set some reasonable goals and expectations, you should have a great chance for success.

Time is one of the key considerations in business planning. Lord Chesterfield, an eighteenth-century British writer once said, "I

▼▼

You Know You're a Knitaholic When* . . .

- You own three cedar chests and five dressers, and you still don't have room for all your sweaters.
- You go on vacation and plan ahead to learn what yarn stores are in the area.
- Your mantra has become "only one more row."
- The dog looks at you with pitiful eyes, begging you to take her for a walk.
- You've got six projects going at once.
- You're planning your next six projects.
- You've seen every movie at the video store as you work on those six projects.
- You own more yarn than you can possibly knit in a lifetime.
- You're seriously considering building an addition to the house to store all that yarn.
- Your eyes are so blurry you need an 8x magnifier to see the pattern, but you keep going anyway.
- Your friends just shake their heads as you arrive for lunch in yet another new creation.

*©1999 Barbara Breiter. Reprinted with permission from Barbara Breiter, a guide at About.com, Inc. To follow the series online, go to www.knitting.about.com

▲▲

recommend to you to take care of the minutes; for the hours will take care of themselves." Are you willing to commit your "minutes" to a new business? How well do you manage your time? Are you already overly committed? How many hours a day can you reasonably spend on knitting? You'll need to honestly answer these questions, and others, in order to get a grasp of how much discretionary time you have.

But you can still start your business, even with a limited amount of time. Take it slowly; devote just a few evenings per week to knitting. Many successful knitters begin part time to get their feet wet and build a yarn inventory.

Finances affect everything you do—especially your business investments. Before you start a business, you'll need to consider the almighty dollar. Fortunately, knitting doesn't require a large cash investment. Your main start-up expenses will be the cost of your yarn, plus any advertising you may choose to do.

Plan Your Work and Work Your Plan

The following questionnaire contains some issues you must consider before starting a knitting business. You'll soon realize that knitting provides many ways to earn a living. Once you figure out your avenue, start small to measure how the public responds to your items and ideas. Above all, pay close attention to what's selling (see chapter 8 for some examples).

How I Would Like to Make Money with Knitting

- ☐ Sell finished, handknitted items
- ☐ Design for yarn companies or magazines
- ☐ Teach classes in my own community
- ☐ Sell knitting supplies by mail
- ☐ Knit for designers or other knitters
- ☐ Sell on the Internet
- ☐ Representative for yarn company
- ☐ Yarn/knitting demonstrator
- ☐ Fashion show coordinator
- ☐ Yarn shop
  - ☐ Owner
  - ☐ Employee
- ☐ Other _____

Keeping It in the Family

Barry Klein, president of the National Needlework Association, which is the premier needlework association in the U.S., also owns Trendsetter Yarns. Beginning at the age of nine, Barry went to his mother's retail needlework and knitting store daily where he slowly learned to needlepoint and knit from the ladies who worked in the store. "Working at Mom's shop kept me from getting into trouble and fighting with my sister," says Barry.

In 1978, his mother started a knitting company called Fantacia Yarns, which was one of the first novelty yarn companies to bring fantasy fibers and fun yarns into the U.S. market. Although Barry was still in high school at the time, he began designing sweaters and publishing pattern books for his mother's company. In order to go to private college, he became a sales representative for Fantacia and enrolled in business and advertising classes at the same time.

Barry started his company, Trendsetter, in 1988 during a trip to Italy and France with his mother so they could work with factories on designing fun and exciting yarns with lots of textures. These types of yarn allow the knitter to do basic knitting, but the textures make an incredible difference in the finished garment. Trendsetter started with a small warehouse in Van Nuys, California, and now has around 4000 square feet of floor space. They currently promote over 40 exclusive Trendsetter Yarns, and distribute Ornaghi Filati, which has 100 percent classic fibers available in large color ranges that

How Much Income Would I Like?

- ☐ Just enough to cover my expenses
- ☐ Part-time income
- ☐ Enough money to live on

How Much Time Can I Dedicate to Knitting?

What Time of Day Can I Work?

- ☐ Daytime
- ☐ Evenings
- ☐ Weekends

work with the novelty fibers in the Trendsetter collection. In addition, they sell over 25,000 different varieties of handmade, natural fiber buttons from over 25 different countries.

Barry loves being a man in what is generally considered a woman's industry: "I've made some incredible friends with the many store owners that I work with, and I've also been teaching classes and doing trunk shows all over the United States," says Barry. This allows him to develop relationships with the very customers that buy his product.

"What makes Trendsetter different than other companies is that we have full control over our product line," explains Barry. "It takes about two years for one of our products to go from inception to distribution, and we have our hands on it the entire way."

As the head of The National Needlework Association (TNNA), Barry has made it his personal mission to bring more store owners together at their semi-annual shows. "It's important that they know about all of the different items available to them before they do their buying," he says. "This creates stronger stores, stronger companies, and a stronger industry."

The National Needlework Association (TNNA) also exposes knitting to people who may not already knit through articles in papers, consumer shows around the U.S., and by putting knitting and knitwear into the movies and television. "It's a really exciting time, because we are seeing lots of youth coming into their work, and this means that there is a long future ahead of us," says Barry.

MY PROJECTED SCHEDULE:

Day of Week	Time	Hours

What Will I Create and Sell?

Clothing

☐ High fashion

☐ Traditional

For Whom?

- ☐ Babies
- ☐ Children
- ☐ Women
- ☐ Men
- ☐ Dolls

Clothing/Accessories

- ☐ Sweaters and jackets
- ☐ Dresses or skirts
- ☐ Mittens and gloves
- ☐ Socks
- ☐ Hats
- ☐ Scarves
- ☐ Shawls
- ☐ Pocketbooks
- ☐ Other _____

Household Items

- ☐ Afghans/blankets
- ☐ Pillows
- ☐ Doilies
- ☐ Tablecloths
- ☐ Small accessories
- ☐ Kitchen items
- ☐ Other _____

Other

- ☐ Toys
- ☐ Stuffed animals

How Am I Going to Sell These Items?

☐ Craft shows
☐ Mall shows
☐ Consignment shops
☐ Craft co-ops
☐ Special orders
☐ Craft malls
☐ Holiday or seasonal boutiques
☐ Gift shops
☐ Bazaars
☐ Home shows
☐ Tourist attractions and shops
☐ Art galleries
☐ Direct sales
☐ Yard/Garage sales
☐ Flea markets
☐ Internet
☐ Mail order
☐ Word of mouth
☐ Classified ads

Teaching and Writing

Where Might I Teach?

☐ At home
☐ Yarn shop
☐ Community college
☐ Adult education
☐ Community recreation department
☐ Senior citizen center

☐ Retirement community
☐ Girl Scouts or youth group
☐ Knitting guild
☐ Knitting workshops at conferences
☐ At trade shows
☐ Other _____

Where Can I Submit My Writing?

☐ Magazines
☐ Newsletters
☐ Knitting books

Part Two

For Profit

Profiting from Your Talent

▼▼

WHEN I STARTED KNITTING as a hobby, I never imagined where it could lead, or that it would be so profitable and rewarding. I'm no different from you, and the fact that I've achieved success in my knitting means that you can also.

Because there are so many career choices in knitting, you may feel a little overwhelmed and confused about where to start. Don't worry, the most important step is to get started somewhere.

As the questionnaire in chapter 6 points out, you have four essential objectives for a knitting business: selling, teaching, designing, and writing. Let's explore these and other important business issues in this chapter.

Selling Your Handknitted Items

Selling your knitted items can be a lot of fun if you approach it realistically. The items you sell and the market you target, relate directly to how much you can charge for your time. An elegant, knitted sweater will take many hours to complete, but a lacy face cloth won't. Depending on the market, you will probably earn more for the face

JANET'S STORY

Janet Johnson Stephens takes advantage of several opportunities available to knitters. She teaches adult education courses and in yarn shops; gives private lessons; works knitting conventions; and volunteers at the Craft Yarn Council of America. She also writes articles about knitting, and has published several designs in various magazines. For several years she wrote the column "Janet's Knits" for *Knitting World*. Janet also  participates in direct sales and was the first female sales representative for the yarn company Phildar. In addition, she once did custom knitting and finishing work and acted as a consultant to yarn shop owners.

After her children grew up and moved out, Janet returned to college and received a degree in textiles and communications. She also took some graduate courses in art history and historic needlework. At present, her particular field of interest is historic needlework.

cloth. Exceptions to this rule are niche markets in which specialty items are greatly coveted and command a much higher price.

Understanding Copyrights

As you prepare to sell your knitting, pay attention to copyright laws governing the sale of pattern reproductions. It's one thing for someone to approach you with a pattern and ask you to knit it for them; but knitting a copyrighted pattern stitch-by-stitch for resale purposes is different. If you're not careful, you can run into problems related to the legal rights of designers and publishers.

You may get away with selling just one designer sweater or afghan from a copyrighted pattern at local show, but watch out! If the pattern bears a copyright notice restricting it to personal use then don't risk selling it. Let patterns give you ideas, but don't copy them—personalize them (see sidebar, Changing Things, on page 228). They can guide you on the number of stitches to cast on, but feel free to change the cable, or use a different design stitch, or change the yarn color, or modify the sleeves or collar. (See chapter 11 for detailed information about copyrights and how you can avoid copyright problems when you start to sell your work.)

Sharing Your Knowledge Through Teaching

Knitters must encourage adults and children to knit so our industry can continue to thrive.

In the introduction, you read how elementary school children learned to knit during World War II. Unfortunately, children today are not taught knitting or other needlecrafts in U.S. schools unless they're lucky enough to have a volunteer demonstrate knitting for them. An acquaintance once asked me to teach knitting to a high school home economics class, which I found gratifying. I wish more teachers would work with volunteers so our young people could learn to knit. The Craft Yarn Council of America currently instructs individuals in the basics of teaching knitting. Take advantage of this wonderful opportunity (see Resources for their address).

You will be ready to teach others when you feel comfortable with knitting and understand the basics. Teaching can provide a steady source of income for you, but you need some teaching experience first. Acquire this experience through volunteer work. Check with your church, senior center, YMCA, or other informational organizations. Most of these welcome volunteer knitting teachers.

After you've done enough volunteer work, you'll have the necessary qualifications for paid teaching jobs. Frequently teaching improves your teaching skills, enabling you to demand more money for your time. Be careful not to forsake your own study while teaching. You don't want to be left behind when a new technique becomes popular. Always look for classes or tutorials that can improve your knitting skills. Given enough time, you'll be teaching these same techniques to your own students.

Once you plan to teach knitting, start by teaching a small group of friends in the comfort of your own home. Teaching your friends will help develop your self-confidence and your teaching technique. When you have a little experience under your belt, you can approach local yarn shops, the adult education department of the local Board of Education, community colleges, senior centers, and so on.

After you've gained some teaching experience in your local community, you may be asked to travel to a nearby community to teach. If possible, take advantage of these opportunities because you can add each experience to your résumé and eventually land that "big" teaching opportunity.

As you gain recognition in the knitting industry, you will be able to command more money. Take advantage of all opportunities that come your way.

Preparations for Teaching

A little class preparation will go a long way toward making you a successful teacher. Review and practice areas that trouble you. Keep up to date on the latest yarns, colors, and fashion trends.

Teachers must know how to communicate effectively with others. Talk slowly and pronounce your words clearly. When talking to the class, try to use the words "we" and "you" instead of "I." Move around the room as you teach; don't stand in one place. Avoid making excessive movements, talking too much with your hands, or rocking back and forth.

Be professional and avoid gossiping with students. Many students, especially women, come to class for companionship as much as they do to learn. Talk with them, but never talk about your other students. Save your personal problems for somewhere else; you're there to teach, not to complain.

Teaching requires a receptiveness to different personalities. Treat each student as an individual and avoid picking favorites. Be patient, cheerful, enthusiastic, and approachable. Make sure the students feel free to ask questions, and repeat directions more than once. What might seem easy to you is often new and difficult for students.

A sense of humor helps. Each week, bring in something new to pique their interest, even if it's just a knitting article that you want to share with them.

Remember that teaching a knitting class differs from teaching school subjects. Knitting students enroll because they're self-motivated, and may be looking for a way to get out of the house and have a good time. Always encourage your students. Show optimism, even if there are a lot of mistakes.

A successful teacher listens and makes each student feel important. Motivate and compliment each student in the best way possible. With classes of mixed knitting abilities, I mix up the students whenever possible. All beginners should know how to cast on and knit before they leave the first class. If necessary, explain to the more advanced knitters that they may not get as much attention during the first session, but that you'll make it up to them in future classes. The more advanced students often help the beginners.

Handy Hint

Develop the self-confidence of your students by getting to know them. Have an introductory session in the first class and allow each student to give his or her name and describe a previous knitting experience.

Writing Lesson Plans and Handouts

Handouts help students because they give them something to refer to at home when they have a problem. Give clear, concise instructions in your handouts and make sure you hand out copies of decent quality. Following is an example of what a lesson plan should look like.

Home Economics 300: Knitting 1

- Course Description: As a beginner, learn basic stitches and procedures necessary to make a sweater or an afghan.
- Course Length: 10 two-hour sessions (20 hours)
- Supplies Required of Students

1. For first class session

   a. One pair of 10- or 12-inch, size 8 knitting needles

   b. For project: materials specified in pattern

- Materials Fee: None
- Textbook: None
- Objectives:
  1. Locate and select appropriate knitting supplies and materials.
  2. Perform basic knitting skills.
  3. Knit, block, join and finish easy-to-knit items.
  4. Utilize art principles in design and construction of projects.
  5. Compare cost and construction processes of ready-made with student-made items of similar design.
  6. Interpret the information (terms) printed on yarn wrappers, hang tags, and care labels.
  7. Use appropriate laundering techniques and storage care for items made.

8. Incorporate management skills during construction of projects.

Course Outline

Week 1: Introduction

- Overview
- Needle sizes and types
- Yarn types and uses
- Supplies
- Notions used in knitting
- How and where to obtain yarn and knitting supplies
- How to cast on
- How to knit

Week 2: Review cast-on stitching

- Garter stitch
- Purl

Week 3: Review

- Ribbing

Week 4: Pattern reading

- Basic abbreviations
- Symbols
- Knitting terminology

Week 5: Increase and decrease

Week 6: Gauge

- Getting garments to fit

Week 7: Stitches

- Cables
- Seed stitch

- Yarn overs
- Slip stitches

Week 8: Identify and correct errors and dropped stitches

Week 9: Finishing
- Shaping necklines and picking up stitches
- Buttonholes

Week 10: More finishing and . . .
- Seams
- Laundering
- Storage

Designing

Designers gain inspiration from the world around them. They can walk through a store, flip through a magazine, or visit a museum and get struck by a great design concept. Once inspired, their ideas become reality with the help of some great computer design software, such as Stitch Painter and Garment Styler from Cochenille, and the Sweater Wizard from Patternworks. (See Resources for their addresses.)

Can you imagine how exciting it must be to publish your own original knitting pattern? Knitting magazines and yarn companies regularly seek new designs and designers. First, you should write to some of the knitting magazines and yarn companies and request information about design submittal policies. Persistence will pay off eventually, and once you publish a design, your confidence will surely grow.

Selling Your Knitting Patterns and Designs

One of the best ways to make some money in knitting is to sell some of your designs to yarn companies or knitting magazines. Before submitting your designs for consideration, you should write to the editors and company representatives for a copy of their guidelines. Your design *must* be original.

Writing for Profit

If you like to write, you may want to consider writing about knitting or some aspect of knitting. Perhaps you have researched ethnic knitting and have mastered a special technique, or found a unique way to market your knitting. Knitting publications, newsletters, and Web sites are interested in articles with an ethnic angle. There will always be new and exciting things to write about in the world of knitting.

Review each publication that you'd like to write for so you can see the style and type of articles that they print. Don't forget to write for their guidelines before submitting anything.

If you're really serious about writing, I recommend starting a knitting journal. When you discover new approaches or shortcuts that improve your knitting, write them down. When you find a good knitting book or Web site, make a note of it. Who knows, you may write a knitting book one day, in which case you'll find that your journal is an invaluable source of information.

Buying Supplies Wholesale

Knitters have a real advantage when it comes to the cost of their material. Often, once a knitter has the basic needles and other necessary supplies, the only real project cost is yarn. And when you purchase your yarn wholesale, you're saving even more.

In fact, buying your supplies wholesale can increase your bottom-line profits because you'll cut your costs by as much as 50 percent. Quite a few companies sell supplies wholesale to crafters, and *Craft Supply Magazine* (see Resources) is a good source

The Multitalented Knitter

When designer Charlene Anderson-Shea was knitting a nd weaving for production she had decent luck selling her products, but *only* through high-end galleries or exclusive women's clothing shops. Expensive knitting does not normally sell well at "crafty" type shops or at your average weekend craft fair. "My best luck was selling at a high-end gallery that featured my work in several one-woman shows. They made a big production of it all, with a runway in the middle of the mall, professional models, full-color post-card invitations, etc." The knitting that Charlene sold was considered wearable art.

"When I was selling, I usually sold complete ensembles: a handwoven skirt and jacket with a handknitted sweater, so it all coordinated. I also sold a fair number of shawls." Most of her selling was done in Hawaii when she lived there.

In recent years, Charlene has found her niche in writing articles and designing for magazines. Her articles and/or designs have appeared in *Handwoven, Honolulu Magazine, Interweave Knits, Knitting NOW, Needle Arts, Open Chain, Professional Quilter, The Creative Machine Newsletter, Quilt, Quilter's Newsletter Magazine, Shuttle Spindle and Dyepot, Spin-Off, Stitch* and *Sew Quilt*. She commented that she finds that she can write and design just as well as she sold her products, and she doesn't have to do all the production work.

for finding them. To open a wholesale account you will need a tax resale number, a business checking account, and sometimes, business references (see chapter 11 for more information about tax issues and business checking accounts).

Like most wholesale companies, yarn companies require minimum orders for wholesale purchases. They sell their yarn by the bag only, and the entire bag must be of one color. In the beginning stages of your business, you probably won't need this much yarn, so it's more cost efficient to purchase yarn locally or by mail. You should also check out some of the discount chain stores. I find their prices often comparable to wholesale prices, and you won't be required to buy an entire bag of yarn.

Networking to Advance Your Business

Networking through industry organizations can be very important for your business. Many of my major accomplishments stem from my association with the following organizations. You will find their contact information in Resources.

The Knitting Guild of America

The Knitting Guild of America (TKGA) is an organization for all knitters, from beginners to professionals. They publish a magazine called *Cast On,* and hold one large national convention and several regional seminars every year. Accompanying their conventions and seminars is a wonderful knitting market with all sorts of delightful yarns for sale. TKGA also offers several correspondence courses and a Master Knitting program to help improve your knitting skills. Their Web site contains some great information for knitters plus a fun chat room.

The Professional Knitwear Designers Guild

The Professional Knitwear Designers Guild (PKDG) is an organization for knitwear designers, authors, teachers, and producers. An independent organization dedicated to the business and promotion of knitting, PKDG provides networking and professional accreditation for freelance designers worldwide. Their bimonthly newsletter lists many opportunities in the knitting industry. There are two levels of membership, associate and professional. As an associate, you can request the assignment of a mentor (a PKDG professional member) who will give you advice and assistance as you prepare for the professional level. Until you establish yourself professionally in the field, I suggest that you join as an associate member, after which you must wait at least two years before applying for the professional level.

The Society of Craft Designers

The Society of Craft Designers (SCD) offers an established network of professional craft designers, editors, publishers, and manufacturers who work together to advance their industry. Many successful craft designers belong to this organization. Every year the SCD sponsors an educational seminar with a designer showcase giving designers a chance to "show their stuff" to buyers who attend including editors, publishers, and manufacturers. SCD also publishes a bimonthly newsletter and offers a certification program, referral service, and a registry of craft designers.

The National Craft Association

Another organization for professional crafters, the National Craft Association, has guidelines for just about anything you might need for your craft business including pricing, merchant credit cards, marketing, displaying, advertising, and so on. Their monthly newsletter is full of wonderful tips for crafters.

Craft Business Network, Country Sampler Group

The Craft Business Network is in the process of establishing local chapters to promote the crafting profession. They offer wholesale purchasing and reduced rate subscriptions to business publications. (This organization used to be called the American Professional Crafter's Guild.)

Your Résumé and Portfolio

Serious knitting entrepreneurs must have a concise résumé. Your résumé should include the traditional information as well as the following facts:

- A list of your awards and achievements
- Your knitting experience
- Knitting and professional organizations you belong to
- Anything else relating to knitting or other crafts

You will also need a *portfolio*. This portfolio can start as a notebook and later expand into actual garments or swatches. When I applied for the professional level with PKDG, I compiled a notebook that contained my résumé, knit swatches, photos of my knitting, copies of my newsletter and leaflets, and so on. This type of portfolio goes a long way toward conveying a professional image.

You Can Have a Multifaceted Knitting Career

Sometimes a career will chart its own course, meaning that you will start in one area and quickly expand into others. That is exactly what happened to me.

Working from Home

A home-based business offers many monetary advantages, but it also requires knowledge of some key issues that you must address, including the following:

- Local zoning laws, permits, and registrations
- Taxes and record keeping
- The installation of a business telephone line
- Business checking account and credit card use
- The need for insurance

See chapter 11 for a detailed discussion of these important topics.

When I decided to open a knitting, needlework, and gift shop after many years of knitting for pleasure, I felt that an industry affiliation could enrich my business, so I joined the Knitting Guild of America. The guild was advertising for teachers, so I decided to submit a teaching proposal. To my pleasant surprise, they accepted my proposal, and I became a faculty member at their first annual convention. It didn't take long before I became more involved with the guild. In fact, I was instrumental in forming the Master Knitting program and had the pleasure of teaching at several national conventions and regional seminars. I also wrote over thirty articles for their publication, *Cast On.*

My career grew over the years, and I became involved in many other knitting activities, most of which have been discussed in this book. I self-published leaflets, started my own knitting newsletter, judged knitting and other craft contests, led knitting workshops, sold my work at craft shows, exhibited at trade shows, held fashion shows, taught for other national needlework and craft organizations, and led adult education courses in several states. All of this from a humble beginning as the owner of a small yarn shop! With time and determination, you too can enjoy the same level of success. Don't be afraid to dream.

Pricing Your Knitting

▼▼▼

WHAT DO I CHARGE for my knitting, you ask? Before you can determine the selling price for your knitting, you'll need to spend some time researching your local market and answering the following questions:

- What is the average market price of my product?
- What is my time worth and what do I need to charge to make a profit?
- What are the costs of my materials?
- Is this a one-of-a-kind piece? If so, what is the perceived value?

Checking the Market for Knitted Products

The average market price of a product is the price that similar items sell for in stores. Determine the average market price of your product by visiting craft shows, craft malls, and consignment shops in your area. Look for comparable items and list all of the prices you find. Divide this figure by the number of items in the list to get the

Pricing for Your Target Market

Sally Crandall, who I introduced to you in the Introduction and chapter 1, charges $20 for baby blankets, $15 for Christmas stockings, and $75 for full-size Icelandic afghans. Although she is happy with her pricing, she recently found some Christmas stockings selling in a local shop for $150. This is a good example of price variation. The target market sets the price. That shop undoubtedly has a high-end clientele for whom price isn't an issue.

average selling price of your item. As you gain experience in the market, you will better understand price variations.

The area you live in makes a big difference because some geographic regions have completely different markets. Part of the year, I live in Wilmington, North Carolina, which is a beach tourist area. Tourists are great craft buyers, but the proximity to the Atlantic Ocean incites their interest in beach crafts instead of high-end knitwear. On the other hand, my husband and I also own a condo in the mountains of northwestern North Carolina where the colder weather necessitates woolen handknits for much of the year. The craft buyers in that part of the state are more interested in higher quality crafts.

Figuring the Value of Your Time

Determining the value of one's time perplexes many knitters. Although knitting is labor-intensive, knitters often don't charge the proper amount for their efforts; some aren't concerned with earnings at all. I've heard it many times: "I would spend the time knitting and watching TV anyway, so if I can knit something and sell it later, then I'm happy!"

Many knitters correctly reject this attitude. Tina Sanders knits children's sweaters and vests and has been very successful with her pricing strategy: "I charge between $6 to $8 per hour, per sweater," she explains. "It's always hard to determine price. I take into consideration the cost of the yarn and the time it takes to knit the sweater or vest. For instance, the sweater I'm working on right now is a size three toddler. The cost of my yarn was $6.50 total, and it is going to take me about eight hours of solid knitting to complete. I will charge $55 for this sweater."

Tina only uses cotton yarn and wool to keep her yarn costs down. "I've been very successful in selling my wares, and most women don't mind paying the price if they know it's handknitted and an original design."

Understanding "Perceived Value"

The perceived value of an item varies tremendously from person to person and market to market. Some people place a higher value on an item than others.

Bonita Edwards (see chapter 7) targets a market that places a high value on one-of-a-kind designer items, thus she can charge higher prices for each item. On the other hand, the general public can't afford her clothes. Why? Because wealthier geographic areas contain people with higher costs of living—and higher salaries, thus their perception of what handmade items are worth may also be higher.

Pricing Tips

■ When I price my own handknitted items, I try to gauge the selling price based on different circumstances. For instance,

I raised the price of Christmas stockings from $25 to $35 and more after adding lining and decorations. Each year, I have raised the price with no objection from buyers. This amounts to more than three times the cost of the yarn and other materials. Shoppers who want handknitted stockings are willing to pay a little more.

■ The best general guideline for selling knitting is to multiply the retail cost of your yarn by 2, 2.5, or 3. Doubling or tripling the cost of their yarn thrills most knitters because one item can fund several new projects.

Handy Hint

Relax. Remember that prices aren't set in stone. Feel free to adjust them up or down according to your needs and the needs of your customers.

■ You can always start lower and gradually raise your prices. But just as high prices can affect sales, low prices can hurt business, too. You don't want customers to think that you don't value your work. Surprisingly, most crafters charge too little for their work. I find that items sell faster after I raise the price. In short, charge the highest price that the market will bear.

■ The type of craft show in which you exhibit can affect your pricing, as well. I learned this quickly while exhibiting at a local senior center. The group next to me—a local craft club whose yarn was donated—sold handknitted hats for $2 each. Unfortunately, my hats started at $15. You'll find some special tips on this topic in chapter 9.

Selling Your Knitting

▼▼▼

THERE ARE SEVERAL WAYS to sell your knitting, and each has its own advantages and disadvantages. You should explore each option and decide which one works best for you. This chapter explains how to sell from your own home, on commission, through arts and crafts shows, and in shops and galleries.

So where do you start selling? Begin with friends and family. You've probably spoiled them with knitted gifts already, so they're quite aware of the quality of your work. They can also help advertise your business by handing out your business card and telling their friends. Don't underestimate the power of "word of mouth" sales; it's the best way to launch and build a business.

Additionally, craft shows or bazaars are a good place to sell your knitting. Advice on obtaining craft show space is discussed later in this chapter. I recommend including more of the smaller, less time-consuming items in your inventory. Not only can you offer these for a lower price, but you'll produce larger quantities in less time.

There are many other avenues for selling your handknitted creations, all of which are discussed in detail later in this chapter.

Selling from Your Home

In the early stages of your knitting, I recommend that you make some handknitted samples and hold an open house. Tell your friends that you're excited about your new business, and that you want to introduce your products to them. Send out invitations and encourage everyone to invite their friends. It shouldn't be a structured, stuffy affair; rather, make it simultaneously professional and fun. Serve refreshments and consider giving out your own knitted creations as door prizes (hair scrunchies, face cloths, ornaments, etc.).

One advantage to an open house is that your friends won't feel obligated to buy anything, and you won't feel like you're imposing on them. If your friends aren't interested, they'll conveniently schedule another appointment on the day of the open house; if they can't attend but genuinely seem interested, then maybe they will arrange to see you at another time.

When setting up for a home show, you should arrange your items in appropriate categories, such as sweaters, household items, and so forth. Let your customers know what's available and assist them in placing special orders. If possible, have yarn samples available.

Sally Crandall, whom I introduced you to earlier holds an annual home show in the fall to which she invites everyone on her customer list, plus many other people. She sells enough knitted afghans, Christmas stockings, and other items to keep her very busy.

A successful home show can secure many future orders and goes a long way toward building your reputation as a knitwear designer and manufacturer.

Commissions and Special Orders

I have a customer who has purchased several Christmas stockings from me over the years. In fact, just last year she ordered another one for a brand new grandchild. She originally approached me because she knew that I enjoyed knitting, and she thought I might know someone who sold knitted Christmas stockings. When I told her that I sold my knitting, she gave me three special orders on the spot. In other words, spread the word! Let everyone know that you're a knitter because you'll never know who might be your next customer.

Special orders can present problems, however, if the finished item doesn't fit, or if the customer decides not to accept it. When I knit a large special-order item, I request a nonrefundable deposit from the customer, and I have the customer sign a contract. One time, I knitted a fisherman sweater for a man who later decided it didn't fit (even though I knitted it to the size measurements he gave me). Because he gave me a $25 deposit and signed a purchase order, I was able to keep the deposit and wear the sweater myself.

Selling at Shows

Most new crafters and many seasoned professionals begin to make money at arts and crafts shows. Often, professionals sponsor craft shows or volunteer at them to raise money for different causes. You'll find both indoor and outdoor shows of all varieties. Over 25% of craft shows are sponsored by civic organizations as fundraisers. Professionally sponsored shows usually cost more to rent space, often between $200 and $500.

Expenses

Expenses are a key issue when considering participation in a craft show. You must weigh the costs of the booth and any required travel expenses carefully. Of course, your expenses relate directly to your potential sales. Does the show have the potential to net $400 or

Best-Selling Craft Show Items

Most shoppers at local craft shows and bazaars look for affordable gifts. On occasion, you may find someone willing to spend several hundred dollars for an item, but most shoppers have limited budgets.

You can sell the following knitted items for moderate prices at minimal effort:

- Knitted wash cloths
- Knitted hair scrunchies
- Hats and mitten sets for children
- Hats and scarves for adults
- Decorative face cloths
- Socks
- Decorated slippers (such as snowflakes or holly leaves at Christmas)
- Knitted items for babies and children
- Afghans and throws
- Dolls and doll clothes
- Pot holders

$2,000 in sales? Until you have a really good idea about the buying potential at a particular show, you won't be able to decide if the booth rental price is reasonable or not. There are times when you can combine a craft show with a vacation. I've tried this several times and had a lot of fun, plus I enjoyed the benefits of business deductions as well.

Shows to Avoid

First-time shows are unknown entities, and many knitters stay away from them until they have proven themselves. I've seen several first-time shows fail, but I've also seen several of them succeed.

A lot depends on the sponsor, location, and their promotion plans. Ask a lot of questions and be wary of organizers who beg you to exhibit (they may have many empty booths). Don't aim for the professional shows immediately because they're extremely competitive, and chances are slim that you will be accepted. Many of these shows turn away more crafters than they accept. You need to find the show that's best for you and your product.

Preparation for a Craft Show

You certainly don't want to wait until the last minute to get ready for a show, so start to assemble your merchandise, check that it's clean and ready-to-wear, and make sure you label each item properly with the size, the type of material, and a price tag (read more about labels and their requirements on page 215).

You should set up your booth ahead of time. Practice by setting up all your tables and other booth equipment in your living room, family room, or garage. You'll probably sell some clothing, so you'll want a mirror in your booth. If possible, set aside an area for a dressing room. Jot down the dimensions of the booth space so that you can fit everything in it. Most shows require you to bring your own tables and chairs, but some show promoters will rent tables, chairs, electricity, floor coverings, and other supplies for a nominal fee.

Classier shows usually require floor-length table coverings, so purchase several yards of a solid color fabric for this purpose. Even if they're not required, table coverings make your booth look more professional. They also offer much needed storage space because you can hide all your extra products and other things under them.

Above all, be comfortable and dress cleanly and neatly. Shorts may not always be appropriate unless you're outside on a hot,

Did you know???

The first craft show in the U.S. was the League of New Hampshire Craftsmen's Annual Fair, which is still held annually.

summer day. You will have a long day at the show and you'll want to dress accordingly. Whenever possible, wear some of your own handknits in a show so customers can see your products.

Selling Factors for Craft Shows

Unusual items will catch a buyer's eye. Buyers can almost become blind to products after shopping at a craft show for a while because they've seen so many similar items that nothing jumps out at them unless it's completely unique. If you can add one or two very unusual items to your booth, then you'll have a better chance of drawing more customers.

If you've done your homework about the show, you'll know what to expect from its audience, and you can plan your crafts accordingly. For instance, a show held near a ski resort sells warm and fuzzy items that cater to skiers.

Try to price items within the expected audience's range. Items priced at $30 or less often sell the best at many of the smaller shows. This doesn't mean that you shouldn't create higher-priced items, but it helps to have some lower-priced items, too, because selling a few of them will often pay off your booth fee.

Craft Show Attendance Factors

Many factors affect the attendance at a craft show. Probably the most important is the weather. Perfect weather can hurt a show because people want to stay home and work in their yards, or go to the beach, and so on. The very best day for an indoor show is a dreary day with a little rain. Too much rain will keep people away because no one wants to get soaked.

The economy of a particular area, conflicting events in the area, the number of craft shows held in the area during the past few weeks, and tourism all affect craft show attendance.

The seasons and holidays also contribute to the success or failure of a craft show. More crafts are sold during the three or four months before Christmas than at any other time of the year. Other holidays that may be good for shows are Valentine's Day, Easter, St. Patrick's Day, the Fourth of July, Halloween, and Thanksgiving.

Different Types of Shows

It's important to understand the different types of shows so you'll know which one best suits the products you plan to sell.

Juried Shows

Professionals, civic organizations, church groups, and amateurs sponsor juried arts and crafts shows. A juried show consists of a panel of judges who decide which crafters will be invited to exhibit. The judges base their decisions on photos of products and booth setup submitted by crafters—the more professional in appearance, the better. The show usually has certain standards, such as restrictions on the number of exhibitors allowed with the same type of craft.

Good slides or photos are an important business tool and will make all the difference in the jurying process. If you want to gain entrance into a high-class professional show, then you must have professional slides. You can submit 35mm photos to the smaller shows, but you'll want to make sure that they show the details of your best work. Blurry pictures won't help you secure a booth anywhere. One photo should be of your booth, and the other photos of the crafts you plan to sell.

Did you know???

When applying for a juried show, you'll be asked to list each type of item that you're bringing to the show. Be sure to list everything because some juried show organizers will only allow you to display and sell the items you listed. I've seen show organizers ask crafters to remove items from their booths that weren't listed on their application.

Items to Pack for a Craft Show

You will need the following items to exhibit at a craft show:

- Cash box with change (both coins and bills)
- Display tables
- Extra price tags
- Table coverings
- Trash bags
- Sales books
- Pens
- Pencils
- Paper clips
- Scotch tape

At some point, you may have to present your work to the judges in person. Of course, you'll want to make a good impression, so bring your best items. Make sure that your finishing work is complete and that the item is clean. I've been a judge on several occasions, and you wouldn't believe how many soiled items get submitted!

You're not likely to be accepted into every juried show that you apply for. Just remember that failing to gain entrance into a juried craft show isn't a reflection of your knitting quality. There are many variables involved in the jurying process that probably have nothing to do with your work. You may be rejected simply because the show's promoters don't want any knitting, or they may have already filled their quota of knitters. Don't allow a rejection to discourage you. As you develop greater skill in knitting, your chances for acceptance at a show will increase.

Dishcloth

Lacy Baby Sweater

Argyle Socks

Fisherman's Hat

- Stapler
- Straight and safety pins
- Business cards
- Guest book
- Credit card machine and forms
- Cellular phone
- Paper or plastic merchandise bags
- Hanging rack and hangers for hanging clothing
- Thermos with a drink for yourself
- A lunch, especially if you are going to be alone in your booth

For Christmas shows you may also need the following:

- Christmas tree for hanging ornaments
- Tree skirt

Local Shows

Amateurs, craft clubs, or civic leaders often stage local shows. Many of these shows are juried, but the jury process for a local organization show is usually not as critical as for the professional shows. The products sold at local shows range in price from $1 to $100 with a few higher-priced items. Booth space for local shows usually costs less than space at professional shows, but this is not always the case.

Theme Fairs

Theme fairs are events such as "Renaissance fairs," or pioneer/early American shows, usually organized by historic groups or communities. To consider this type of event, your product will need to fit within the fair's guidelines. If you're a knitter who also hand-spins,

The Jurying Process

I've been a judge on several occasions. Judges must not be partial and should avoid relying on personal opinions. The following are some of the qualities that judges look for:

- Is the knitting technique and finishing of high quality?
- Do the decreases match?
- Are the seams neat and even?
- Are the tails worked in?
- Is this something that the public would be interested in buying?

Questions you may want to ask the jurors:

- How are specific items selected?
- Who is on the jury? Are they knitters?
- When will I be notified of acceptance or rejection?

you may find space in such an event, particularly if it's a historical event. Craftspeople who can demonstrate their art or craft are always in demand.

Mall Shows

The management for shopping malls often produce what are called mall shows. These shows usually limit what you can sell because you cannot compete with the stores in the mall. This ruling usually eliminates knitting because most of what you'll sell is clothing. Many crafters feel that mall shows aren't good for sales because customers come to malls for specific reasons and usually won't stop at booths in the mall corridors. This may not be true, but before doing a mall show, always check with other crafters who have exhibited there.

Other Shows

You can also profit from other types of shows. For instance, you should consider participating in fashion shows in your area, especially if your inventory consists of handknitted garments.

Some crafters like to participate in flea markets, although I usually advise against this. Flea markets are full of used goods for sale, and most of the customers that attend these shows are looking for a bargain—not nice handknitted items. Of course, like anything else, this does not always hold true and might be worth trying.

Indoor Shows

Indoor shows are held in a wide variety of locations such as church social halls, school gymnasiums, coliseums, and large city convention centers. The cost of these shows usually depends on the location and the sponsor. Shows sponsored by amateurs and civic groups are normally less expensive than those sponsored by professionals.

A big advantage to indoor shows is the nighttime security that's usually provided, which makes it safe to leave your products out overnight. Most crafters cover their products with a sheet or some other covering when they leave at night anyway, but always take your cash box, cellular phone, and other valuables home with you.

In some of the better craft shows, it doesn't matter where your booth is located, but in others, the location of your booth can make all the difference. Usually corner spaces and booths near the entrance and exits are good, but these spaces often cost more.

Avoid booths near the food area because food booths can be noisy and have long lines. In addition, you don't want customers stopping by your booth with food, drinks, and dirty hands. Stay away from entertainment areas that can be noisy and distracting, as well.

Tips for Exhibiting Outdoors

Outdoor shows represent one of the oldest ways of selling your products. They are held in parking lots, garages, fields, shopping areas, parks, people's front yards—everywhere. Outdoor shows are usually less costly to enter and the booths offer a lot more space than indoor booths. Most crafters that participate in outdoor shows have some form of covering, such as a tent or canopy. Without a covering, your items can be damaged or destroyed by the sun, wind, or rain. These coverings take up extra room in your vehicle, so you may need a station wagon or van for transportation.

Consider the weather and take appropriate clothing. You'll be miserable if you wear a long-sleeved shirt in 90-degree weather, and you'll freeze if you forget a sweater and the temperature drops.

Security for outdoor shows is another consideration. When a show runs for more than one day, you usually need to remove your products each night, because the chance of your items being stolen or damaged is too great a risk to take. You may be able to leave your tent and tables out overnight, but never leave your merchandise. Some show organizers have a large tent under which you can display your items, but you still need to take your items home each night, which is a great nuisance.

Finding the Best Shows

The best way to find a good show in your area is to ask fellow crafters. If possible, personally visit the craft show during its operation. If you're unable to attend the show, have a friend check it out for you. While you're at the show, talk with other crafters and get their opinions concerning the event. Are they happy with the show and do they plan to come back next year? Are they happy with the show's promoters, advertising, exhibit space, entry process, and the attendance?

While show attendance is an important consideration, it can sometimes be misleading. Some shows may have too many people. I experienced this at a show in which there were so many people that no one could even get close to my booth because the aisles just weren't big enough to handle the crowds.

If you've never participated in a craft show, you should do your first show close to home to avoid the extra expense of long-distance travel and hotel rooms. If you're planning a show out of town, try to go to one in a city where you have friends to stay with.

To find out about shows in your area, check with your chamber of commerce and the local and state arts councils. To find shows in other areas, subscribe to craft show periodicals listed in Resources. Craft show publications have no knitting information about shows such as how to advertise at the show, what the show's theme is, if there is a jury process, what type of products are sold, the show's location, parking facilities, admission fees, commissions, security, entry fees, and so on. *Sunshine Artist* lists thousands of shows nationally and contains reports on shows written by crafters. *The Crafts Report* features some of the bigger shows.

Selling in Shops, Galleries, and Craft Malls

Following is a brief introduction to your selling opportunities in retail shops and stores.

Consignment Shops

Consignment shops are retail shops in which you leave your merchandise to be sold. When the items sell, the shop takes a sales commission of 30 to 50%. Consignment selling is a convenient way for you to display your knitting to the public, because you don't have to worry about show fees or being present to sell your knitting. Consignment has its advantages, especially for new knitters, but before leaving your items, you should visit the shop personally *several times*. Drop in unannounced so you can see the shop "in action." How many customers are there? How does the staff treat the customers? How is the merchandise displayed? Does the shop's theme fit in with your type of knitting? Look into the shop's business practices. How long has it been in existence? Check with other crafters. What is the sales volume? Check their record with the chamber of commerce or the Better Business Bureau, too.

Make sure you sign a consignment agreement that describes the condition of the merchandise you're leaving with them, the

Accepting Credit Cards

It's proven that you will make more sales if you accept credit cards. Setting up a merchant account can be as simple as contacting your local bank. If your local bank can't help you, look for business organizations that offer credit card accounts to crafters (see chapter 11 for details).

A few years ago, I purchased a credit card machine (the kind you see in most stores) for $300, which seemed pricey to me, but it turned out to be quite handy. I never have to worry about making a trip to the bank or mailing in forms, which sometimes take several days to clear before the money is deposited to my account. Even without taking the machine to a craft show, I can still accept charges by calling the 800 number on my cellular phone and getting preauthorization, after which I punch the information into my machine at home.

sales commission you will pay, and other important details. Do they pay their consignors regularly? Also find out how quickly they pay after a sale. Will they notify you when it's time to restock or are you supposed to check that yourself? Essentially, you're leaving knit-wear that you have spent a lot of time knitting, and you should do everything possible to verify that the shop owner or manager takes good care of it (see the Business & Legal section in chapter 11 for more cautionary tips about consignment selling).

Galleries and Boutiques

Galleries and boutiques are another wonderful way to sell knitting, especially if you make *haute couture*. These shops usually prefer to take your items on consignment rather than purchasing them outright. You can find galleries by reading the ads in crafts magazines, such as *The Crafts Report,* or by looking for contests in the back of art magazines. Match the gallery to your style because galleries differ in taste. Poochie Myers, who you met in an earlier chapter, sells many items in galleries and boutiques: Her advice is to have a thick skin, stick with it, be patient, and it will pay off.

Craft Malls and Rent-a-Space Shops

Craft malls and rent-a-space shops are appearing all over the coun-try. *The Crafts Report* and *Sunshine Artist* not only list craft shows all around the U.S., but have ads from large craft malls where you can sell knitting and other crafts. (A few of these are listed in Re-sources.) Some of these malls have been in business for a long time, but others are fairly new. One advantage to a craft mall is that you can display your knitting on a national scale instead of just a local one by mailing your items to the mall.

> ### Did you know???
>
> There seem to be more craft shows, fairs, and galleries in New England than any other place in the U.S. The fact that they've survived for so long there is testament to the quality of these shows.

As always, make sure to check out each shop very carefully before putting your items in them. Most craft malls charge high monthly fees and sales are not always good enough to cover the rent. I personally checked out a large, really nice, two-story shop last summer that impressed me. However, their monthly rent fees were quite exorbitant—the least expensive was a little spot for jewelry for $65 per month! A section with three shelves that was only about 6 feet wide was $150 per month. Rental fees like these require a lot of sales just to make your monthly rent. Few knitters can make enough sales to justify selling this way, unless they offer a variety of craft items for sale.

The Art of Selling

Many of us refrain from calling ourselves "salespeople." Luckily enough, your products will usually do the selling for you because you have personally knitted the item and know everything about it.

Let's summarize some of the points previously discussed. One of the first keys to successful selling in any outlet is to create a desirable product line. Always keep the customer foremost in your mind when designing and planning your knitting. You want to knit some popular, trendy items, so always be aware of what's fashionable and plan your knitting designs accordingly.

When you're selling directly to customers at shows, *always* listen and make them feel important. Make eye contact, and don't look preoccupied with something else. The worst thing you can do at a craft show is read a book or a newspaper, because this signals "Do Not Disturb" to the customer. If you need to keep your hands busy, sit in your booth and knit. In fact, knitting in your booth is a great way to promote your products and customers will love watching you work.

Selling on the Internet

Increasingly, knitters are selling their products and patterns online. The availability of Web site development software, books, and so on, has made it very easy for a small business to have a Web presence. It's affordable, open 24 hours a day, and adds a bit of credibility to your business. A Web site address printed on your business card tells your customers that you're serious about your business. In addition, your customers will appreciate viewing pictures of your current designs and patterns at any time. When the customer sees a product or pattern they're interested in, they can e-mail you or phone you to get more information.

Always be enthusiastic, even if you're feeling exhausted after a very long day because you must maintain your interest level with each and every customer.

If you're selling knitted garments, wear one of your outfits. You are the best model for your knitted clothing, and customers will recognize your pride in yourself and your products if you wear them. No one likes a pushy salesperson, so don't be overly aggressive. You'll want to nurture sales in a pleasant way by encouraging people to touch your knitting. Make sure you have a mirror nearby so they can hold the garment against their face to see if the color compliments them. Be honest when they ask your opinion because you certainly don't want to sell them something they will be unhappy with. You can do it—it's fun!

Marketing Your Knitting

▼▼

RUNNING A SUCCESSFUL KNITTING business requires more than just understanding how to knit. You must also devote some time to business and marketing strategies. If you don't spread the word, how will anyone know that you're in business?

Quite simply, you can't succeed if you're not willing to take risks. Even one new idea, design, or marketing venture can make the difference between success and failure. You can expand your horizons only if you're willing to take advantage of the opportunities surrounding you. Remember that successful marketing is a combination of many good ideas.

This chapter discusses your advertising options and explains how to promote your business through publicity and other promotional efforts.

Your Advertising Options

A customer's first impression of you is the most important, and often times ads *are* the customer's first impression. You'll want to create a positive image with your business cards, brochures, and/or classified advertisements. Wording is very important in all your printed materials, so pay special attention to it. Get the help and advice of a business professional if necessary.

You should consider the following methods when advertising your business:

- Word of mouth
- Business cards
- Brochures
- Letterhead and envelopes
- Press releases
- Feature articles
- Classified advertisements
- Promotional newsletters
- The Internet/World Wide Web sites
- Mailings to customers/prospect lists
- Tags and labels for your products

Word of Mouth

There is nothing better for your business than word-of-mouth publicity. When someone hears about your work and comes to you with an order, it's always a pleasant surprise. You can encourage this type of advertising by knitting in public, wearing what you make, and talking about your knitting to everyone.

Business Cards

You should purchase business cards as soon as you start your knitting business. Be sure to carry them with you and give them to friends, acquaintances, and anyone you meet who could become a potential customer. You never know

Handy Hint

Go to your local library to research how to write advertising text. One book that contains helpful guidelines is *Homemade Money* by Barbara Brabec (Betterway Books, 1997).

when opportunity will present itself, and you don't want to miss a chance for free publicity. I once handed out a business card on the interstate while stuck in a several-mile-long traffic jam!

You can order business cards at your local printer or make your own with some of the computer software programs available.

Brochures

You should vary the size of your brochures. Full-page brochures are flimsy, whereas prospective buyers can just slip smaller brochures into their pockets. I find that small brochures—3¾ inches × 8½ inch size (one third of an 8½ × 11-inch sheet of paper)—work best.

An eye-catching brochure will add to your professional image by showing why your work is different and what the buyer will gain by purchasing your unique item. A brochure or flyer can also advertise any classes you may be teaching.

Letterhead and Envelopes

You can have letterhead and envelopes printed professionally at your local printer or office center, or you can print them yourself with a computer and printer. You can purchase many charming address labels commercially, including some with yarn and needles, or you can design the labels yourself using one of the many computer software applications available.

Press Releases

A press release (also called a news release) is a two-page announcement that you send to publication editors. Editors are always looking for information of interest to their readers, and a press release can be a great way to advertise your business for free. Editors receive a lot of junk mail, so to get their attention you'll want your information to be timely and exciting.

BONITA'S STORY

Bonita Edwards, a professional and very successful knitter, targets a niche market with her clothes line. Bonita learned to knit as a young girl, and it wasn't long before she began experimenting with colors and patterns. Her knitting skills progressed to the point where she envisioned a design and knitted it quickly and easily.

But Bonita didn't capitalize on her talent until several years later when her coworkers began requesting sweaters. They inadvertently launched her freelance career.

When Bonita decided to target the celebrity market, she did a lot of research before making her contacts. Her hard work paid off. "My first celebrity client was Bill Cosby, whom I got to work for by researching, finding, and contacting the show's costumer," says Bonita. "Most of my work came as a result of my initiative to look for, and persistently contact, my desired clients. The other shows came pretty much the same way. I got a job working on Eddie Murphy's movie *Boomerang* because I sent a sample of my work to his PR person."

There was no stopping her after these initial clients. "I built, and continue to build, my clientele by word of mouth," explains Bonita. "I research and contact people in my target market, and I also try very hard to do quality work which lends itself to referrals."

Her philosophy and work ethic are obviously a winning combination; in addition to Bill Cosby and Eddie Murphy, Bonita's clients include

When writing a press release, think of the type of information *you* would like to see in an article, including who, what, when, where, and why. Here are some general rules to follow:

1. **Include your name and contact information at the top of the release.**

Malcolm Jamal Warner, Meredith Baxter, Cree Summer, Dawn Lewis, Grace Jones, Halle Berry, David Alan Grier, Debbie Allen, and Lawrence Fishburne.

Bonita's preference for natural fibers and imported novelty yarns yield timeless, original garments. Sometimes her clients request remakes of 10-year-old designs!

Because of the quality of her designs, Bonita charges more for her products. Her handknitwear starts at $450 and rises to $4,500+ for a coat. Sweaters range from $495 to $995 and shawls start at $495. Accessories, such as hats, go for $195 to $875.

When asked to describe herself, Bonita replied, "I view myself as a success in progress. I am an innovator, and I have an innate need to express creativity. I'm inspired by color and the naturalness of a fiber, and get a thrill out of creating something that never existed before."

In addition to maintaining her celebrity clientele, Bonita designs coats and sweaters for *Knit 'n Style* magazine (formally *Fashion Knitting* magazine), and the Knitting Guild of America's Winter '99 issue of *Cast On* also featured her work.

Bonita is a true inspiration for anyone wanting to design clothing. (See Resources for Bonita's contact information.)

2. Your headline, which summarizes the press release, must immediately catch the eye of the reader.

3. All of the important information should be in the first paragraph.

4. The release must be typed and double-spaced.

5. Be brief, but include all the facts.
6. Personalize your press release with a photo if possible.
7. Timing is important. If you submit timely, interesting information, then your press releases are more apt to be printed.
8. Obtain a copy of the publication's editorial deadlines. Many editors have closing dates two to three months in advance of publication.
9. Don't call and ask the editor to send you a copy of the article after it has been published. Get your own copies, and save at least one original copy of each press release for your files.

Feature Articles

You can submit ideas for feature articles about you or your business to newspapers, newsletters, magazines, or journals. If you've knitted something unusual, it may be worthy of an article. Local newspapers often look for a "hometown artist" to write about. If you let them know what you're knitting, you may find yourself featured in an upcoming issue.

What would be newsworthy enough for your local paper to publicize? You might announce a prize you've won at the state fair, or a knitting class you'll be teaching. If you're ever featured in a national magazine, send a press release to your newspaper. You never know, they may do a feature on it.

Classified Advertisements

You pay for classified advertising by the word, so you don't want to use more words than necessary. Consider your budget when planning an advertisement. Don't go overboard.

The advertising rate usually grows as the circulation of the magazine increases. I have advertised in several of the major knitting magazines for years and find that it works quite well.

Writing an Advertisement

You should remember the following three rules when writing advertisement copy for a classified ad:

1. Word order is important. The most important words should come first, meaning, whatever you're selling should be the first thing someone reads.

2. Be concise. Don't waste words. People just want the facts.

3. Tailor your material to your projected audience.

Display advertising is quite expensive, thus it's probably not something you will use when you're just starting out in your knitting business.

Promotional Newsletters

Many craftspeople with computers publish free newsletters for their customers. This kind of promotional newsletter can double as a brochure, and may be simple or complex, ranging from one to four pages. Once you acquire a list of customers, you can send out brief free newsletters from time to time to announce new products or services. Include information about your latest activities and announce shows or other events that you're participating in.

The Internet/World Wide Web Sites

The Internet is one of the best places to sell your merchandise today. Some Internet servers offer free Web sites, but these sites are usually for private individuals and are unavailable for businesses. Check with your local server for availability.

A Web site has the advantage of 24-hour service, plus there are no printing or mailing costs. The more people that visit your Web site, the better your chances of selling products or services. Once you have a Web site, let everyone know about it. Be sure to include the Web site address on all of your printed materials.

I recently joined the National Craft Association, which offers Web pages for members at a small cost. In fact, the NCA created my Web page. The NCA's purpose is to assist crafters in their arts and crafts business. See Resources for more information about the NCA.

Mailings to Customers/Prospect Lists

A mailing list is a great way to advertise. Whenever you do craft shows or home shows you should always have a guest book for compiling names and addresses to add to your mailing list.

You'll want your mailed item to stand out from the rest, so I recommend hand addressing them if you're sending only a few at a time. Using colored envelopes is another good way of gaining attention.

Paying for first class postage is much better than bulk mailing, because first class mail travels faster, is more reliable than bulk mail, and costs very little more.

Tags and Labels for Your Products

Tags and labels come in many different shapes, styles, and sizes. The following examples are just a few of them.

Hang Tags

Hang tags are tags or cards that hang from your knitting products. They can be any size and should list your name, address, phone number, e-mail address, Web site if available, and a brief description of you and your work. Including your personal story and details about any special techniques you used on the garment is a nice touch. The important thing is to make your name as a knitter synonymous with quality. You can make your own hang tags or order them from one of the suppliers listed in Resources.

Name Labels

Name labels are essentially fabric labels with your name on them: "Handknit by Shirley MacNulty." These labels are also a good way to advertise. I once received a special order because of the name label I attached to an item. (Check Resources for name labels. I have ordered over the years from several of the companies listed. Also, see chapter 11 for more information about labels.)

How to Get Free Publicity

Success begins with hard work and publicizing your business. The following describe ways to obtain free publicity.

Give Demonstrations

There is no easier way to get publicity than by giving a demonstration. When you're starting out, I suggest that you give the first few demonstrations at no charge. It's a wonderful way to gain publicity,

Made in the USA

To challenge the mass marketing and foreign importing power of major companies, you must knit with distinction. Be different! Advertise the fact that your items have been "Made in the USA" by sewing labels on your items. See Resources for the names of several companies that offer such labels.

and it may lead to future contacts. You can give a demonstration for your neighbors, church group, local Girl Scout group, women's club, and others.

Announce Classes

Teaching a class is always a great way to increase your exposure. Always send a press release to your local newspaper to announce your new classes. This way, your name will appear in the newspaper, and you'll have the opportunity to interact with your students. If you make a good impression, they will tell their friends about you. You may want to progress from teaching locally to teaching nationally. Some organizations require certification, which is available from the Professional Knitwear Designers Guild (see Resources for contact information).

Enter Competitions

If your local area has a county fair—and many areas of the country have these—you should enter one or more of your best handknitted pieces. Adding "Blue Ribbon Winner" to your résumé enhances your reputation and improves your marketability. In addition to the county fair in my area, our senior center sponsors the local portion of the statewide "senior games." Senior games are open to anyone over 55. They include sporting events, crafts, and art. I have judged county fairs in three different states in addition to the local senior games. These competitions have had very few knitted items submitted, so this sounds like a great way to have a chance of winning a ribbon.

Give to Charity

Donating something you have made to charity, such as an afghan, is another great way to publicize your business. Many churches and nonprofit organizations have auctions or similar affairs and often look for items to donate. You can also get a tax write-off along with the free publicity.

Appear on Television

If you live in an area that has its own TV stations, it may be possible to get some free TV news coverage if you do something locally. I had an opportunity to be on our local NBC television station several years ago because someone saw my name label inside one of my Christmas neckties. From this, I got a TV interview plus orders for several ties. For the TV program, which was a special segment of the evening news, they filmed me at my kitchen table wearing one of my handknitted outfits, sewing my neckties and, of course, knitting other projects.

Join Local Craft Organizations

As I discussed earlier, there is no better way to promote your business than being a member of both professional and nonprofessional organizations, locally and nationally. Memberships enable you to network with other knitters and crafters, take classes, attend seminars, and learn what's new in the industry. Resources lists several national organizations you may want to join. Note that the Knitting Guild of America offers opportunities to form local chapters. If this is something you'd like to do, contact the organization for more information. By joining guilds, you'll meet other knitters and if you're the organizer, you'll probably become the president or one of the other officers.

Contact your local chamber of commerce to see which organizations are available locally. Also check your local telephone book and yellow pages under "local organizations." If there is a yarn shop in your community, the owners or employees may know the name of craft guilds in your community.

Most communities have a local craft or art association that you can join. The size of a city or town doesn't necessarily reflect the size of the guild. Often the smallest county has the most active groups. The local group that I presently belong to, Coastal Crafts Originals, sponsors one large show yearly. It's held at our local university coliseum, which has room for about 100 booths. Because I'm a member, my show fee is about 50% less than exhibitors who aren't members.

The more recognition you gain in the yarn industry, the better chance you have of becoming recognized. I was asked to make a needlepoint Christmas ornament for the White House Blue Room Christmas Tree in 1997 because of my membership in The National Needlepoint Association (TNNA). Also, Hallmark Cards and the United Way of America approached me to participate in a needlepoint project through the TNNA.

The strongest advice I can give you is to *stay visible;* let others know that you have started a business and take advantage of any free publicity that comes your way. You'll never know where your new business will take you.

A Mini-Course in Crafts-Business Basics

by Barbara Brabec

▼▼

THIS SECTION OF THE BOOK will familiarize you with important areas of legal and financial concern and enable you to ask the right questions if and when it is necessary to consult with an attorney, accountant, or other business adviser. Although the tax and legal information included here has been carefully researched by the author and is accurate to the best of her knowledge, it is not the business of either the author or publisher to render professional services in the area of business law, taxes, or accounting. Readers should therefore use their own good judgment in determining when the services of a lawyer or other professional would be appropriate to their needs.

Information presented applies specifically to businesses in the United States. However, because many U.S. and Canadian laws are similar, Canadian readers can certainly use the following information as a start-up business plan and guide to questions they need to ask their own local, provincial, or federal authorities.

Contents

7. Insurance Tips

Homeowner's or Renter's Insurance
Liability Insurance
Insurance on Crafts Merchandise
Auto Insurance

8. Important Regulations Affecting Artists and Craftspeople

Consumer Safety Laws
Labels Required by Law
The Bedding and Upholstered Furniture Law
FTC Rule for Mail-Order Sellers

9. Protecting Your Intellectual Property

Perspective on Patents
What a Trademark Protects
What Copyrights Protect
Copyright Registration Tips
Respecting the Copyrights of Others
Using Commercial Patterns and Designs

10. To Keep Growing, Keep Learning

Motivational Tips

A "Things to Do" Checklist with Related Resources

- Business Start-Up Checklist
- Government Agencies
- Crafts and Home-Business Organizations
- Recommended Craft Business Periodicals
- Other Services and Suppliers
- Recommended Business Books
- Helpful Library Directories

1. Starting Right

In preceding chapters of this book, you learned the techniques of a particular art or craft and realized its potential for profit. You learned what kind of products are likely to sell, how to price them, and how and where you might sell them.

Now that you've seen how much fun a crafts business can be (and how profitable it might be if you were to get serious about selling what you make!) you need to learn about some of the "nitty-gritty stuff" that goes hand in hand with even the smallest business based at home. It's easy to start selling what you make and it's satisfying when you earn enough money to make your hobby self-supporting. Many crafters go this far and no further, which is fine. But even a hobby seller must be concerned about taxes and local, state, and federal laws. And if your goal is to build a part- or full-time business at home, you must pay even greater attention to the topics discussed in this section of the book.

Everyone loves to make money . . . but actually starting a business frightens some people because they don't understand what's involved. It's easy to come up with excuses for why we don't do certain things in life; close inspection of those excuses usually boils down to fear of the unknown. We get the shivers when we step out of our comfort zone and try something we've never done before. The simple solution to this problem lies in having the right information at the right time. As someone once said, "Knowledge is the antidote to fear."

The quickest and surest way to dispel fear is to inform yourself about the topics that frighten you. With knowledge comes a sense of power, and that power enables you to move. Whether your goal is merely to earn extra income from your crafts hobby or launch a genuine home-based business, reading the following information will help you get started on the right legal foot, avoid financial pitfalls, and move forward with confidence.

When you're ready to learn more about art or crafts marketing or the operation of a home-based crafts business, a visit to your library or bookstore will turn up many interesting titles. In addition to the special resources listed by this book's author, you will find my list of recommended business books, organizations, periodicals, and other helpful resources in section 10 of this chapter. This information is arranged in a checklist you can use as a plan to get your business up and running.

Before you read my "Mini-Course in Crafts-Business Basics," be assured that I understand where you're coming from because I was once there myself.

For a while I sold my craft work, and this experience led me to write my first book, *Creative Cash*. Now, twenty years later, this crafts-business classic ("my baby") has reached its sixth edition. Few of those who are totally involved in a crafts business today started out with a business in mind. Like me, most began as hobbyists looking for something interesting to do in their spare time, and one thing naturally led to another. I never imagined those many years

Social Security Taxes

When your craft business earnings are more than $400 (net), you must file a Self-Employment Tax form (Schedule SE) and pay into your personal Social Security account. This could be quite beneficial for individuals who have some previous work experience but have been out of the workplace for a while. Your re-entry into the business world as a self-employed worker, and the additional contributions to your Social Security account, could result in increased benefits upon retirement.

Because so many senior citizens are starting home-based businesses these days, it should be noted that there is a limit on the amount you can earn before losing Social Security benefits. The good news is that this dollar limit increases every year, and once you are past the age of 70, you can earn any amount of income and still receive full benefits. For more information, contact your nearest Social Security office.

ago when I got serious about my crafts hobby that I was putting myself on the road to a full-time career as a crafts writer, publisher, author, and speaker. Since I and thousands of others have progressed from hobbyists to professionals, I won't be at all surprised if someday you, too, have a similar adventure.

2. Taxes and Record Keeping

"Ambition in America is still rewarded . . . with high taxes," the comics quip. Don't you long for the good old days when Uncle Sam lived within his income and without most of yours?

Seriously, taxes are one of the first things you must be concerned about as a new business owner, no matter how small your endeavor. This section offers a brief overview of your tax responsibilities as a sole proprietor.

Is Your Activity a "Hobby" or a "Business?"

Whether you are selling what you make only to get the cost of your supplies back, or actually trying to build a profitable business, you need to understand the legal difference between a profitable hobby and a business, and how each is related to your annual tax return.

The IRS defines a hobby as "an activity engaged in primarily for pleasure, not for profit." Making a profit from a hobby does not automatically place you "in business" in the eyes of the Internal Revenue Service, but the activity will be *presumed* to have been engaged in for profit if it results in a profit in at least three years out of five. Or, to put it another way, a "hobby business" automatically becomes a "real business" in the eyes of the IRS at the point where you can state that you are (1) trying to make a profit, (2) making regular business transactions, and (3) have made a profit three years out of five.

As you know, all income must be reported on your annual tax return. How it's reported, however, has everything to do with the amount of taxes you must pay on this income. If hobby income is under $400, it must be entered on the 1040 tax form, with taxes payable accordingly. If the amount is greater than this, you must file a Schedule C form with your 1040 tax form. This is to your advantage, however, since taxes are due only on your *net profit*. Since you can deduct expenses up to the amount of your hobby income, there may be little or no tax at all on your hobby income.

Self-Employment Taxes

Whereas a hobby cannot show a loss on a Schedule C form, a business can. Business owners must pay not only state and federal income taxes on their profits, but self-employment taxes as well. (See sidebar, "Social Security Taxes," page 177.) Because self-employed people pay Social Security taxes at twice the level of regular, salaried workers, you should strive to lower your annual gross profit figure on the Schedule C form through every legal means possible. One way to do this is through careful record keeping of all expenses related to the operation of your business. To quote IRS publications, expenses are deductible if they are "ordinary, necessary, and somehow connected with the operation and potential profit of your business." In addition to being able to deduct all expenses related to the making and selling of their products, business owners can also depreciate the cost of tools and equipment, deduct the overhead costs of operating a home-based office or studio (called the Home Office Deduction), and hire their spouse or children.

Given the complexity of our tax laws and the fact that they are changing all the time, a detailed discussion of all the tax deductions currently available to small business owners cannot be included in a book of this nature. Learning, however, is as easy as reading a book such as *Small Time Operator* by Bernard Kamoroff (my favorite tax and accounting guide), visiting the IRS Web site, or consulting your regular tax adviser.

You can also get answers to specific tax questions 24 hours a day by calling the National Association of Enrolled Agents (NAEA). Enrolled agents (EAs) are licensed by the Treasury Department to represent taxpayers before the IRS. Their rates for doing tax returns are often less than what you would pay for an accountant or CPA. (See my checklist for NAEA's toll-free number you can call to ask for a referral to an EA in your area.)

An important concept to remember is that even the smallest business is entitled to deduct expenses related to its business, and the same tax-saving strategies used by "the big guys" can be used by small business owners. Your business may be small now or still in the dreaming stage, but it could be larger next year and surprisingly profitable a few years from now. Therefore it is in your best interest always to prepare for growth, profit, and taxes by learning all you

Keeping Tax Records

Once you're in business, you must keep accurate records of all income and expenses, but the IRS does not require any special kind of bookkeeping system. Its primary concern is that you use a system that clearly and accurately shows true income and expenses. For the sole proprietor, a simple system consisting of a checkbook, a cash receipts journal, a cash disbursements ledger, and a petty cash fund is quite adequate. Post expenses and income regularly to avoid year-end pile-up and panic.

If you plan to keep manual records, check your local office supply store or catalogs for the *Dome* series of record-keeping books, or use the handy ledger sheets and worksheets included in *Small Time Operator.* (This classic tax and accounting guide by CPA Bernard Kamoroff includes details on how to keep good records and prepare financial reports.) If you have a computer, there are a number of accounting software programs available, such as Intuit Quicken, MYOB (Mind Your Own Business) Accounting, and Intuit Quick-

can about the tax laws and deductions applicable to your business. (See also sidebar, "Keeping Tax Records.")

Sales Tax Is Serious Business

If you live in a state that has a sales tax (all but five states do), and sell products directly to consumers, you are required by law to register with your state's Department of Revenue (Sales Tax division) for a resale tax number. The fee for this in most states ranges from $5 to $25, with some states requiring a bond or deposit of up to $150.

Depending on where you live, this tax number may also be called a Retailer's Occupation Tax Registration Number, resale license, or use tax permit. Also, depending on where you live, the place you must call to obtain this number will have different names. In California, for example, you would contact the State Board of Equalization; in Texas, it's called the State Comptroller's Office.

Books, the latter of which is one of the most popular and best bookkeeping systems for small businesses. The great advantage of computerized accounting is that financial statements can be created at the press of a key after accounting entries have been made.

Regardless which system you use, always get a receipt for everything and file receipts in a monthly envelope. If you don't want to establish a petty cash fund, spindle all of your cash receipts, tally them at month's end, and reimburse your personal outlay of cash with a check written on your business account. On your checkbook stub, document the individual purchases covered by this check.

At year's end, bundle your monthly tax receipt envelopes and file them for future reference, if needed. Since the IRS can audit a return for up to three years after a tax return has been filed, all accounting and tax records should be kept at least this long, but six years is better. Personally, I believe you should keep all your tax returns, journals, and ledgers throughout the life of your business.

Within your state's revenue department, the tax division may have a name such as Sales and Use Tax Division or Department of Taxation and Finance. Generally speaking, if you check your telephone book under "Government," and look for whatever listing comes closest to "Revenue," you can find the right office.

If your state has no sales tax, you will still need a reseller's permit or tax exemption certificate to buy supplies and materials at wholesale prices from manufacturers, wholesalers, or distributors. Note that this tax number is only for supplies and materials used to make your products, not for things purchased at the retail level or for general office supplies.

Once registered with the state, you will begin to collect and remit sales and use tax (monthly, quarterly, or annually, as determined by your state) on all *taxable sales*. This does not mean *all* of your gross income. Different states tax different things. Some states put a sales tax on certain services, but generally you will never have to pay sales tax on income from articles sold to magazines, on teaching or consulting fees, or subscription income (if you happen to publish a newsletter). In addition, sales taxes are not applicable to:

- **items sold on consignment through a charitable organization, shop, or other retail outlet, including craft malls and rent-a-space shops (because the party who sells directly to the consumer is the one who must collect and pay sales tax.)**

- **products you wholesale to others who will be reselling them to consumers. (Be sure to get their tax-exemption ID number for your own files, however, in case you are ever questioned as to why you did not collect taxes on those sales.)**

As you sell throughout the year, your record-keeping system must be set up so you can tell which income is taxable and which is tax-exempt for reporting on your sales tax return.

Collecting Sales Tax at Craft Shows

States are getting very aggressive about collecting sales tax, and agents are showing up everywhere these day, especially at the larger craft fairs, festivals, and small business conferences. As I was writing this chapter, a post on the Internet stated that in New Jersey the sales tax department is routinely contacting show promoters about a month before the show date to get the names and addresses of exhibitors. It is expected that other states will soon be following suit. For this reason, you should always take your resale or tax collection certificate with you to shows.

Although you must always collect sales tax at a show when you sell in a state that has a sales tax, how and when the tax is paid to the state can vary. When selling at shows in other states, you may find that the show promoter has obtained an umbrella sales tax certificate, in which case vendors would be asked to give management a check for sales tax at the end of the show for turning over to a tax agent. Or you may have to obtain a temporary sales tax certificate for a show, as advised by the show promoter. Some sellers who regularly do shows in two or three states say it's easier to get a tax ID number from each state and file an annual return instead of doing taxes on a show-by-show basis. (See sidebar, "Including Tax in the Retail Price," page 184.)

Collecting Sales Tax at a Holiday Boutique

If you're involved in a holiday boutique where several sellers are offering goods to the public, each individual seller will be responsible for collecting and remitting his or her own sales tax. (This means someone has to keep very good records during the sale so each seller receives a record of the sale and the amount of tax on that sale.) A reader who regularly has home boutiques told me that in her community she must also post a sign at her "cash station" stating that sales tax is being collected on all sales, just as craft fair sellers must do in some states. Again, it's important that you get complete details from your own state about its sales tax policies.

Collecting Tax on Internet Sales

Anything you sell that is taxable in your state is also taxable on the Internet. This is simply another method of selling, like craft fairs or mail-order sales. You don't have to break out Internet sales separately; simply include them in your total taxable sales.

3. The Legal Forms of Business

Every business must take one of four legal forms:

Sole Proprietorship
Partnership
LLC (Limited Liability Company)
Corporation

Including Tax in the Retail Price

Is it okay to incorporate the amount of sales tax into the retail price of items being sold directly to consumers? I don't know for sure because each state's sales tax law is different.

Crafters like to use round-figure prices at fairs because this encourages cash sales and eliminates the need for taking coins to make change. Some crafters tell their customers that sales tax has been included in their rounded-off prices, but you should not do this until you check with your state. In some states, this is illegal; in others, you may find that you are required to inform your customers, by means of a sign, that sales tax has been included in your price. Your may also have to print this information on customer receipts as well.

If you make such a statement and collect taxes on cash sales, be sure to report those cash sales as taxable income and remit the tax money to the state accordingly. Failure

As a hobby seller, you automatically become a sole proprietor when you start selling what you make. Although most professional crafters remain sole proprietors throughout the life of their business, some do form craft partnerships or corporations when their business begins to generate serious money, or if it happens to involve other members of their family. You don't need a lawyer to start a sole proprietorship, but it would be folly to enter into a partnership, corporation, or LLC without legal guidance. Here is a brief look at the main advantages and disadvantages of each type of legal business structure.

Sole Proprietorship

No legal formalities are involved in starting or ending a sole proprietorship. You're your own boss here, and the business starts when you say it does and ends automatically when you stop running it. As discussed earlier, income is reported annually on a Schedule C form

to do this would be a violation of the law, and it's easy to get caught these days when sales tax agents are showing up at craft fairs across the country.

Even if rounding off the price and including the tax within that figure turns out to be legal in your state, it will definitely complicate your bookkeeping. For example, if you normally sell an item for $5 or some other round figure, you must have a firm retail price on which to calculate sales tax to begin with. Adding tax to a round figure makes it uneven. Then you must either raise it or lower the price, and if you lower it, what you're really doing is paying the sales tax for your customer out of your profits. This is no way to do business.

I suggest that you set your retail prices based on the pricing formulas given in this book, calculate the sales tax accordingly, and give your customers change if they pay in cash. You will be perceived as a professional when you operate this way, whereas crafters who insist always on "cash only" sales are sending signals to buyers that they don't intend to report this income to tax authorities.

and taxed at the personal level. The sole proprietor is fully liable for all business debts and actions. In the event of a lawsuit, personal assets are not protected.

Partnership

There are two kinds of partnerships: general and limited.

A *general partnership* is easy to start, with no federal requirements involved. Income is taxed at the personal level and the partnership ends as soon as either partner withdraws from the business. Liability is unlimited. The most financially dangerous thing about a partnership is that the debts incurred by one partner must be assumed by all other partners. Before signing a partnership agreement, make sure the tax obligations of your partner are current.

In a *limited partnership,* the business is run by general partners and financed by silent (limited) partners who have no liability beyond an investment of money in the business. This kind of partnership is more complicated to establish, has special tax withholding regulations, and requires the filing of a legal contract with the state.

LLC (Limited Liability Company)

This legal form of business reportedly combines the best attributes of other small business forms while offering a better tax advantage than a limited partnership. It also affords personal liability protection similar to that of a corporation. To date, few craft businesses appear to be using this business form.

Corporation

A corporation is the most complicated and expensive legal form of business and not recommended for any business whose earnings are less than $25,000 a year. If and when your business reaches this point, you should study some books on this topic to fully understand the pros and cons of a corporation. Also consult an accountant or attorney for guidance on the type of corporation you should select—a "C" (general corporation) or an "S" (subchapter S corporation). One book that offers good perspective on this topic is *INC Yourself—How to Profit by Setting Up Your Own Corporation*.

The main disadvantage of incorporation for the small business owner is that profits are taxed twice: first as corporate income and again when they are distributed to the owner-shareholders as dividends. For this reason, many small businesses elect to incorporate as subchapter S corporations, which allows profits to be taxed at owners' regular individual rates. (See sidebar, "The Limited Legal Protection of a Corporation," below.)

The Limited Legal Protection of a Corporation

Business novices often think that by incorporating their business they can protect their personal assets in the event of a lawsuit. This is true if you have employees who do something wrong and cause your business to be sued. As the business owner, however, if you personally do something wrong and are sued as a result, you might in some cases be held legally responsible, and the "corporation door" will offer no legal protection for your personal assets.

Or, as CPA Bernard Kamoroff explains in *Small Time Operator*, "A corporation will not shield you from personal liability that you normally should be responsible for, such as not having car insurance or acting with gross negligence. If you plan to incorporate solely or primarily with the intention of limiting your legal liability, I suggest you find out first exactly how limited the liability really is for your particular venture. Hire a knowledgeable lawyer to give you a written opinion." (See section 7, "Insurance Tips.")

4. Local and State Laws and Regulations

This section will acquaint you with laws and regulations that affect the average art or crafts business based at home. If you've unknowingly broken one of these laws, don't panic. It may not be as bad as you think. It is often possible to get back on the straight and narrow merely by filling out a required form or by paying a small fee of some kind. What's important is that you take steps now to comply with the laws that pertain to your particular business. Often, the fear of being caught when you're breaking a law is often much worse than doing whatever needs to be done to set the matter straight. In the end, it's usually what you don't know that is most likely to cause legal or financial problems, so never hesitate to ask questions about things you don't understand.

Even when you think you know the answers, it can pay to "act dumb." It is said that Napoleon used to attend meetings and pretend to know nothing about a topic, asking many probing questions. By feigning ignorance, he was able to draw valuable information and insight out of everyone around him. This strategy is often used by today's small business owners, too.

Business Name Registration

If you're a sole proprietor doing business under any name other than your own full name, you are required by law to register it on both the local and state level. In this case, you are said to be using an "assumed," "fictitious," or "trade" name. What registration does is enable authorities to connect an assumed name to an individual who can be held responsible for the actions of a business. If you're doing business under your own name, such as Kay Jones, you don't have to register your business name on either the local or state level. If your name is part of a longer name, however (for example, Kay Jones Designs), you should check to see if your county or state requires registration.

Local Registration

To register your name, contact your city or county clerk, who will explain what you need to do to officially register your business on the local level. At the same time, ask if you need any special municipal or county licenses or permits to operate within the law. (See next section, "Licenses and Permits.") This office can also tell you how and where to write to register your name at the state level. If you've been operating under an assumed name for a while and are worried because you didn't register the name earlier, just register it now, as if the business were new.

Registration involves filling out a simple form and paying a small fee, usually around $10 to $25. At the time you register, you will get details about a classified ad you must run in a general-circulation newspaper in your county. This will notify the public at large that you are now operating a business under an assumed name. (If you don't want your neighbors to know what you're doing, simply run the ad in a newspaper somewhere else in the county.) After publication of this ad, you will receive a Fictitious Name Statement that you must send to the county clerk, who in turn will file it with your registration form to make your business completely legitimate. This name statement or certificate may also be referred to as your DBA ("doing business as") form. In some areas, you cannot open a business checking account if you don't have this form to show your bank.

State Registration

Once you've registered locally, contact your secretary of state to register your business name with the state. This will prevent its use by a corporate entity. At the same time, find out if you must

Picking a Good Business Name

If you haven't done it already, think up a great name for your new business. You want something that will be memorable—catchy, but not too cute. Many crafters select a simple name that is attached to their first name, such as "Mary's Quilts" or "Tom's Woodcrafts." This is fine for a hobby business, but if your goal is to build a full-time business at home, you may wish to choose a more professional-sounding name that omits your personal name. If a name sounds like a hobby business, you may have difficulty getting wholesale suppliers to take you seriously. A more professional name may also enable you to get higher prices for your products. For example, the above names might be changed to "Quilted Treasures" or "Wooden Wonders."

Don't print business cards or stationery until you find out if someone else is already using the name you've chosen. To find out if the name has already been registered, you

obtain any kind of state license. Generally, home-based craft businesses will not need a license from the state, but there are always exceptions. An artist who built an open-to-the-public art studio on his property reported that the fine in his state for operating this kind of business without a license was $50 a day. In short, it always pays to ask questions to make sure you're operating legally and safely.

Federal Registration

The only way to protect a name on the federal level is with a trademark, discussed in section 8.

Licenses and Permits

A "license" is a certificate granted by a municipal or county agency that gives you permission to engage in a business occupation. A "permit" is similar, except that it is granted by local authorities. Until recently, few craft businesses had to have a license or permit

can perform a trademark search through a search company or hire an attorney who specializes in trademak law to conduct the search for you. And if you are planning to eventually set up a Web site, you might want to do a search to see if that domain name is still available on the Internet. Go to www.networksolutions.com to do this search. Business names have to be registered on the Internet, too, and they can be "parked" for a fee until you're ready to design your Web site.

It's great if your business name and Web site name can be the same, but this is not always possible. A crafter told me recently she had to come up with 25 names before she found a domain name that hadn't already been taken. (Web entrepreneurs are grabbing every good name they can find. Imagine my surprise when I did a search and found that two different individuals had set up Web sites using the titles of my two best-known books, *Creative Cash* and *Homemade Money*.)

of any kind, but a growing number of communities now have new laws on their books that require home-based business owners to obtain a "home occupation permit." Annual fees for such permits may range from $15 to $200 a year. For details about the law in your particular community or county, call your city or country clerk (depending on whether you live within or outside city limits).

Use of Personal Phone for Business

Although every business writer stresses the importance of having a business telephone number, craftspeople generally ignore this advice and do business on their home telephone. While it's okay to use a home phone to make outgoing business calls, you cannot advertise a home telephone number as your business phone number without being in violation of local telephone regulations. That means you cannot legally put your home telephone number on a business card or business stationery or advertise it on your Web site.

That said, let me also state that most craftspeople totally ignore this law and do it anyway. (I don't know what the penalty for breaking this law is in your state; you'll have to call your telephone company for that information and decide if this is something you want to do.) Some phone companies might give you a slap on the wrist and tell you to stop, while others might start charging you business line telephone rates if they discover you are advertising your personal phone number.

The primary reason to have a separate phone line for your business is that it enables you to freely advertise your telephone number to solicit new business and invite credit card sales, custom order inquiries, and the like. Further, you can deduct 100 percent of the costs of a business telephone line on your Schedule C tax form, while deductions for the business use of a home phone are severely limited. (Discuss this with your accountant.)

If you plan to connect to the Internet or install a fax machine, you will definitely need a second line to handle the load, but most crafters simply add an additional personal line instead of a business line. Once on the Internet, you may have even less need for a business phone than before since you can simply invite contact from buyers by advertising your e-mail address. (Always include your e-mail and Internet address on your business cards and stationery.)

If your primary selling methods are going to be consignment shops, craft fairs, or craft malls, a business phone number would be necessary only if you are inviting orders by phone. If you present a holiday boutique or open house once or twice a year, there should be no problem with putting your home phone number on promotional fliers because you are, in fact, inviting people to your home and not your business (similar to running a classified ad for a garage sale).

If and when you decide a separate line for your business is necessary, you may find it is not as costly as you think. Telephone companies today are very aware of the number of people who are working at home, and they have come up with a variety of affordable packages and second-line options, any one of which might be perfect for your craft business needs. Give your telephone company a call and see what's available.

Zoning Regulations

Before you start any kind of home-based business, check your home's zoning regulations. You can find a copy at your library or at city hall. Find out what zone you're in and then read the information under "home occupations." Be sure to read the fine print and note the penalty for violating a zoning ordinance. In most cases, someone who is caught violating zoning laws will be asked to cease and desist and a penalty is incurred only if this order is ignored. In other cases, however, willful violation could incur a hefty fine.

Zoning laws differ from one community to another, with some of them being terribly outdated (actually written back in horse-and-buggy days). In some communities, zoning officials simply "look the other way" where zoning violations are concerned because it's easier to do this than change the law. In other places, however, zoning regulations have recently been revised in light of the growing number of individuals working at home, and these changes have not always been to the benefit of home-based workers or self-employed individuals. Often there are restrictions as to (1) the amount of space in one's home a business may occupy (impossible to enforce, in my opinion), (2) the number of people (customers, students) who can come to your home each day, (3) the use of non-family employees, and so on. If you find you cannot advertise your home as a place of business, this problem can be easily solved by renting a P.O. box or using a commercial mailbox service as your business address.

Although I'm not suggesting that you violate your zoning law, I will tell you that many individuals who have found zoning to be a problem do ignore this law, particularly when they have a quiet business that is unlikely to create problems in their community.

Zoning officials don't go around checking for people who are violating the law; rather, they tend to act on complaints they have received about a certain activity that is creating problems for others. Thus, the best way to avoid zoning problems is to keep a low profile by not broadcasting your home-based business to neighbors. More important, never annoy them with activities that emit fumes or odors, create parking problems, or make noise of any kind.

While neighbors may grudgingly put up with a noisy hobby activity (such as sawing in the garage), they are not likely to tolerate the same noise or disturbance if they know it's related to a home-based business. Likewise, they won't mind if you have a garage sale every year, but if people are constantly coming to your home to buy from your home shop, open house, home parties, or holiday boutiques every year, you could be asking for trouble if the zoning laws don't favor this kind of activity.

5. General Business and Financial Information

This section offers introductory guidelines on essential business basics for beginners. Once your business is up and running, however, you need to read other craft-business books to get detailed information on the following topics and many others related to the successful growth and development of a home-based art or crafts business.

Making a Simple Business Plan

As baseball star Yogi Berra once said, "If you don't know where you are going, you might not get there." That's why you need a plan.

Like a road map, a business plan helps you get from here to there. It doesn't have to be fancy, but it does have to be in written form. A good business plan will save you time and money while helping you stay focused and on track to meet your goals. The kind of business plan a craftsperson makes will naturally be less complicated than the business plan of a major manufacturing company, but the elements are basically the same and should include:

- *History*—how and why you started your business
- *Business description*—what you do, what products you make, why they are special
- *Management information*—your business background or experience and the legal form your business will take
- *Manufacturing and production*—how and where products will be produced and who will make them; how and where supplies and materials will be obtained, and their estimated costs; labor costs (yours or other helpers); and overhead costs involved in the making of products
- *Financial plan*—estimated sales and expense figures for one year
- *Market research findings*—a description of your market (fairs, shops, mail order, Internet, etc.), your customers, and your competition
- *Marketing plan*—how you are going to sell your products and the anticipated cost of your marketing (commissions, advertising, craft fair displays, etc.)

If this all seems a bit much for a small crafts business, start managing your time by using a daily calendar/planner and start a notebook you can fill with your creative and marketing ideas, plans, and business goals. In it, write a simple mission statement that answers the following questions:

- What is my primary mission or goal in starting a business?
- What is my financial goal for this year?
- What am I going to do to get the sales I need this year to meet my financial goal?

The most important thing is that you start putting your dreams, goals, and business plans on paper so you can review them regularly.

It's always easier to see where you're going if you know where you've been.

When You Need an Attorney

Many business beginners think they have to hire a lawyer the minute they start a business, but that would be a terrible waste of money if you're just starting a simple art or crafts business at home, operating as a sole proprietor. Sure, a lawyer will be delighted to hold your hand and give you the same advice I'm giving you here (while charging you $150 an hour or more for his or her time). With this book in hand, you can easily take care of all the "legal details" of small business start-up. The day may come, however, when you do need legal counsel, such as when you:

Form a Partnership or Corporation

As stated earlier, an attorney's guidance is necessary in the formation of a partnership. Although many people have incorporated without a lawyer using a good how-to book on the topic, I wouldn't recommend doing this because there are so many details involved here, not to mention different types of corporate entities.

Defend an Infringement of a Copyright or Trademark

You don't need an attorney to get a simple copyright, but if someone infringes on one of your copyrights, you will probably need legal help to stop the infringer from profiting from your creativity. You can file your own trademark application (if you are exceedingly careful about following instructions), but it would be difficult to protect your trademark without legal help if someone tries to steal it. In both cases, you would need an attorney who specializes in copyright, patent, and trademark law. (If you ever need a good attorney who understands the plight of artists and crafters, contact me by e-mail at barbara@crafter.com and I'll refer you to

Get a Safety Deposit Box

The longer you are in business, the more important it will be to safeguard your most valuable business records. When you work at home, there is always the possibility of fire or damage from some natural disaster, be it a tornado, earthquake, hurricane, or flood. You will worry less if you keep your most valuable business papers, records, computer disks, and so forth off-premises, along with other items that would be difficult or impossible to replace. Some particulars I have always kept in my business safety deposit box include master software disks and computer back-up tapes; original copies of my designs and patterns, business contracts, copyrights, insurance policies, and a photographic record of all items insured on our homeowner's policy. Remember: Insurance is worthless if you cannot prove what you owned in the first place.

the attorney who has been helpful to me in protecting my common-law trademark to *Homemade Money*, my home-business classic. The 6th edition of this book includes the details of my trademark infringement story.)

Negotiate a Contract

Many craft hobbyists of my acquaintance have gone on to write books and sell their original designs to manufacturers, suddenly finding themselves with a contract in hand that contains a lot of confusing legal jargon. When hiring an attorney to check any kind of contract, make sure he or she has experience in the particular field involved. For example, a lawyer specializing in real estate isn't going to know a thing about the inner workings of a book publishing company and how the omission or inclusion of a particular clause or phrase might impact the author's royalties or make it difficult to get publishing rights back when the book goes out of print. Although I have no experience in the licensing industry, I presume the same thing holds true here. What I do know for sure is that the problem with most contracts is not so much what's *in* them, as what *isn't*. Thus you need to be sure the attorney you hire for specialized contract work has done this kind of work for other clients.

Hire Independent Contractors

If you ever grow your business to the point where you need to hire workers and are wondering whether you have to hire employees or can use independent contractors instead, I suggest you to seek counsel from an attorney who specializes in labor law. This topic is very complex and beyond the scope of this beginner's guide, but I do want you to know that the IRS has been on a campaign for the past several years to abolish independent contractors altogether. Many small businesses have suffered great financial loss in back taxes and penalties because they followed the advice of an accountant or regular attorney who didn't fully understand the technicalities of this matter.

If and when you do need a lawyer for general business purposes, ask friends for a reference, and check with your bank, too, since it will probably know most of the attorneys with private practices in your area. Note that membership in some small business organizations will also give you access to affordable prepaid legal services. If you ever need serious legal help but have no funds to pay for it, contact the Volunteer Lawyers for the Arts (see resources in section 10).

Why You Need a Business Checking Account

Many business beginners use their personal checking account to conduct the transactions of their business, *but you must not do this* because the IRS does not allow co-mingling of business and personal income. If you are operating as a business, reporting income on a Schedule C form and taking deductions accordingly, the lack of a separate checking account for your business would surely result in an IRS ruling that your endeavor was a hobby and not a business. That, in turn, would cost you all the deductions previously taken on earlier tax returns and you'd end up with a very large tax bill. Don't you agree that the cost of a separate checking account is a small price to pay to protect all your tax deductions?

You do not necessarily need one of the more expensive business checking accounts; just a *separate account* through which you run all business income and expenditures. Your business name does not have to be on these checks so long as only your name (not your spouse's) is listed as account holder. You can save money on your checking account by first calling several banks and savings and loan institutions and comparing the charges they set for imprinted checks, deposits, checks written, bounced checks, and other services. Before you open your account, be sure to ask if the bank can set you up to take credit cards (merchant account) at some point in the future.

Accepting Credit Cards

Most of us today take credit cards for granted and expect to be able to use them for most everything we buy. It's nice to be able to offer credit card services to your craft fair customers, but it is costly and thus not recommended for beginning craft sellers. If you get into selling at craft fairs on a regular basis, however, at some point you may find you are losing sales because you don't have "merchant status" (the ability to accept credit cards as payment).

Some craftspeople have reported a considerable jump in sales once they started taking credit cards. That's because some people who buy with plastic may buy two or three items instead of one, or are willing to pay a higher price for something if they can charge it. Thus, the higher your prices, the more likely you are to lose sales if you can't accept credit cards. As one jewelry maker told me, "I always seem to get the customers who have run out of cash and left their checkbook at home. But even when they have a check, I feel uncomfortable taking a check for $100 or more."

A list follows of the various routes you can travel to get merchant status. You will have to do considerable research to find out which method is best for you. All will be costly, and you must have sufficient sales, or the expectation of increased sales, to consider taking credit cards in the first place. Understand, too, that taking credit cards in person (called face-to-face transactions where you have the card in front of you) is different from accepting credit cards by phone, by mail, or through a Web site (called non–face-to-face transactions). Each method of selling is treated differently by bankcard providers.

Merchant Status from Your Bank

When you're ready to accept credit cards, start with the bank where you have your business checking account. Where you bank, and where you live, has everything to do with whether you can get merchant status from your bank or not. Home-business owners in small towns often have less trouble than do those in large cities. One crafter told me Bank of America gave her merchant status with no problem, but some banks simply refuse to deal with anyone who doesn't operate out of a storefront. Most banks now insist that credit card sales be transmitted electronically, but a few still offer manual printers and allow merchants to send in their sales slips by mail. You will be given details about this at the time you apply for merchant status. All banks will require proof that you have a going business and will want to see your financial statements.

Merchant Status Through a Crafts Organization

If you are refused by your bank because your business is home based or just too new, getting bankcard services through a crafts or home-business organization is the next best way to go. Because such organizations have a large membership, they have some negotiating power with the credit card companies and often get special deals for their members. As a member of such an organization, the chances are about 95 percent that you will automatically be accepted into an its bankcard program, even if you are a brand new business owner.

One organization I can recommend to beginning sellers is the National Craft Association. Managing Director Barbara Arena tells me that 60 percent of all new NCA members now take the MasterCard/VISA services offered by her organization. "Crafters who are unsure about whether they want to take credit cards over a long period of time have the option of renting equipment," says Barbara. "This enables them to get out of the program with a month's notice. NCA members can operate on a software basis through their personal computer (taking their laptop computer to shows and calling in sales on their cell phone), or use a swipe machine. Under NCA's program, crafters can also accept credit card sales on their Internet site."

For more information from NCA and other organizations offering merchant services, see "Knitting, Craft, and Business Organizations" on page 272.

Merchant Status from Credit Card Companies

If you've been in business for a while, you may find you can get merchant status directly from American Express or Novus Services, Inc., the umbrella company that handles the Discover, Bravo, and Private Issue credit cards. American Express says that in some cases it can grant merchant status immediately upon receipt of some key information given on the phone. As for Novus, many crafters have told me how easy it was to get merchant status from this company. Novus says it only needs your Social Security number and information to check your credit rating. If Novus accepts you, it can also get you set up to take VISA and MasterCard as well if you meet the special acceptance qualifications of these two credit card companies. (Usually, they require you to be in business for at least two years.)

Merchant Status from an Independent
Service Organization Provider (ISO)

ISOs act as agents for banks that authorize credit cards, promoting their services by direct mail, through magazine advertising, telemarketing, and on the Internet. Most of these bankcard providers are operating under a network marketing program (one agent representing one agent representing another, and so on). They are everywhere on the Internet, sending unsolicited e-mail messages to Web site owners. In addition to offering the merchant account service itself, many are also trying to get other Web site owners to promote the same service in exchange for some kind of referral fee. I do not recommend that you get merchant status through an ISO because I've heard too many horror stories about them. If you want to explore this option on the Internet, however, use your browser's search button and type "credit cards + merchant" to get a list of such sellers.

In general, ISOs may offer a low discount rate but will sock it to you with inflated equipment costs, a high application fee, and extra fees for installation, programming, and site inspection. You will also have to sign an unbreakable three- or four-year lease for the electronic equipment.

As you can see, you must really do your homework where bankcard services are concerned. In checking out the services offered by any of the providers noted here, ask plenty of questions. Make up a chart that lets you compare what each one charges for application and service fees, monthly charges, equipment costs, software, discount rates, and transaction fees.

Transaction fees can range from 20 to 80 cents per ticket, with discount rates running anywhere from 1.67 percent to 5 percent. Higher rates are usually attached to non–face-to-face credit card transactions, paper transaction systems, or a low volume of sales. Any rate higher than 5 percent should be a danger signal since you could be dealing with an unscrupulous seller or some kind of illegal third-party processing program.

I'm told that a good credit card processor today may cost around $800, yet some card service providers are charging two or three times that amount in their leasing arrangements. I once got a quote from a major ISO and found it would have cost me $40 a month to lease the terminal—$1,920 over a period of four years—or I could buy it for just $1,000. In checking with my bank, I learned I could get the same equipment and the software to run it for just $350!

In summary, if you're a nervous beginner, the safest way to break into taking credit cards is to work with a bank or organization that offers equipment on a month-by-month rental arrangement. Once you've had some experience in taking credit card payments, you can review your situation and decide whether you want to move into a leasing arrangement or buy equipment outright.

6. Minimizing the Financial Risks of Selling

This book contains a good chapter on how and where to sell your crafts, but I thought it would be helpful for you to have added perspective on the business management end of selling through various outlets, and some things you can do to protect yourself from financial loss and legal hassles.

First you must accept the fact that all businesses occasionally suffer financial losses of one kind or another. That's simply the nature of business. Selling automatically carries a certain degree of risk in that we can never be absolutely sure that we're going to be paid for anything until we actually have payment in hand. Checks may bounce, wholesale buyers may refuse to pay their invoices, and consignment shops can close unexpectedly without returning merchandise to crafters. In the past few years, a surprising number

State Consignment Laws

Technically, consigned goods remain the property of the seller until they are sold. When a shop goes out of business, however, consigned merchandise may be seized by creditors in spite of what your consignment agreement may state. You may have some legal protection here, however, if you live in a state that has a consignment law designed to protect artists and craftspeople in such instances. I believe such laws exist in the states of CA, CO, CT, IL, IA, KY, MA, NH, NM, NY, OR, TX, WA, and WI. Call your secretary of state to confirm this or, if your state isn't listed here, ask whether this law is now on the books. Be sure to get full details about the kind of protection afforded by this law because some states have different definitions for what constitutes "art" or "crafts."

of craft mall owners have stolen out of town in the middle of the night, taking with them all the money due their vendors, and sometimes the vendors' merchandise as well. (This topic is beyond the scope of this book, but if you'd like more information on it, see my *Creative Cash* book and back issues of my *Craftsbiz Chat* newsletter on the Internet at www.crafter.com/brabec).

Now I don't want you to feel uneasy about selling or suspicious of every buyer who comes your way, because that would take all the fun out of selling. But I *do* want you to know that bad things sometimes happen to good craftspeople who have not done their homework (by reading this book, you are doing *your* homework). If you will follow the cautionary guidelines that follow, you can avoid some common selling pitfalls and minimize your financial risk to the point where it will be negligible.

Selling to Consignment Shops

Never consign more merchandise to one shop than you can afford to lose, and do not send new items to a shop until you see that payments are being made regularly according to your written consignment agreement. It should cover the topics of:

- insurance (see "Insurance Tips," section 7)
- pricing (make sure the shop cannot raise or lower your retail price without your permission)
- sales commission (40 percent is standard; don't work with shop owners who ask for more than this. It makes more sense to wholesale products at 50 percent and get payment in 30 days)
- payment dates
- display of merchandise
- return of unsold merchandise (some shops have a clause stating that if unsold merchandise is not claimed within 30 to 60 days after a notice has been sent, the shop can dispose of it any way it wishes)

Above all, make sure your agreement includes the name and phone number of the shop's owner (not just the manager). If a shop fails and you decide to take legal action, you want to be sure your lawyer can track down the owner. (See sidebar, "State Consignment Laws," page 204.)

Selling to Craft Malls

Shortly after the craft mall concept was introduced to the crafts community in 1988 by Rufus Coomer, entrepreneurs who understood the profit potential of such a business began to open malls all over the country. But there were no guidebooks and everyone was flying by the seat of his or her pants, making up operating rules along the way. Many mall owners, inexperienced in retailing, have since gone out of business, often leaving crafters holding the bag. The risks of selling through such well-known chain stores as Coomers or American Craft Malls are minimal, and many independently owned malls have also established excellent reputations in the industry. What you need to be especially concerned about here are new malls opened by individuals who have no track record in this industry.

I'm not telling you *not* to set up a booth in a new mall in your area—it might prove to be a terrific outlet for you—but I am cautioning you to keep a sharp eye on the mall and how it's being operated. Warning signs of a mall in trouble include:

- less than 75 percent occupancy
- little or no ongoing advertising
- not many shoppers
- crafters pulling out (usually a sign of too few sales)
- poor accounting of sales
- late payments

If a mall is in trouble, it stands to reason that the logical time for it to close is right after the biggest selling season of the year, namely Christmas. Interestingly, this is when most of the shady mall owners have stolen out of town with crafters' Christmas sales in their pockets. As stated in my *Creative Cash* book:

> If it's nearing Christmastime, and you're getting uncomfortable vibes about the financial condition of a mall you're in, it might be smart to remove the bulk of your merchandise—especially expensive items—just before it closes for the holidays. You can always restock after the first of the year if everything looks rosy.

Avoiding Bad Checks

At a crafts fair or other event where you're selling directly to the public, if the buyer doesn't have cash and you don't accept credit cards, your only option is to accept a check. Few crafters have bad check problems for sales held in the home (holiday boutique, open house, party plan, and such), but bad checks at craft fairs are always possible. Here are several things you can do to avoid accepting a bad check:

- Always ask to see a driver's license and look carefully at the picture on it. Write the license number on the check.

- If the sale is a for a large amount, you can ask to see a credit card for added identification, but writing down the number will do no good because you cannot legally cover a bad check with a customer's credit card. (The customer has a legal right to refuse to let you copy the number as well.)

- Look closely at the check itself. Is there a name and address printed on it? If not, ask the customer to write in this information by hand, along with his or her phone number.

- Look at the sides of the check. If at least one side is not perforated, it could be a phony check.

- Look at the check number in the upper right-hand corner. Most banks who issue personalized checks begin the numbering system with 101 when a customer reorders new checks. The Small Business Administration says to be more cautious with low sequence numbers because there seems to be a higher number of these checks that are returned.

- Check the routing number in the lower left-hand corner and note the ink. If it looks shiny, wet your finger and see if the ink rubs off. That's a sure sign of a phony check because good checks are printed with magnetic ink that does not reflect light.

Collecting on a Bad Check

No matter how careful you are, sooner or later, you will get stuck with a bad check. It may bounce for three reasons:

> nonsufficient funds (NSF)
> account closed
> no account (evidence of fraud)

I've accepted tens of thousands of checks from mail-order buyers through the years and have rarely had a bad check I couldn't collect with a simple phone call asking the party to honor his or her obligation to me. People often move and close out accounts before all checks have cleared, or they add or subtract wrong, causing their account to be overdrawn. Typically, they are embarrassed to have caused a problem like this.

When the problem is more difficult than this, your bank can help. Check to learn its policy regarding bounced checks. Some automatically put checks through a second time. If a check bounces at this point, you may ask the bank to collect the check for you. The check needs to be substantial, however, since the bank fee may be $15 or more if they are successful in collecting the money.

If you have accepted a check for a substantial amount of money and believe there is evidence of fraud, you may wish to do one of the following:

- **notify your district attorney's office**
- **contact your sheriff or police department (since it is a crime to write a bad check)**
- **try to collect through small claims court**

For more detailed information on all of these topics, see *The Crafts Business Answer Book.*

7. Insurance Tips

As soon as you start even the smallest business at home, you need to give special attention to insurance. This section offers an introductory overview of insurance concerns of primary interest to crafts-business owners.

Homeowner's or Renter's Insurance

Anything in the home being used to generate income is considered to be business-related and thus exempt from coverage on a personal policy. Thus your homeowner's or renter's insurance policy will not cover business equipment, office furniture, supplies, or inventory of finished goods unless you obtain a special rider. Such riders, called a "Business Pursuits Endorsement" by some companies, are inexpensive and offer considerable protection. Your insurance agent will be happy to give you details.

As your business grows and you have an ever-larger inventory of supplies, materials, tools, and finished merchandise, you may find it necessary to buy a special in-home business policy that offers broader protection. Such policies may be purchased directly from insurance companies or through craft and home-business organizations that offer special insurance programs to their members.

Liability Insurance

There are two kinds of liability insurance. *Product* liability insurance protects you against lawsuits by consumers who have been injured while using one of your products. *Personal* liability insurance protects you against claims made by individuals who have suffered bodily injury while on your premises (either your home or the place where you are doing business, such as in your booth at a crafts fair).

Your homeowner's or renter's insurance policy will include some personal liability protection, but if someone were to suffer bodily injury while on your premises for *business* reasons, that coverage might not apply. Your need for personal liability insurance will be greater if you plan to regularly present home parties, holiday boutiques, or open house sales in your home where many people might be coming and going throughout the year. If you sell at craft fairs, you would also be liable for damages if someone were to fall and be injured in your booth or if something in your booth falls and injures another person. For this reason, some craft fair promoters now require all vendors to have personal liability insurance.

As for product liability insurance, whether you need it or not depends largely on the type of products you make for sale, how careful you are to make sure those products are safe, and how and where you sell them. Examples of some crafts that have caused injury to consumers and resulted in court claims in the past are stuffed toys with wire or pins that children have swallowed; items made of yarn or fiber that burned rapidly; handmade furniture that collapsed when someone put an ordinary amount of weight on them; jewelry with sharp points or other features that cut the wearer, and so on. Clearly, the best way to avoid injury to consumers is to make certain your products have no health hazards and are safe to use. (See discussion of consumer safety laws in section 8.)

Few artists and craftspeople who sell on a part-time basis feel they can afford product liability insurance, but many full-time craft professionals, particularly those who sell their work wholesale, find it a necessary expense. In fact, many wholesale buyers refuse to buy from suppliers that do not carry product liability insurance.

I believe the least expensive way to obtain both personal and product liability insurance is with one of the comprehensive in-home or craft business policies offered by a craft or home-business organization. Such policies generally offer a million dollars of both personal and product liability coverage. (See "Things to Do" Checklist on page 237 and Resources for some organizations you can contact for more information. Also check with your insurance agent about the benefits of an umbrella policy for extra liability insurance.)

Insurance on Crafts Merchandise

As a seller of art or crafts merchandise, you are responsible for insuring your own products against loss. If you plan to sell at craft fairs, in craft malls, rent-a-space shops, or consignment shops, you may want to buy an insurance policy that protects your merchandise both at home or away. Note that while craft shops and malls generally have fire insurance covering the building and its fixtures, this coverage cannot be extended to merchandise offered for sale because it is not the property of the shop owner. (Exception: Shops and malls in shopping centers are mandated by law to buy fire insurance on their contents whether they own the merchandise or not.)

This kind of insurance is usually part of the home-business/crafts-business insurance policies mentioned earlier.

Auto Insurance

Be sure to talk to the agent who handles your car insurance and explain that you may occasionally use your car for business purposes. Normally, a policy issued for a car that's used only for pleasure or driving to and from work may not provide complete coverage for an accident that occurs during business use of the car, particularly if the insured is to blame for the accident. For example, if you were delivering a load of crafts to a shop or on your way to a crafts fair and had an accident, would your business destination and the "commercial merchandise" in your car negate your coverage in any

Insuring Your Art or Crafts Collection

The replacement cost insurance you may have on your personal household possessions does not extend to "fine art," which includes such things as paintings, antiques, pictures, tapestries, statuary, and other articles that cannot be replaced with new articles. If you have a large collection of art, crafts, memorabilia, or collector's items, and its value is more than $1,500, you may wish to have your collection appraised so it can be protected with a separate all-risk endorsement to your homeowner's policy called a "fine arts floater."

way? Where insurance is concerned, the more questions you ask, the better you'll feel about the policies you have.

8. Important Regulations Affecting Artists and Craftspeople

Government agencies have a number of regulations that artists and craftspeople must know about. Generally, they relate to consumer safety, the labeling of certain products and trade practices. Following are regulations of primary interest to readers of books in Prima's FOR FUN & PROFIT series. If you find a law or regulation related to your particular art or craft interest, be sure to request additional information from the government agency named there.

Consumer Safety Laws

All product sellers must pay attention to the Consumer Product Safety Act, which protects the public against unreasonable risks of injury associated with consumer products. The Consumer Product Safety Commission (CPSC) is particularly active in the area of toys and consumer goods designed for children. All sellers of handmade products must be doubly careful about the materials they use for children's products since consumer lawsuits are common where products for children are concerned. To avoid this problem, simply comply with the consumer safety laws applicable to your specific art or craft.

Toy Safety Concerns

To meet CPSC's guidelines for safety, make sure any toys you make for sale are:

- too large to be swallowed
- not apt to break easily or leave jagged edges

- free of sharp edges or points
- not put together with easily exposed pins, wires, or nails
- nontoxic, nonflammable, and nonpoisonous

The Use of Paints, Varnishes, and Other Finishes

Since all paint sold for household use must meet the Consumer Product Safety Act's requirement for minimum amounts of lead, these paints are deemed to be safe for use on products made for children, such as toys and furniture. Always check, however, to make sure the label bears a nontoxic notation. Specialty paints must carry a warning on the label about lead count, but "artist's paints" are curiously exempt from CPS's lead-in-paint ban and are not required to bear a warning label of any kind. Thus you should *never* use such paints on products intended for use by children unless the label specifically states they are *nontoxic* (lead-free). Acrylics and other water-based paints, of course, are nontoxic and completely safe for use on toys and other products made for children. If you plan to use a finishing coat, make sure it is nontoxic as well.

Fabric Flammability Concerns

The Flammable Fabrics Act is applicable only to those who sell products made of fabric, particularly products for children. It prohibits the movement in interstate commerce of articles of wearing apparel and fabrics that are so highly flammable as to be dangerous when worn by individuals, and for other purposes. Most fabrics comply with the above act, but if you plan to sell children's clothes or toys, you may wish to take an extra step to be doubly sure the fabric you are using is safe. This is particularly important if you plan to wholesale your products. What you should do is ask your fabric supplier for a *guarantee of compliance with the Flammability Act*. This guarantee is generally passed along to the buyer by a statement on the invoice that reads "continuing guaranty under the Flammable Fabrics Act." If you do not find such a statement on your invoice, you should ask the fabric manufacturer, wholesaler, or distributor to furnish you with their "statement of compliance" with the flammability standards. The CPSC can also tell you if a particular manufacturer has filed a continuing guarantee under The Flammable Fabrics Act.

Labels Required by Law

The following information applies only to crafters who use textiles, fabrics, fibers, or yarn products to make wearing apparel, decorative accessories, household furnishings, soft toys, or any product made of wool.

Different governmental agencies require the attachment of certain tags or labels to products sold in the consumer marketplace, whether manufactured in quantity or handmade for limited sale. You don't have to be too concerned about these laws if you sell only at local fairs, church bazaars, and home boutiques. As soon as you get out into the general consumer marketplace, however—doing large craft fairs, selling through consignment shops, craft malls, or wholesaling to shops—it would be wise to comply with all the federal labeling laws. Actually, these laws are quite easy to comply with because the required labels are readily available at inexpensive prices, and you can even make your own if you wish. Here is what the federal government wants you to tell your buyers in a tag or label:

- **What's in a product, and who has made it. The Textile Fiber Products Identification Act (monitored both by the Bureau of Consumer Protection and the Federal Trade Commission) requires that a special label or hangtag be attached to all textile wearing apparel and household furnishings, with the exception of wall hangings. "Textiles" include products made of any fiber, yarn, or fabric, including garments and decorative accessories, quilts, pillows, place mats, stuffed toys, rugs, etc. The tag or label must include**

(1) the name of the manufacturer and (2) the generic names and percentages of all fibers in the product in amounts of 5 percent or more, listed in order of predominance by weight.

■ How to take care of products. Care Labeling Laws are part of the Textile Fiber Products Identification Act, details about which are available from the FTC. If you make wearing apparel or household furnishings of any kind using textiles, suede, or leather, you must attach a permanent label that explains how to take care of the item. This label must indicate whether the item is to be dry-cleaned or washed. If it is washable, you must indicate whether in hot or cold water, whether bleach may or may not be used, and the temperature at which it may be ironed.

■ Details about products made of wool. If a product contains wool, the FTC requires additional identification under a separate law known as the Wool Products Labeling Act of 1939. FTC rules require that the labels of all wool or textile products clearly indicate when imported ingredients are used. Thus, the label for a skirt knitted in the U.S. from wool yarn imported from England would read, "Made in the USA from imported products" or similar wordage. If the wool yarn was spun in the U.S., a product made from that yarn would simply need a tag or label stating it was "Made in the USA" or "Crafted in USA" or some similarly clear terminology.

The Bedding and Upholstered Furniture Law

This is a peculiar state labeling law that affects sellers of items that have a concealed filling. It requires the purchase of a license, and products must have a tag that bears the manufacturer's registry number.

Bedding laws have long been a thorn in the side of crafters because they make no distinction between the large manufacturing company that makes mattresses and pillows, and the individual crafts producer who sells only handmade items. "Concealed filling" items include not just bedding and upholstery, but handmade pillows and quilts. In some states, dolls, teddy bears, and stuffed soft sculpture items are also required to have a tag.

Fortunately, only twenty-nine states now have this law on the books, and even if your state is one of them, the law may be arbitrarily enforced. (One exception is the state of Pennsylvania, which is reportedly sending officials to craft shows to inspect merchandise to see if it is properly labeled.) The only penalty that appears to be connected with a violation of this law in any state is removal of merchandise from store shelves or craft fair exhibits. That being the case, many crafters choose to ignore this law until they are challenged. If you learn you must comply with this law, you will be required to obtain a state license that will cost between $25 and $100, and you will have to order special "bedding stamps" that can be attached to your products. For more information on this complex topic, see *The Crafts Business Answer Book*.

FTC Rule for Mail-Order Sellers

Even the smallest home-based business needs to be familiar with Federal Trade Commission (FTC) rules and regulations. A variety of free booklets are available to business owners on topics related to advertising, mail-order marketing, and product labeling (as discussed earlier). In particular, crafters who sell by mail need to pay attention to the FTC's Thirty-Day Mail-Order Rule, which states that one must ship customer orders within thirty days of receiving payment for the order. This rule is strictly enforced, with severe financial penalties for each violation.

Unless you specifically state in your advertising literature how long delivery will take, customers will expect to receive the product within thirty days after you get their order. If you cannot meet this shipping date, you must notify the customer accordingly, enclosing a postage-paid reply card or envelope, and giving them the option to cancel the order if they wish. Now you know why so many catalog sellers state, "Allow six weeks for delivery." This lets them off the hook in case there are unforeseen delays in getting the order delivered.

9. Protecting Your Intellectual Property

"Intellectual property," says Attorney Stephen Elias in his book, *Patent, Copyright & Trademark,* "is a product of the human intellect that has commercial value."

This section offers a brief overview of how to protect your intellectual property through patents and trademarks, with a longer discussion of copyright law, which is of the greatest concern to individuals who sell what they make. Since it is easy to get patents, trademarks, and copyrights mixed up, let me briefly define them for you:

- A *patent* is a grant issued by the government that gives an inventor the right to exclude all others from making, using, or selling an invention within the United States and its territories and possessions.

- A *trademark* is used by a manufacturer or merchant to identify his or her goods and distinguish them from those manufactured or sold by others.

- A *copyright* protects the rights of creators of intellectual property in five main categories (described in this section).

Perspective on Patents

A patent may be granted to anyone who invents or discovers a new and useful process, machine, manufacture or composition of matter, or any new and useful improvement thereof. Any new, original, and ornamental design for an article of manufacture can also be patented. The problem with patents is that they can cost as much as

$5,000 or more to obtain, and once you've got one, they still require periodic maintenance through the U.S. Patent and Trademark Office. To contact this office, you can use the following Web sites: www.uspto.com or www.lcweb.loc.gov.

Ironically, a patent doesn't even give one the right to sell a product. It merely excludes anyone else from making, using, or selling your invention. Many business novices who have gone to the trouble to patent a product end up wasting a lot of time and money because a patent is useless if it isn't backed with the right manufacturing, distribution, and advertising programs. As inventor Jeremy

A Proper Copyright Notice

Although a copyright notice is not required by law, you are encouraged to put a copyright notice on every original thing you create. Adding the copyright notice does not obligate you to formally register your copyright, but it does serve to warn others that your work is legally protected and makes it difficult for anyone to claim they have "accidentally stolen" your work. (Those who actually do violate a copyright because they don't understand the law are called "innocent infringers" by the Copyright Office.)

A proper copyright notice includes three things:

1. the word "copyright," its abbreviation "copr.," or the copyright symbol, ©

2. the year of first publication of the work (when it was first shown or sold to the public)

3. the name of the copyright owner. Example: © 2000 by Barbara Brabec. (When the words "All Rights Reserved" are added to the copyright notation, it means that copyright protection has been extended to include all of the Western Hemisphere.)

The copyright notice should be positioned in a place where it can easily be seen. It can be stamped, cast, engraved, painted, printed, wood-burned, or simply written by hand in permanent ink. In the case of fiber crafts, you can attach an inexpensive label with the copyright notice and your business name and logo (or any other information you wish to put on the label).

Gorman states in *Homemade Money*, "Ninety-seven percent of the U.S. patents issued never earn enough money to pay the patenting fee. They just go on a plaque on the wall or in a desk drawer to impress the grandchildren fifty years later."

What a Trademark Protects

Trademarks were established to prevent one company from trading on the good name and reputation of another. The primary function of a trademark is to indicate origin, but in some cases it also serves as a guarantee of quality.

You cannot adopt any trademark that is so similar to another that it is likely to confuse buyers, nor can you trademark generic or descriptive names in the public domain. If, however, you come up with a particular word, name, symbol, or device to identify and distinguish your products from others, you may protect that mark by trademark provided another company is not already using a similar mark. Brand names, trade names, slogans, and phrases may also qualify for trademark protection.

Many individual crafters have successfully registered their own trademarks using a how-to book on the topic, but some would say never to try this without the help of a trademark attorney. It depends on how much you love detail and how well you can follow directions. Any mistake on the application form could cause it to be rejected, and you would lose the application fee in the process. If this is something you're interested in, and you have designed a mark you want to protect, you should first do a trademark search to see if someone else is already using it. Trademark searches can be done using library directories, an online computer service (check with your library), through private trademark search firms, or directly on the Internet through the Patent & Trademark Office's online search service (see checklist and resources). All of these searches together could still be inconclusive, however, because many companies have a stash of trademarks in reserve waiting for just the right product. As I understand it, these "nonpublished" trademarks are in a special file that only an attorney or trademark search service could find for you.

Like copyrights, trademarks have their own symbol, which looks like this: ®. This symbol can only be used once the trademark has been formally registered through the U.S. Patent and Trademark Office. Business owners often use the superscript initials "TM" with a mark to indicate they've claimed a logo or some other mark, but this offers no legal protection. While this does not guarantee trademark protection, it does give notice to the public that you are claiming this name as your trademark. However, after you've used a mark for some time, you do gain a certain amount of common-law protection for that mark. I have, in fact, gained common-law protection for the name of my *Homemade Money* book and successfully defended it against use by another individual in my field because this title has become so closely associated with my name in the home-business community.

Whether you ever formally register a trademark or not will have much to do with your long-range business plans, how you feel about protecting your creativity, and what it would do to your business if someone stole your mark and registered it in his or her own name. Once you've designed a trademark you feel is worth protecting, get additional information from the Patent & Trademark Office and read a book or two on the topic to decide whether this is something you wish to pursue. (See "Things to Do" Checklist and Resources.)

What Copyrights Protect

As a serious student of the copyright law, I've pored through the hard-to-interpret copyright manual, read dozens of related articles and books, and discussed this subject at length with designers, writers, teachers, editors, and publishers. I must emphasize, however, that I am no expert on this topic, and the following information does not constitute legal advice. It is merely offered as a general guide to a very complex legal topic you may wish to research further on your own at some point. In a book of this nature, addressed to hobbyists and beginning crafts-business owners, a discussion of copyrights must be limited to three basic topics:

- what copyrights do and do not protect
- how to register a copyright and protect your legal rights
- how to avoid infringing on the rights of other copyright holders

One of the first things you should do now is send for the free booklets offered by the Copyright Office (see checklist and resources). Various free circulars explain copyright basics, the forms involved in registering a copyright, and how to submit a copyright application and register a copyright. They also discuss what you cannot copyright. Rather than duplicate all the free information you can get from the Copyright Office with a letter or phone call, I will only briefly touch on these topics and focus instead on addressing some of the particular copyright questions crafters have asked me in the past.

Things You Can Copyright

Some people mistakenly believe that copyright protection extends only to printed works, but that is not true. The purpose of the copyright law is to protect any creator from anyone who would use his creative work for his own profit. Under current copyright law, claims are now registered in seven classes, five of which pertain to crafts:

1. *Serials* (Form SE)—periodicals, newspapers, magazines, bulletins, newsletters, annuals, journals, and proceedings of societies.
2. *Text* (Form TX)—books, directories, and other written works, including the how-to instructions for a crafts project. (You

could copyright a letter to your mother if you wanted to—
or your best display ad copy, or any other written words that
represent income potential.)

3. *Visual Arts* (Form VA)—pictorial, graphic, or sculptural
   works, including fine, graphic, and applied art; photographs,
   charts; technical drawings; diagrams; and models. (Also included in this category are "works of artistic craftsmanship
   insofar as their form but not their mechanical or utilitarian
   aspects are concerned.")

4. *Performing Arts* (Form PA)—musical works and accompanying words, dramatic works, pantomimes, choreographic
   works, motion pictures, and other audiovisual works.

5. Sound Recordings (Form SR)—musical, spoken, or other
   sounds, including any audio- or videotapes you might
   create.

Selling How-To Projects to Magazines

If you want to sell an article, poem, or how-to project to a magazine, you need not
copyright the material first because copyright protection exists from the moment you
create that work. Your primary consideration here is whether you will sell "all rights"
or only "first rights" to the magazine.

The sale of first rights means you are giving a publication permission to print your article, poem, or how-to project once, for a specific sum of money. After publication, you
then have the right to resell that material or profit from it in other ways. Although it is
always desirable to sell only "first rights," some magazines do not offer this choice.

If you sell all rights, you will automatically lose ownership of the copyright to your
material and you can no longer profit from that work. Professional designers often
refuse to work this way because they know they can realize greater profits by publishing their own pattern packets or design leaflets and wholesaling them to shops.

Things You Cannot Copyright

You can't copyright ideas or procedures for doing, making, or building things, but the *expression* of an idea fixed in a tangible medium may be copyrightable—such as a book explaining a new system or technique. Brand names, trade names, slogans, and phrases cannot be copyrighted, either, although they might be entitled to protection under trademark laws.

The design on a craft object can be copyrighted, but only if it can be identified separately from the object itself. Objects themselves (a decorated coffee mug, a box, a tote bag) cannot be copyrighted.

Copyright Registration Tips

First, understand that you do not have to formally copyright anything because copyright protection exists from the moment a work is created, whether you add a copyright notice or not.

So why file at all? The answer is simple: If you don't file the form and pay the fee (currently $30), you'll never be able to take anyone to court for stealing your work. Therefore, in each instance where copyright protection is considered, you need to decide how important your work is to you in terms of dollars and cents, and ask yourself whether you value it enough to pay to protect it. Would you actually be willing to pay court costs to defend your copyright, should someone steal it from you? If you never intend to go to court, there's little use in officially registering a copyright; but since it costs you nothing to add a copyright notice to your work, you are foolish not to do this. (See sidebar, "A Proper Copyright Notice," page 218.)

If you do decide to file a copyright application, contact the Copyright Office and request the appropriate forms. When you file the copyright application form (which is easy to complete), you must include with it two copies of the work. Ordinarily, two actual copies of copyrighted items must be deposited, but certain items are exempt from deposit requirements, including all three-dimensional sculptural works and any works published only as reproduced in or on jewelry, dolls, toys, games, plaques, floor coverings, textile and other fabrics, packaging materials, or any useful article. In these cases, two photographs or drawings of the item are sufficient.

Note that the Copyright Office does not compare deposit copies to determine whether works submitted for registration are similar to any material already copyrighted. It is the sender's responsibility to determine the originality of what's being copyrighted. (See discussion of "original" in the next section, under "Respecting the Copyrights of Others.")

Protecting Your Copyrights

If someone ever copies one of your copyrighted works, and you have registered that work with the Copyright Office, you should defend it as far as you are financially able to do so. If you think you're dealing with an innocent infringer—another crafter, perhaps, who has probably not profited much (if at all) from your work—a strongly worded letter on your business stationery (with a copy to an attorney, if you have one) might do the trick. Simply inform the copyright infringer that you are the legal owner of the work and the only one who has the right to profit from it. Tell the infringer that he or she must immediately cease using your copyrighted work, and ask for a confirmation by return mail.

If you think you have lost some money or incurred other damages, consult with a copyright attorney before contacting the infringer to see how you can best protect your rights and recoup any financial losses you may have suffered. This is particularly important if the infringer appears to be a successful business or corporation. Although you may have no intention of ever going to court on this matter, the copyright infringer won't know that, and one letter from a competent attorney might immediately resolve the matter at very little cost to you.

Mandatory Deposit Requirements

Although you do not have to officially register a copyright claim, it *is* mandatory to deposit two copies of all "published works" for the collections of the Library of Congress within three months after publication. Failure to make the deposit may subject the copyright owner to fines and other monetary liabilities, but it does not affect copyright protection. No special form is required for this mandatory deposit.

Note that the term "published works" pertains not just to the publication of printed matter, but to the public display of any item. Thus you "publish" your originally designed craftwork when you first show it at a craft fair, in a shop, on your Web site, or any other public place.

Respecting the Copyrights of Others

Just as there are several things you must do to protect your "intellectual creations," there are several things you must not do if you wish to avoid legal problems with other copyright holders.

Copyright infringement occurs whenever anyone violates the exclusive rights covered by copyright. If and when a copyright case goes to court, the copyright holder who has been infringed upon must prove that his or her work is the original creation and that the two works are so similar that the alleged infringer must have copied it. This is not always an easy matter, for "original" is a difficult word to define. Even the Copyright Office has trouble here, which is why so many cases that go to court end up setting precedents.

In any copyright case, there will be discussions about "substantial similarity," instances where two people actually have created the same thing simultaneously, loss of profits, or damage to one's business or reputation. If you were found guilty of copyright infringement, at the very least you would probably be ordered to pay to the original creator all profits derived from the sale of the copyrighted work to date. You would also have to agree to refund any orders you might receive for the work in the future. In some copyright cases where the original creator has experienced considerable financial loss, penalties for copyright infringement have been as high as $100,000. As you can see, this is not a matter to take lightly.

This is a complex topic beyond the scope of this book, but any book on copyright law will provide additional information if you should ever need it. What's important here is that you fully understand the importance of being careful to respect the legal rights of others. As a crafts business owner, you could possibly infringe on someone else's designs when you (1) quote someone in an article, periodical, or book you've written; (2) photocopy copyrighted materials; or (3) share information on the Internet. Following is a brief discussion of the first three topics and a longer discussion of the fourth.

1. **Be careful when quoting from a published source.** If you're writing an article or book and wish to quote someone's words from any published source (book, magazine, Internet, and so on), you should always obtain written permission first. Granted, minor quotations from published sources are okay when they fall under the Copyright Office's Fair Use Doctrine, but unless you completely understand this doctrine, you should protect yourself by obtaining permission before you quote anyone in one of your own written works. It is not necessarily the quantity of the quote, but the value of the quoted material to the copyright owner.

   In particular, never *ever* use a published poem in one of your written works. To the poet, this is a "whole work," much the same as a book is a whole work to an author. While the use of one or two lines of a poem, or a paragraph from a book may be considered "fair use," many publishers now require written permission even for this short reproduction of a copyrighted work.

2. **Photocopying can be dangerous.** Teachers often photocopy large sections of a book (sometimes whole books) for distribution to their students, but this is a flagrant violation of the copyright law. Some publishers may grant photocopying of part of a work if it is to be used only once as a teaching aid, but written permission must always be obtained first.

   It is also a violation of the copyright law to photocopy patterns for sale or trade because such use denies the creator the profit from a copy that might have been sold.

3. **Don't share copyrighted information on the Internet.** People everywhere are lifting material from *Reader's Digest* and other copyrighted publications and "sharing" them on the Internet through e-mail messages, bulletin boards, and the like. *This is a very dangerous thing to do.* "But I didn't see a copyright notice," you might say, or "It indicated the author was anonymous." What you must remember is that *everything* gains copyright protection the moment it is created, whether a copyright notice is attached to it or not. Many "anonymous" items on the Internet are actually copyrighted poems and articles put there by someone who not only violated the copyright law but compounded the matter by failing to give credit to the original creator.

   If you were to pick up one of those "anonymous" pieces of information and put it into an article or book of your own, the original copyright owner, upon seeing his or her work in your publication, would have good grounds for a lawsuit. Remember, pleading ignorance of the law is never a good excuse.

   Clearly there is no financial gain to be realized by violating the rights of a copyright holder when it means that any day you might be contacted by a lawyer and threatened with a lawsuit. As stated in my *Crafts Business Answer Book & Resource Guide:*

▼▼

Changing Things

Many crafters have mistakenly been led to believe that they can copy the work of others if they simply change this or that so their creation doesn't look exactly like the one they have copied. But many copyright court cases have hinged in someone taking "a substantial part" of someone else's design and claiming it as their own. As explained earlier, if your "original creation" bears even the slightest resemblance to the product you've copied—and you are caught selling it in the commercial marketplace—there could be legal problems.

Crafters often combine the parts of two or three patterns in an attempt to come up with their own original patterns, but often this only compounds the possible copyright problems. Let's imagine you're making a doll. You might take the head from one pattern, the arms and legs from another, and the unique facial features from another. You may think you have developed an original creation (and perhaps an original pattern

▲▲

The best way to avoid copyright infringement problems is to follow the "Golden Rule" proposed by a United States Supreme Court justice: "Take not from others to such an extent and in such a manner that you would be resentful if they so took from you."

Using Commercial Patterns and Designs

Beginning crafters who lack design skills commonly make products for sale using commercial patterns, designs in books, or how-to instructions for projects found in magazines. The problem here is that all of these things are published for the general consumer market and offered for *personal use* only. Because they are all protected by copyright, that means only the copyright holder has the right to profit from their use.

That said, let me ease your mind by saying that the sale of products made from copyrighted patterns, designs, and magazine how-to projects is probably not going to cause any problems *as long*

you might sell), but you haven't. Since the original designer of any of the features you've copied might recognize her work in your "original creation" or published pattern, she could come after you for infringing on "a substantial part" of her design. In this case, all you've done is multiply your possibilities for a legal confrontation with three copyright holders.

"But I can't create my own original designs and patterns!" you moan. Many who have said this in the past were mistaken. With time and practice, most crafters are able to develop products that are original in design, and I believe you can do this, too. Meanwhile, check out Dover Publications' *Pictorial Archive* series of books (see the "Things to Do" Checklist and Resources). Here you will find thousands of copyright-free designs and motifs you can use on your craft work or in needlework projects. And don't forget the wealth of design material in museums and old books that have fallen into the public domain. (See sidebar, "What's in the Public Domain?" on page 232.)

as sales are limited, and they yield a profit only to you, the crafter. That means no sales through shops of any kind where a sales commission or profit is received by a third party, and absolutely no wholesaling of such products.

It's not that designers and publishers are concerned about your sale of a few craft or needlework items to friends and local buyers; what they are fighting to protect with the legality of copyrights is their right to sell their own designs or finished products in the commercial marketplace. You may find that some patterns, designs, or projects state "no mass production." You are not mass producing if you make a dozen handcrafted items for sale at a craft fair or holiday boutique, but you would definitely be considered a mass-producer if you made dozens, or hundreds, for sale in shops.

Consignment sales fall into a kind of gray area that requires some commonsense judgment on your part. This is neither wholesaling nor selling direct to consumers. One publisher might consider such sales a violation of a copyright while another might not.

Whenever specific guidelines for the use of a pattern, design, or how-to project is not given, the only way to know for sure if you are operating on safe legal grounds is to write to the publisher and get written permission on where you can sell reproductions of the item in question.

Now let's take a closer look at the individual types of patterns, designs, and how-to projects you might consider using once you enter the crafts marketplace.

Craft, Toy, and Garment Patterns

Today, the consumer has access to thousands of sewing patterns plus toy, craft, needlework, and woodworking patterns of every kind and description found in books, magazines, and design or project leaflets. Whether you can use such patterns for commercial use depends largely on who has published the pattern and owns the copyright, and what the copyright holder's policy happens to be for how buyers may use those patterns.

To avoid copyright problems when using patterns of any kind, the first thing you need to do is look for some kind of notice on the pattern packet or publication containing the pattern. In checking some patterns, I found that those sold by *Woman's Day* state specifically that reproductions of the designs may not be sold, bartered, or traded. *Good Housekeeping*, on the other hand, gives permission to use their patterns for "income-producing activities." When in doubt, ask!

Whereas the general rule for selling reproductions made from commercial patterns is "no wholesaling and no sales to shops," items made from the average garment pattern (such as an apron, vest, shirt, or simple dress) purchased in the local fabric store *may* be an exception. My research suggests that selling such items in your local consignment shop or craft mall isn't likely to be much of a problem because the sewing pattern companies aren't on the lookout for copyright violators the way individual craft designers and major corporations are. (And most people who sew end up changing those patterns and using different decorations to such a degree that pattern companies might not recognize those patterns even if they were looking for them. See sidebar, "Changing Things," page 228.)

On the other hand, commercial garment patterns that have been designed by name designers should never be used without permission. In most cases, you would have to obtain a licensing agreement for the commercial use of such patterns.

Be especially careful about selling reproductions of toys and dolls made from commercial patterns or design books. Many are likely to be for popular copyrighted characters being sold in the commercial marketplace. In such cases, the pattern company will have a special licensing arrangement with the toy or doll manufacturer to sell the pattern, and reproductions for sale by individual crafters will be strictly prohibited.

Take a Raggedy Ann doll, for example. The fact that you've purchased a pattern to make such a doll does not give you the right to sell a finished likeness of that doll any more than your purchase of a piece of artwork gives you the right to re-create it for sale in some other form, such as notepaper or calendars. Only the original creator has such rights. You have simply purchased the *physical property* for private use.

How-To Projects in Magazines and Books

Each magazine and book publisher has its own policy about the use of its art, craft, or needlework projects. How those projects may be used depends on who owns the copyright to the published projects. In some instances, craft and needlework designers sell their original designs outright to publishers of books, leaflets, or magazines. Other designers authorize only a one-time use of their projects, which gives them the right to republish or sell their designs to another market or license them to a manufacturer. If guidelines about selling finished products do not appear somewhere in the magazine or on the copyright page of a book, you should always write and get permission to make such items for sale. In your letter, explain how many items you would like to make, and where you plan to sell them, as that could make a big difference in the reply you receive.

In case you missed the special note on the copyright page of this book, you *can* make and sell all of the projects featured in this and any other book in Prima's FOR FUN & PROFIT series.

As a columnist for *Crafts Magazine,* I can also tell you that its readers have the right to use its patterns and projects for money-making purposes, but only to the extent that sales are limited to places where the crafter is the only one who profits from their use. That means selling directly to individuals, with no sales in shops of any kind where a third party would also realize some profit from a sale. Actually, this is a good rule-of-thumb guideline to use if you plan to sell only a few items of any project or pattern published in any magazine, book, or leaflet.

What's in the Public Domain?

For all works created after January 1, 1978, the copyright lasts for the life of the author or creator plus 50 years after his or her death. For works created before 1978, there are different terms, which you can obtain from any book in your library on copyright law.

Once material falls into the public domain, it can never be copyrighted again. As a general rule, anything with a copyright date more than 75 years ago is probably in the public domain, but you can never be sure without doing a thorough search. Some characters in old books—such as Beatrix Potter's *Peter Rabbit*—are now protected under the trademark law as business logos. For more information on this, ask the Copyright Office to send you its circular on "How to Investigate the Copyright Status of a Work."

Early American craft and needlework patterns of all kind are in the public domain because they were created before the copyright law was a reality. Such old patterns may

In summary, products that aren't original in design will sell, but their market is limited, and they will never be able to command the kind of prices that original-design items enjoy. Generally speaking, the more original the product line, the greater one's chances for building a profitable crafts business.

As your business grows, questions about copyrights will arise, and you will have to do a little research to get the answers you need. Your library should have several books on this topic and there is a wealth of information on the Internet. (Just use your search button and type "copyright information.") If you have a technical copyright question, remember that you can always call the Copyright Office and speak to someone who can answer it and send you additional information. Note, however, that regulations prohibit the Copyright Office from giving legal advice or opinions concerning the rights of persons in connection with cases of alleged copyright infringement.

show up in books and magazines that are copyrighted, but the copyright in this case extends only to the book or magazine itself and the way in which a pattern has been presented to readers, along with the way in which the how-to-make instructions have been written. The actual patterns themselves cannot be copyrighted by anyone at this point.

Quilts offer an interesting example. If a contemporary quilt designer takes a traditional quilt pattern and does something unusual with it in terms of material or colors, this new creation would qualify for a copyright, with the protection being given to the quilt as a work of art, not to the traditional pattern itself, which is still in the public domain. Thus you could take that same traditional quilt pattern and do something else with it for publication, but you could not publish the contemporary designer's copyrighted version of that same pattern.

10. To Keep Growing, Keep Learning

Everything we do, every action we take, affects our life in one way or another. Reading a book is a simple act, indeed, but trust me when I say that your reading of this particular book *could ultimately change your life.* I know this to be true because thousands of men and women have written to me over the years to tell me how their lives changed after they read one or another of my books and decided to start a crafts business. My life has changed, too, as a result of reading books by other authors.

Many years ago, the purchase of a book titled *You Can Whittle and Carve* unleashed a flood of creativity in me that has yet to cease. That simple book helped me to discover unknown craft talents, which in turn led me to start my first crafts business at home. That experience prepared me for the message I would find a decade later in the book, *On Writing Well* by William Zinsser. This author changed my life by giving me the courage to try my hand at writing professionally. Dozens of books later, I had learned a lot about the art and craft of writing well and making a living in the process.

Now you know why I believe reading should be given top priority in your life. Generally speaking, the more serious you become about anything you're interested in, the more reading you will need to do. This will take time, but the benefits will be enormous. If a crafts business is your current passion, this book contains all you need to know to get started. To keep growing, read some of the wonderful books recommended in the resource section of this book. (If you don't find them in your local library, ask your librarian to obtain them for you through the inter-library loan program.) Join one or more of the organizations recommended. Subscribe to a few periodicals or magazines, and "grow your business" through networking with others who share your interests.

Motivational Tips

As you start your new business or expand a money-making hobby already begun, consider the following suggestions:

- *Start an "Achievement Log."* Day by day, our small achievements may seem insignificant, but viewed in total after several weeks or months, they give us important perspective. Reread your achievement log periodically in the future, especially on days when you feel down in the dumps. Make entries at least once a week, noting such things as new customers or accounts acquired, publicity you've gotten, a new product you've designed, the brochure or catalog you've just completed, positive feedback received from others, new friendships, and financial gains.

- *Live your dream.* The mind is a curious thing—it can be trained to think success is possible or to think that success is only for other people. Most of our fears never come true, so allowing our minds to dwell on what may or may not happen cripples us, preventing us from moving ahead, from having confidence, and from living out our dreams. Instead of "facing fear," focus on the result you want. This may automatically eliminate the fear.

- *Think positively.* As Murphy has proven time and again, what can go wrong will, and usually at the worst possible moment. It matters little whether the thing that has gone wrong was caused by circumstances beyond our control or by a mistake in judgment. What does matter is how we deal with the problem at hand. A positive attitude and the ability to remain flexible at all times are two of the most important ingredients for success in any endeavor.

- *Don't be afraid to fail.* We often learn more from failure than from success. When you make a mistake, chalk it up to experience and consider it a good lesson well learned. The more you learn, the more self-confident you will become.

- *Temper your "dreams of riches" with thoughts of reality.* Remember that "success" can also mean being in control of your own life, making new friends, or discovering a new world of possibilities.

Online Help

Today, one of the best ways to network and learn about business is to get on the Internet. The many online resources included in the "Things to Do Checklist" in the next section will give you a jump-start and lead to many exciting discoveries.

For continuing help and advice from Barbara Brabec, be sure to visit her Web site at www.crafter.com/brabec. There you will find her monthly *Craftsbiz Chat* newsletter, reprints of some of her crafts marketing and business columns, recommended books, and links to hundreds of other arts and craft sites on the Web. Reader questions may be e-mailed to barbara@crafter.com for discussion in her newsletter, but questions cannot be answered individually by e-mail.

You can also get Barbara's business advice in her monthly columns in *Crafts Magazine* and *The Crafts Report*.

Until now you may have lacked the courage to get your craft ideas off the ground, but now that you've seen how other people have accomplished their goals, I hope you feel more confident and adventurous and are ready to capitalize on your creativity. By following the good advice in this book, you can stop dreaming about all the things you want to do and start making plans to do them!

I'm not trying to make home-business owners out of everyone who reads this book, but my goal is definitely to give you a shove in that direction if you're teetering on the edge, wanting something more than just a profitable hobby. It's wonderful to have a satisfying hobby, and even better to have one that pays for itself; but the nicest thing of all is a real home business that lets you fully utilize your creative talents and abilities while also adding to the family income.

"The things I want to know are in books," Abraham Lincoln once said. "My best friend is the person who'll get me a book I ain't read." You now hold in your hands a book that has taught you many things you wanted to know. To make it a *life-changing book,* all you have to do is act on the information you've been given.

I wish you a joyful journey and a potful of profits!

"Things to Do" Checklist

INSTRUCTIONS: Read through this entire section, noting the different things you need to do to get your crafts business "up and running." Use the checklist as a plan, checking off each task as it is completed and obtaining any recommended resources. Where indicated, note the date action was taken so you have a reminder about any follow-up action that should be taken.

Business Start-Up Checklist

__Call city hall or county clerk

    __to register fictitious business name

    __to see if you need a business license or permit

    __to check on local zoning laws
    (info also available in your library)

    *Follow up:*_____

__Call state capitol

    __secretary of state: to register your business name;
    ask about a license

    __Department of Revenue: to apply for sales tax number

    *Follow up:*_____

__Call your local telephone company about

    __cost of a separate phone line for business

    __cost of an additional personal line for Internet access

    __any special options for home-based businesses

    *Follow up:*_____

__Call your insurance agent(s) to discuss

  __business rider on house insurance
  (or need for separate in-home insurance policy)
  __benefits of an umbrella policy for extra liability insurance
  __using your car for business
  (how this may affect your insurance)

  *Follow up:*_____

__Call several banks or S&Ls in your area to

  __compare cost of a business checking account
  __ get price of a safe-deposit box for valuable business records

  *Follow up:*_____

__Visit office and computer supply stores to check on

  __manual bookkeeping systems, such as the
  Dome Simplified Monthly
  __accounting software
  __standard invoices and other helpful business forms

  *Follow up:*_____

__Call National Association of Enrolled Agents at (800) 424-4339

  __to get a referral to a tax professional in your area
  __to get answers to any tax questions you may have (no charge)

  *Follow up:*_____

__Contact government agencies for information
relative to your business.

  (See "Government Agencies" checklist.)

__Request free brochures from organizations

  (See "Craft and Home Business Organizations.")

__Obtain sample issues or subscribe to selected publications

  (See "Recommended Craft Business Periodicals.")

__Obtain other information of possible help to your business

(See "Other Services and Suppliers.")

__Get acquainted with the business information available to you in your library.

(See list of "Recommended Business Books" and "Helpful Library Directories.")

Government Agencies

__Consumer Product Safety Commission (CPSC), Washington, DC 20207. Toll-free hotline: (800) 638-2772. Information Services: (301) 504-0000. Web site: www.cpsc.gov. (Includes a "Talk to Us" e-mail address where you can get answers to specific questions.) If you make toys or other products for children, garments (especially children's wear), or use any kind of paint, varnish, lacquer, or shellac on your products, obtain the following free booklets:

__*The Consumer Product Safety Act of 1972*
__*The Flammable Fabrics Act*

Date Contacted:_____Information Received:_____

*Follow up:*_____

__Copyright Office, Register of Copyrights, Library of Congress, Washington, DC 20559. To hear recorded messages on the Copyright Office's automated message system (general information, registration procedures, copyright search info, etc.), call (202) 707-3000. You can also get the same information online at www.loc.gov/copyright.

To get free copyright forms, a complete list of all publications available, or to speak personally to someone who will answer your special questions, call (202) 797-9100. In particular, ask for:

__Circular R1, *The Nuts and Bolts of Copyright*
__Circular R2 (a list of publications available)

Date Contacted:_____Information Received:_____

*Follow up:*_____

__Department of Labor. If you should ever hire an employee
or independent contractor, contact your local Labor Department, Wage & Hour Division, for guidance on what you must
do to be completely legal. (Check your phone book under
"U.S. Government.")

Date Contacted:_____Information Received:_____

*Follow up:*_____

__Federal Trade Commission (FTC), 6th Street & Pennsylvania
Avenue., N.W., Washington, DC 20580. Web site: www.ftc.gov. Request
any of the following booklets relative to your craft or business:

__*Textile Fiber Products Identification Act*

__*Wool Products Labeling Act of 1939*

__*Care Labeling of Textile Wearing Apparel*

__*The Hand Knitting Yarn Industry* (booklet)

__*Truth-in-Advertising Rules*

__*Thirty-Day Mail Order Rule*

Date Contacted:_____Information Received:_____

Follow up _____

__Internal Revenue Service (IRS). Check the Internet at www
.irs.gov to read the following information online or call your
local IRS office to get the following booklets and other free tax
information:

__*Tax Guide for Small Business—#334*

__*Business Use of Your Home—#587*

__*Tax Information for Direct Sellers*

Date Contacted:_____Information Received:_____

*Follow up*_____

__Patent and Trademark Office (PTO), Washington, DC 20231.
Web site: www.uspto.gov

For patent and trademark information 24 hours a day, call
(800) 786-9199 (in northern Virgina, call (703) 308-9000) to hear
various messages about patents and trademarks or to order the
following booklets:

__*Basic Facts about Patents*
__*Basic Facts about Trademarks*

To search the PTO's online database of all registered trademarks,
go to www.uspto.gov/tmdb/index.html.

Date Contacted:_____Information Received:_____

*Follow up:*_____

__Social Security Hotline. (800) 772-1213. By calling this number,
you can hear automated messages, order information booklets,
or speak directly to someone who can answer specific questions.

Date Contacted:_____Information Received:_____

*Follow up*_____

__U.S. Small Business Administration (SBA). (800) U-ASK-SBA.
Call this number to hear a variety of prerecorded messages on
starting and financing a business. Weekdays, you can speak personally to an SBA adviser to get answers to specific questions
and request such free business publications as:

__*Starting Your Business* —#CO-0028

__*Resource Directory for Small Business Management*—#CO-0042
   (a list of low-cost publications available from the SBA)

The SBA's mission is to help people get into business and stay
there. One-on-one counseling, training, and workshops are available through 950 small business development centers across the
country. Help is also available from local district offices of the

SBA in the form of free business counseling and training from SCORE volunteers (see below). The SBA office in Washington has a special Women's Business Enterprise section that provides free information on loans, tax deductions, and other financial matters. District offices offer special training programs in management, marketing, and accounting.

A wealth of business information is also available online at www.sba.gov and www.business.gov (the U.S. Business Adviser site). To learn whether there is an SBA office near you, look under "U.S. Government" in your telephone directory, or call the SBA's toll-free number.

Date Contacted:_____Information Received:_____

*Follow up:*_____

__SCORE (Service Corps of Retired Executives). (800) 634-0245. There are more than 12,400 SCORE members who volunteer their time and expertise to small business owners. Many craft businesses have received valuable in-depth counseling and training simply by calling the organization and asking how to connect with a SCORE volunteer in their area.

In addition, the organization offers e-mail counseling via the Internet at www.score.org. You simply enter the specific expertise required and retrieve a list of e-mail counselors who represent the best match by industry and topic. Questions can then be sent by e-mail to the counselor of your choice for response.

Date Contacted:_____Information Received:_____

*Follow up:*_____

Crafts and Home-Business Organizations

In addition to the regular benefits of membership in an organization related to your art or craft (fellowship, networking, educational conferences or workshops, marketing opportunities, etc.), membership may also bring special business services, such as insurance programs, merchant card services, and discounts on supplies and materials. Each of the following organizations will send you membership information on request.

__The American Association of Home-Based Businesses, P.O. Box 10023, Rockville, MD 20849. (800) 447-9710. Web site: www.aahbb.org. This organization has chapters throughout the country. Members have access to merchant card services, discounted business products and services, prepaid legal services, and more.

Date Contacted:_____Information Received:_____

*Follow up:*_____

__American Crafts Council, 72 Spring Street, New York, NY 10012. (800)-724-0859. Web site: www.craftcouncil.org. Membership in this organization will give you access to a property and casualty insurance policy that will cost between $250 and $500 a year, depending on your city, state, and the value of items being insured in your art or crafts studio. The policy includes insurance for a craftsperson's work in the studio, in transit or at a show; a million dollars' coverage for bodily injury and property damage in studio or away; and a million dollars' worth of product liability insurance. This policy is from American Phoenix Corporation; staff members will answer your specific questions when you call (800) 274-6364, ext. 337.

Date Contacted:_____Information Received:_____

*Follow up:*_____

__Arts & Crafts Business Solutions, 2804 Bishop Gate Drive, Raleigh, NC 27613. (800) 873-1192. This company, known in the industry as the Arts Group, offers a bankcard service specifically for and tailored to the needs of the arts and crafts marketplace. Several differently priced packages are available, and complete information is available on request.

Date Contacted:_____Information Received:_____

*Follow up:*_____

__Home Business Institute, Inc., P.O. Box 301, White Plains, NY 10605-0301. (888) DIAL-HBI; Fax: (914) 946-6694. Web site: www.hbiweb.com. Membership benefits include insurance programs (medical insurance and in-home business policy that includes some liability insurance); savings on telephone services, office supplies, and merchant account enrollment; and free advertising services.

Date Contacted:_____Information Received:_____

*Follow up:*_____

__National Craft Association (NCA), 1945 E. Ridge Road, Suite 5178, Rochester, NY 14622-2647. (800) 715-9594. Web site: www.craft assoc.com. Members of NCA have access to a comprehensive package of services, including merchant account services; discounts on business services and products; a prepaid legal program; a check-guarantee merchant program; checks by fax, phone, or e-mail; and insurance programs. Of special interest to this book's readers is the "Crafters Business Insurance" policy (through RLI Insurance Co.) that includes coverage for business property; art/craft merchandise or inventory at home, in transit or at a show; theft away from premises; up to a million dollars in both personal and product liability insurance; loss of business income, and more. Members have the option to select the exact benefits they need. Premiums range from $150 to $300, depending on location, value of average inventory, and the risks associated with one's art or craft.

Date Contacted:_____Information Received:_____

*Followup:*_____

Recommended Craft Business Periodicals

Membership in an organization generally includes a subscription to a newsletter or magazine that will be helpful to your business. Here are additional craft periodicals you should sample or subscribe to:

__*The Crafts Report—The Business Journal for the Crafts Industry,* Box 1992, Wilmington, DE 19899. (800) 777-7098. On the Internet at www.craftsreport.com. A monthly magazine covering all areas of craft business management and marketing (includes my column, Barbara Brabec's "BusinessWise" column).

__*Craft Supply Magazine—The Industry Journal for the Professional Crafter,* Krause Publications, Inc., 700 East State Street, Iowa, WI 54990-0001. (800) 258-0929. Web site: www.krause.com. A monthly magazine that includes crafts business and marketing articles and wholesale supply sources.

__*Home Business Report,* 2949 Ash Street, Abbotsford, B.C., V2S 4G5 Canada. (604) 857-1788; Fax: (604) 854-3087. Canada's premier home-business magazine, relative to both general and craft-related businesses.

__*SAC Newsmonthly,* 414 Avenue B, P.O. Box 159, Bogalusa, LA 70429-0159. (800) TAKE-SAC; Fax: (504) 732-3744. A monthly national show guide that also includes business articles for professional crafters.

__*Sunshine Artist* magazine, 2600 Temple Drive, Winter Park, FL 32789. (800) 597-2573; Fax: (407) 539-1499. Web site: www.sunshineartist.com. America's premier show and festival guide.

Each monthly issue contains business and marketing articles of interest to both artists and craftspeople.

Other Services and Suppliers

Contact any of the following companies that offer information or services of interest to you.

__American Express. For merchant account information, call the Merchant Establishment Services Department at (800) 445-AMEX.

Date Contacted:_____Information Received:_____

*Follow up:*_____

__Dover Publications, 31 E. 2nd Sreet, Mineola, NY 11501. Your source for thousands of copyright-free designs and motifs you can use in your craftwork or needlecraft projects. Request a free catalog of books in the *Pictorial Archive* series.

Date Contacted:_____Information Received:_____

*Follow up:*_____

__Novus Services, Inc. For merchant account information, call (800) 347-6673.

Date Contacted:_____Information Received:_____

*Follow up:*_____

__Volunteer Lawyers for the Arts (VLA), 1 E. 53rd Street, New York, NY 10022. Legal hotline: (212) 319-2910. If you ever need an attorney, and cannot afford one, contact this nonprofit organization, which has chapters all over the country. In addition to providing legal aid for performing and visual artists and craftspeople (individually or in groups), the VLA also provides a range of educational services, including issuing publications concerning taxes, accounting, and insurance.

Date Contacted:_____Information Received:_____

*Follow up:*_____

__Widby Enterprises USA, 4321 Crestfield Road, Knoxville, TN 37921-3104. (888) 522-2458. Web site: www.widbylabel.com. Standard and custom-designed labels that meet federal labeling requirements.

Date Contacted:_____Information Received:_____

*Follow up:*_____

Recommended Business Books

When you have specific business questions not answered in this beginner's guide, check your library for the following books. Any not on library shelves can be obtained through the library's inter-library loan program.

__*Business and Legal Forms for Crafts* by Tad Crawford (Allworth Press)

__*Business Forms and Contracts (in Plain English) for Crafts People* by Leonard D. DuBoff (Interweave Press)

__*Crafting as a Business* by Wendy Rosen (Chilton)

__*The Crafts Business Answer Book & Resource Guide: Answers to Hundreds of Troublesome Questions about Starting, Marketing & Managing a Homebased Business Efficiently, Legally, & Profitably* by Barbara Brabec (M. Evans & Co.)

__*Creative Cash: How to Profit from Your Special Artistry, Creativity, Hand Skills, and Related Know-How* by Barbara Brabec (Prima Publishing)

__*422 Tax Deductions for Businesses & Self Employed Individuals* by Bernard Kamoroff (Bell Springs Publishing)

__*Homemade Money: How to Select, Start, Manage, Market and Multiply the Profits of a Business at Home* by Barbara Brabec (Betterway Books)

__*How to Register Your Own Trademark with Forms* by Mark Warda, 2nd ed. (Sourcebooks)

__*INC Yourself: How to Profit by Setting Up Your Own Corporation*, by Judith H. McQuown (HarperBusiness)

__*Patent, Copyright & Trademark: A Desk Reference to Intellectual Property Law* by Attorney Stephen Elias (Nolo Press)

__*The Perils of Partners* by Irwin Gray (Smith-Johnson Publisher)

__*Small Time Operator: How to Start Your Own Business, Keep Your Books, Pay Your Taxes & Stay Out of Trouble* by Bernard Kamoroff (Bell Springs Publishing)

__*Trademark: How to Name a Business & Product* by McGrath and Elias (Nolo Press)

Helpful Library Directories

__*Books in Print* and *Guide to Forthcoming Books* (how to find out which books are still in print, and which books will soon be published)

__*Encyclopedia of Associations* (useful in locating an organization dedicated to your art or craft)

__*National Trade and Professional Associations of the U.S.* (more than 7,000 associations listed alphabetically and geographically)

__*The Standard Periodical Directory* (annual guide to U.S. and Canadian periodicals)

__*Thomas Register of American Manufacturers* (helpful when you're looking for raw material suppliers or the owners of brand names and trademarks)

__*Trademark Register of the U.S.* (contains every trademark currently registered with the U.S. Patent & Trademark Office)

Glossary

▼▼

I have researched the following knitting terms and abbreviations for years. You may find them in knitting directions although you may not find them mentioned in this book.

Alternate knit rows: Every other knit row.

Alternate rows: Every other row.

Aran knitting: A combination of several motifs normally including some cable patterns. Another name for fisherman knitting. The patterns are taken from the sweaters of the Aran islands off the west coast of Ireland.

Asterisk (*): A symbol in knitting patterns that marks the sequence of stitches to be repeated across the row or as many times as specified after the *.

Back cable: A cable made when the cable needle has been held to the back of the work. A cable that slants toward the right.

Back of work: The side of the knitting that is away from the knitter.

Bar increase: An increase made by working into the same stitch twice by knitting first into the front loop and then knitting into the back loop.

Bind off: To remove stitches from the needle; to permanently finish off.

Bind off in pattern: Bind off while working whatever stitch would have been made if you worked the row regularly.

Bind off loosely: Don't pull the yarn too tightly when binding off. The bound off edge should stretch as much as the knitting before it.

Blocking: A technique for shaping a knitted piece into its desired shape.

Bobbin: A small implement for holding yarn when working intarsia patterns.

Bobble: A large knot-type stitch that is made by working several times into the same stitch, then knitting and/or purling several times across these stitches and then decreasing back to one stitch. They are used in many decorative patterns, especially in Aran knitting.

Boucle: Two yarns plied at different tensions, held in place by another yarn, forming loops.

Brackets: [ ]: Separates directions within a pattern.

Cable: Twisting selected stitches around each other by use of a cable needle to make a rope-like design.

Cable back: A cable made when the cable needle is held to the back of the work. A cable that slants toward the right.

Cable front: A cable made when the cable needle is held to the front of the work. A cable that slants toward the left.

Cable needle: A double-pointed needle used for working cables.

Cast off: The British term for binding off.

Cast on: Placing the stitches on the needle.

Circular knitting: Knitting in the round.

Color fastness: A color that retains its original color without fading or running.

Continental knitting method: Knitting when the yarn is held in the left hand.

Continue in pattern: Continue working in the same pattern that you have been working.

Cords: Strands twisted or woven together.

Crossed stitches: A pattern made by changing the working order of two or three stitches while taking the knitted loops diagonally.

Crossing stitches: A way to produce certain decorative stitches such as braids, honeycomb, and so on. These crossed stitches appear to have been twisted because they are pulled diagonally either to the right or to the left. They can be made with or without the use of a cable needle.

Decrease: Working two or more stitches together as a means of eliminating stitches.

Decrease round or decrease row: A round or row that contains decreases.

Diagonal knitting: Bias knitting that's made by placing decreases at one end of the fabric and increases at the other end.

Do not turn work: Keep working in the same direction; don't turn the work around to go in the other direction.

Double decrease: Decreases when two stitches are decreased, i.e., *k3 tog.*

Double increase: Increase when two new stitches are formed from one original stitch, i.e., *k1, yo, k1,* all in the same stitch.

Drop stitch: A stitch that has been dropped from the needle.

Drop wrap: To make an elongated stitch the yarn is wrapped more than one time around the needle and on the following row this extra wrap is dropped off the needle.

Duplicate stitch: An embroidery stitch in knitting that covers an already existing knit stitch. An embroidery stitch that, when finished, looks like a knit stitch.

Dye lot: Number or letter assigned to yarn of the same color that has been dyed together.

Edge: Border of a piece (side, top, or bottom).

Elasticity: The ability to recover size and shape after being stretched.

Elongated stitch: A stitch made by wrapping the yarn around the needle more than once, then dropping the extra wraps on the following row.

End with a RS (WS) row: End after working a right side (wrong side) row.

English (American) knitting method: Knitting with yarn held in the right hand.

Entrelacs: A combination of stockinette stitch squares that resemble basketweave. Another name for patchwork knitting.

Every other row: Often pattern stitches, or increases and decreases, are worked only on right side rows. Every right side row would be the same as every other row.

Every 4th row: The pattern is worked on every 4th row, i.e., Row 1, 5, 9, and so on. Another name for alternate knit rows.

Eyelet pattern: An opening in knitting separated from other openings by more than two strands of yarn. A grouping of lace holes can also be referred to as eyelet knitting.

Fabric: Finished material in your knitting project.

Faggot, faggotting: The most basic of lace stitches. It's composed only of a yarn over and a decrease.

Fair Isle: Patterns from the Fair Isles located off the northern tip of Scotland. These patterns normally contain geometric patterns, in several colors, all over the garments. Some Fair Isle patterns have rounded yokes and geometric patterns only at the top and sometimes also on a bottom border.

Fasten off: Finish with the yarn in use. In binding off, pull the yarn through the last loop on the strand.

Felting: The process of the matting of wool fibers together by means of heat, moisture, and pressure or agitation.

Flat knitting: Knitting worked on two needles. Knitting in which the work is turned at the end of every row. Knitting worked in rows in comparison to circular knitting.

Floats: Extra strands of yarn carried along the back of the work.

Forward: The side of the work facing the knitter.

Front cable: A cable made when the cable needle has been held to the front of the work. The resulting cable slants toward the left.

Fulling: The process of intentionally felting or matting a wool garment.

Garter stitch: The result when every stitch on every row is knitted.

Gauge: The number of stitches and/or rows per inch in a given pattern. Gauge is another name for tension. It's often necessary to obtain the correct gauge and to change the needle size one or two sizes larger or smaller than the recommended size. Remember, *it's always necessary to check gauge to obtain a proper fit.*

Gauge swatch: A small sample of knit fabric made by the same person using the same stitches, needles, and yarn that will be used for the garment. It's made to obtain the proper stitch and row gauge.

Grafting: A means of invisible joining of knitted pieces.

Guernsey: A type of sweater originating from the Channel Islands, off the coast of Great Britain. The simple design features a decorative ribbing, set-in sleeves, underarms, side gussets, and often side vents.

Gussets: Diamond-shaped pieces knit separately and inserted at the underarms of a jacket and coat.

Herringbone: A knitting pattern that produces a woven effect on a flat surface and has the look of a traditional herringbone weave or fabric.

I-cord: A knitted cord used in trimming. To make an I-cord, use double-pointed needles. Knit 3 (or 4 or 5) stitches; *do not turn*. Slide stitches toward the opposite end of the needle. Knit 3 (4, 5) stitches. Repeat until the piece is the desired length. This makes a nice cord that can be used as a trim to sew on a garment or used by itself.

Increase: A way to add one or more stitches to those already on the knitting needle. Increases are made to give shape, add pattern, or to give both shape and pattern simultaneously.

In pattern: To follow the directions as written, by knitting if the next stitch is supposed to be knit, and purling if the next stitch is supposed to be purled.

Intarsia: A multiple-color technique in which blocks of color are worked using separate balls of yarn or bobbins.

In the same way: Repeat whatever pattern you're doing.

Irish moss: Another name for moss stitch. The changing of knit to purl and purl to knit stitches is done on every other row instead of every row as in seed stitch.

Jacquard: A form of knitting that has multicolor motifs rather than blocks of solid color as in intarsia. Two or more yarns are carried across each row, although only one of them is worked at any one time. It's usually worked in stockinette stitch. Fair Isle knitting is an example of jacquard knitting.

Join being careful not to twist stitches: In circular knitting, after the first row is worked, the knitting continues around the needle. When joining and starting the second round, be careful that the stitches at the join aren't twisted.

Kitchener stitch: A method of grafting together stitches that are still on the needles, working with an equal amount of stitches on each of two needles. The result resembles an unbroken line of knitting in stockinette.

Knit even: Continue knitting in the present manner without changing anything.

Knit into the back loop: Instead of knitting into the front loop of the stitch as usual, you insert the needle into the back loop and knit, thus twisting the stitch at its base.

Knit into the front and back of the next stitch: A bar increase. Knit the next stitch as usual, but don't remove it from the needle. Take the tip of the right needle to the back, and then knit the stitch through the back loop. Remove both stitches from the needle.

Knit and purl into the next stitch: A moss increase. Knit the next stitch as usual, but don't remove it from the needle. Take the point of the knitting needle around to the back and purl the stitch, and then remove both stitches from the needle.

Knit position: Knitting with the yarn held in the back, away from the knitter.

Knit, purl, knit all into the same stitch: A double increase. Knit the next stitch as usual, but don't remove it from the needle. Bring the yarn between the needle points to the front of the work and purl the same stitch. Take the yarn again between the needle points to the back of the work, and again knit the stitch. Remove all three stitches from the left needle. Three stitches have been made from one original stitch.

Knit the knit stitches and purl the purl stitches: A term used when working rib stitches and some other pattern stitches such as Iris moss stitch. This means that you will knit the knit stitches and purl the purl stitches as they come to you on the needle.

Knit the purl stitches and purl the knit stitches: A term used in moss, seed, and some other patterns. This means that you will work the stitches the opposite of how they are facing you by purling the knit stitches and knitting the purl stitches.

Knit side: The smooth side of the work; looks like a group of *V*s.

Knit stitch: The most basic stitch in knitting. Stitch mode while holding the yarn in the back of the work.

Knit two together: Knit the next two stitches together as if they were one stitch.

Knit, yarn over, knit all into the next stitch: Knit the next stitch as usual, but don't remove it from the needle. Bring the yarn forward between the needle points to the purl position, and with the yarn in this position, knit the same stitch again. A double increase.

Knitting again: Knit two stitches together, leave them on the needle, and then go back and knit the first stitch again.

Knitting on: A British term for casting on.

Knitting up stitches: A British term for picking up stitches.

Knitwise: Working as if you are going to knit with the yarn held to the back of the work.

Lace: Any open-work pattern, usually made with a combination of decreases and yarn overs. Lacework is apt to be looser than stockinette stitching with the same number of stitches.

Left cable: A cable that slants toward the left. A cable made by holding the cable needle in the front of the work.

Left decreases: Decreases that slant toward the left such as *ssk, ssp, sl 1, k1, psso, k2 tog tbl*.

Lifted increase right: Insert the tip of the right needle from the front into the right side of the stitch below the next stitch on the left needle. Knit this loop through the front and then knit the stitch on the needle.

Lifted increase left: Knit the next stitch. Insert the tip of the left needle into the left side of the stitch two rows below the last worked stitch on the right needle. Pull this loop out and knit into the back loop.

Make one: An almost invisible increase. Pick up the horizontal thread lying between the stitch just worked and the following stitch. Insert the tip of the left needle (from the front) under this strand and place the strand on the left needle. Knit into the back loop of the strand to make a new stitch.

Marker: A circular ring-like device that separates patterns or marks a place in your work.

Matching decreases: The decrease on the right side of the work faces in the opposite direction as the decrease on the left side, i.e., *ssk* on the right side and *k2 tog* on the left side or *k2 tog* on the right side and *ssk* on the left side.

Matching increases: The increase on the right side slants in the opposite direction as the increase on the left side, i.e., a make one stitch on the right side and a reverse make one stitch on the left side or a right lifted increase on the right side and a left lifted increase on the left side.

Miss a stitch: A British term for slipping a stitch.

Mock cable rib: Rib stitch that looks like a cable but is made without using a cable needle.

Moss increase: Knit and purl into the next stitch. Knit the next stitch as usual, but don't remove it from the left hand needle. Bring the yarn between the needle points to the front of the work and purl the same stitch. Remove both stitches from the left needle.

Moss stitch: A stitch resembling a seed stitch, but the change from knit to purl and purl to knit takes place every other row instead of on every row.

Multiple: The number of stitches needed for a particular pattern. A multiple of 6 plus 3 would mean any number times 6 and then add 3.

Natural fibers: Fibers that come from either animals or plants.

Nearside: The side of the work facing the knitter at any given time.

Non-working yarn: When using more than one color of yarn, the nonworking yarn is the yarn not being used at the particular time.

Over: A yarn over. Place the yarn over the needle the number of times specified. *Y2on* means to take the yarn two times over the needle.

Paired decrease or paired increase: The same as a matching decrease or increase.

Pass slipped stitch over: The last part of *sl1, k1, psso* or the slipped stitch is picked up and passed over the knit stitch.

Pattern leaflets: Small leaflets (booklets) that contain from one to several dozen knitting patterns.

Picot pattern: A combination of yarn overs and decreases to make a special edge.

Pick up loops: A British term for picking up stitches.

Pilling: The matting of yarn or formation of yarn into little balls.

Place marker on needle: Slide the marker onto the knitting needle in the place specified in the directions. The marker is then slipped from needle to needle each time you come upon it in your work.

Ply: The number of strands that a yarn is composed of.

Popcorn: A small bobble. A pattern stitch in which a small knot shows on the surface of the work.

Purl stitch: Stitch in knitting that's the opposite of a knit stitch; looks like horizontal bumps.

Raised increase: Another name for a make 1 increase.

Repeat from *: Repeat whatever instructions come after the * for as long as specified.

Resilience: Elasticity or stretch of yarn.

Reverse make one: An almost invisible increase made by picking up the strand lying between the stitch just worked and the following stitch by inserting the left needle from the back. Place the strand on the needle and knit the strand through the front loop.

Reverse stockinette stitch: A stockinette stitch in which the purl side is the right side and the knit side is the wrong side.

Reversing shaping: A term used for garments such as cardigans when the shaping required is worked in the opposite direction from the other side (right versus left side of cardigan).

Ribbing: A pattern stitch often used at the bottom, top, and edges of a garment.

Right cable: A cable that slants toward to right. A cable made by holding the cable needle in the back of the work.

Right side row: The side of the knitting that will be on the outside of the project when finished.

Round: A row in circular knitting; each stitch on a set of 4 or 5 double-pointed needles or a circular needle.

Round knitting: Another name for circular knitting. Knitting worked in the round as compared to flat knitting.

Row: A horizontal series of stitches.

Row gauge: The number of rows per inch.

Schematic: A scale drawing that shows specific measurements of all the pieces of a garment.

Seed stitch: A texture knit/purl stitch pattern. On the first row you work *k1, p1*, repeating all the way across the row. On all other rows you will knit the purl stitches and purl the knit stitches.

Selvage: The edge of a piece of fabric that has been finished to prevent raveling.

Short rows: A technique that adds rows in one part of a pattern without changing the total number of stitches on the needle. They are used for shaping.

Slip a stitch as if to knit: Insert the tip of the right needle into the next stitch as if you are going to knit it, but instead just slip it into the right needle without working it. The stitch will lie on the needle in the opposite direction from the other stitches.

Slip a stitch as if to purl: Insert the tip of the right needle into the next stitch from the right as if to purl, but instead of purling it, just slide it to the right needle without working it at all.

Slip, knit, pass: Another term for slip 1, knit 1, pass the slipped stitch over.

Slip knot: The first stitch in a cast on row.

Slipped stitch: A stitch that has been slipped from one needle to the next without being worked.

Slip, slip, knit: A left slanting decrease. Slip the next two stitches, one at a time, from the left needle to the right needle, slipping them as if to knit. Insert the tip of the left needle from the left into the front of these two stitches and knit them together.

Slip, slip, purl: A purl decrease that when worked on the wrong side, has the same appearance from the right side as the *ssk*. Slip the next two stitches from the left needle to the right needle, slipping them one at a time as if to knit. Then slip them back to the left needle, slipping them again one at a time. They will lie on the needle in the opposite direction from the other stitches on the needle. Take the tip of the right needle to the back and insert the tip of the right needle from the left into the back of the second stitch and then into the back of the first stitch and purl them together.

Steek: A temporary insert that makes it possible to continue working around in circular knitting (going right across where the armholes or center front will be later without dividing for the opening). The steek is later cut open and the edges are secured from raveling.

Stitch: Loop of yarn on the needle.

Stitch gauge: The number of stitches per inch.

Stockinette stitch: A stitch formed by knitting one row and purling the next row. The knit side is the right side.

Stocking stitch: Another name for a stockinette stitch.

Stranding: A way to carry the yarn across the back in color patterns.

Swatch: A sample of knitting made to check your gauge or to check the pattern stitches.

Swiss darning: Another name for duplicate stitch.

Symbolcraft: A form of knitting instructions written out in symbols on a grid instead of being written out in words.

Tapestry needle: A blunt-pointed needle with a large eye used for sewing knitted pieces together.

Tension: The resilience of the yarn as it passes over the fingers; another name for gauge.

Texture stitch: A stitch with a surface or textural interest. Texture stitches can be a combination of knit and purl stitches, cables, popcorns, bobbles, twisted stitches, and others.

Through back loop: Work the stitch through its back loop instead of through the usual front loop.

Traveling stitches: Stitches moved from one position to another.

Turn your work around: When you finish a row, you must turn the work (knitting on the left needle) around so the end with the yarn is on the right end of the left needle so you can begin the next row.

Twisted rib: Rib stitch in which the knit stitches are twisted by knitting into the back instead of the front loops, which twists them at the base.

Unknitting: A term for taking out your knitting stitch by stitch.

Weave in ends: Loose ends must be carefully woven in so that they don't unravel. It's best to weave them into seams when there are seams or to use them for seams whenever possible. They must be woven in so that they don't show from the right side, and they should always be woven into yarn of a similar color.

Weight: The actual weight of a skein or ball of yarn, usually given in grams.

With the yarn in the back (wyib): When the yarn is held in the back, away from the knitter. The yarn is held in the knit position.

With the yarn in the front (wyif): The yarn is held in the front toward the knitter. The yarn is held in the purl position.

Work: Another name for the knitting project you are currently working on.

Work across stitches on the holder: Work the stitches from the stitch holder on to the working needle, either knitting or purling them as the directions state.

Work even: Continue to work in whatever stitch or pattern you've been working without changing anything.

Working stitch: The stitch you are presently working on.

Working yarn: The yarn you are using to knit.

Work in pattern: Work the following rows in the specified pattern.

Work straight: The same as work even.

Work to correspond, reversing shaping: Used when two pieces are to be made the same, but with opposite shaping, as in right and left front.

Wrong side row: The side of the knitting that will be on the inside when finished.

Yarn around needle (yrn or wrn): Yarn over between two purl stitches. Take the yarn over the top of the needle from the front to the back, and bring it back again to the front by bringing it between the needle points and purl.

Yarn back: Take the yarn between the needle points to the back.

Yarn forward: Bring the yarn to the front between the needle points.

Yarn forward and around needle (yfrn or wfrn): Bring the yarn forward to the front by bringing it between the needle points. Take it over the top of the right needle, and bring it back again to the front between the needle points and purl.

Yarn forward and over the needle (yfon or wfon): A yarn over between two knit stitches. Bring the yarn forward by bringing it between the needle points to the front of the work. Take it back over the top of the needle and proceed to knit. This means that you're really working a knit stitch with the yarn held in the purl position.

Yarn over: A new stitch made by wrapping the yarn around the needle an extra time.

Yarn over needle (yon or won): A yarn over after a purl and before a knit stitch. Take the yarn from the front to the back by taking it over the top of the needle and knitting with the yarn held in the purl position. When working this yarn over there you use a very small amount of yarn, so to make all the resulting holes the same size, hold the yarn a little loosely when taking it over the top of the needle to knit.

Yarn two times over the needle (y2on): Work the yarn over as you normally would, and then take it over the top of the needle again. This is a double yarn over that's usually worked to make an elongated stitch.

Knitting Abbreviations

alt: alternate

alt row: alternate rows

approx: approximately

as estab: as established

as foll: as follows; work the instructions that follow

b: back, below

B: bobble

beg: beginning

bet: between

bk: back

BL, bl: back loop, below

blw: below

BO (bo): bind off, bobble

but: buttonhole

c: cable

C4B: cable 4 to the back, right slanting cable

C4F: cable 4 to the front, left slanting cable

c, cr: crochet

CC, cc: contrasting color

Ch, ch: chain

circ: circular

cm: centimeter

cn: cable needle

CO, co: cast on

cont in patt: continue in pattern

Cr, cr: cross

Cr L: cross left

Cr R: cross right

d: decrease

dc: double crochet

dec: decrease

Dec 1, dec 1: decrease 1 (not December first)

diag: diagonal

diam: diameter

dir: directions

div: divide

dk: dark

DK: double knitting

dp: double pointed

dpn: double-pointed needle

dw: drop wrap

elon: elongated

eor: every other row

est: established

F, f: front

FC: front cable

fab: fabric

fac: facing

fig: figure

fin: finished

fol, foll: following

Fr, fr: front

from beg: from the beginning

FT, ft: front twist

fwd: forward

g: garter stitch

gm: gram

grp: group

g st: garter stitch

H, hk: hank of yarn

I cord: a knitted cord used for decoration

in(es): inch, inches

inc: increase

incl: including

inc L: increase to the left

inc R: increase to the right

inst: instructions

k: knit

k1: knit 1 stitch

k1, p1: knit one stitch, purl 1 stitch

k1, tbl: Knit through the back loop instead of through the front loop. Makes a twisted stitch.

kfb: Knit into the front and back loops of a stitch

k1b: knit into the stitch below; also knit into back loop

k2: knit 2 stitches

k2 tog: knit the next two stitches together as if they were one stitch; decrease slanting toward the right

k2 tog b: knit the next two stitches together through their back loops; decrease whichever slants toward the left, with the stitches twisted at the base

k2 tog tbl: knit the next stitches together through their back loops

k3 tog: knit the next 3 stitches together

kb 1: knit the next stitch through the back loop

kb 2: knit the next 2 stitches through the back loops

kfb: knit into the front and back loops of a stitch; an increase

k1, yo, k1: knit one, yarn over, knit one all into the same stitch; a double increase (3 stitches made from 1 stitch)

kpk: knit, purl, all into the next stitch; a double increase; (3 stitches made from 1 stitch)

ksb: knit into the stitch in the row below

k-wise: knitwise, as if to knit

L, l: left

LC: left cable, left cross

Lg, lg: large

LH: left hand

LHN: left hand needle

Lp (s): loop, loops

LS: left slant, left side

LT: left twist

M, m: make, marker

mm: millimeter

MB: make bobble

MC: main color

m1: make 1; an increase

m1k: make one knitwise; an increase

m1p: make 1 purlwise; an increase

med: medium

mult: multiple

n, no: number

ndl: needle

o: yarn over

oo: yarn over two times

ooo: yarn three times over the needle

opp: opposite

over: yarn over

oz: ounce

p: purl

p1: purl 1 stitch

p1, k1: Purl 1 stitch, knit 1 stitch

p1 tbl: purl 1 stitch through the back loop

p2: Purl 2 stitches

p2 tog: purl the next 2 stitches together; decrease

p2 tog tbl: purl the next 2 stitches together through their back loops

p3 tog: purl the next 3 stitches together; double decrease

pat: pattern

pbl: purl into the back loop

pfb: purl into the front and then into the back loop of a stitch; an increase; 2 stitches made from 1 stitch

pfl: purl into the front loop (the usual way to purl)

pm: place marker

psso: pass the slipped stitch over

p2sso: pass the two slipped stitches over

prec: preceding

prev: previous

pu: pick up

p-wise: purl wise, as if to purl

R, r: round, row, right

RC, rc: right cable, right cross

RH, rh: right hand

RHN: right hand needle

RS, rs: right side, right slant

RT: right twist

rt: right

rem: remaining

rep: repeat

repeat from *: Repeat the stitch the number of times written after the *. For example, **k8, p5; repeat from *5 more times* tells you to work *k8, p5* six times (counting the first time). If the * wasn't used, the direction would read: *k8, p5, k8, p5, k8, p5, k8, p5, k8, p5, k8, p5*.

rev: reverse

rev st st: reverse stockinette stitch

rib: ribbing

rnd: round

s: stitch

sc: single crochet

sk: skip

skp: slip, knit, pass slipped stitch over

sk2p: slip 1, knit 2 together, pass the slipped stitch over

sl: slip

sl 1 k: slip 1 stitch as if to knit

sl 1, k1, psso: Slip 1 stitch, knit the following stitch, pass the slipped stitch over the knit stitch and off the needle.

sl 1 p: slip 1 stitch as if to purl

sl st: slip stitch

sm: small

sp: space

ss: slip stitch

ssk: slip, slip, knit 2 together

sssk: slip, slip, slip, knit 3 together; double decrease

ssp: slip, slip, purl 2 together

st: stitch

st st: stockinette stitch

T, t: together; twist

T2, t2: twist 2

tbl: through back loop

tfl: through the front loop

tog: together

tw: twist

Tw2 B: twist 2 stitches to the back

Tw2 F: twist 2 stitches to the front

Tw2 L: twist 2 stitches to the left

Tw2 R: twist 2 stitches to the right

UK: United Kingdom

U.S.: United States

W, w: wool

wb: wool (yarn) to the back

wf: wool (yarn) to the front

wfon: wool forward and over the needle

wfrn: wool forward and around the needle

won: wool over the needle

wrn: wool around the needle

Ws, ws: wrong side

wyb: with the yarn in the back

wyf: with the yarn in the front

wyib: with the yarn in the back

wyif: with the yarn in the front

✕: times. For example, 2 × means 2 times.

x lg: extra large

Y, y: yarn

y2on: yarn 2 times over the needle

yb: yarn in the back, yarn back

yf: yarn in the front, yarn forward

[yf] twice, [yf] 2X: yarn forward two times around the needle

yfon: yarn forward and over the needle

yfrd: yarn forward

yfrn: yarn forward and around the needle

yo: yarn over

yon: yarn over the needle

Resources

▼▼

Recommended Books

Knitting Books

Abstracts and Images by Lee Anderson (Rocklin, CA: Vibrant Handknits, 1997).

Aran Knitting by Alice Starmore (Loveland, CO: Interweave Press, 1997). A complete workshop on Aran knitting.

The Art of Fair Isle Knitting: History, Techniques, Color and Patterns by Ann Feitelson (Loveland, CO: Interweave Press, 1996).

The Best of Knitter's Shawls and Scarves, edited by Nancy Thomas (Sioux Falls, SD: XRX Books, 1999).

The Best of Rowan: 50 Designer Knitting Patterns from Rowan, by Stephen Sheard (Loveland, CO: Interweave Press, 1998).

The Casual You: Knitting Designs for the Family by Lee Anderson (Seattle, WA: Eagle Anderson, 1991).

Charted Knitting Designs: A Third Treasury of Knitting Patterns by Barbara Walker (Pittsville, WI: Schoolhouse Press, 1998).

Colorful Knitwear Design by *Threads Magazine* (Newtown, CT: Taunton Press, 1994).

Creative Knitting by Mary Walker Phillips (Loveland, CO: Interweave Press, 1989).

Danish Lace Treasures by Gloria Penning (Herman, MO: Heirloom Lace).

Designing Knitwear by Deborah Newton (Newtown, CT: Taunton Press, 1992).

Folk Knitting in Estonia by Nancy Bush (Loveland, CO: Interweave Press, 1999).

Folk Socks: The History and Techniques of Handknitted Footwear by Nancy Bush (Loveland, CO: Interweave Press, 1995).

Gossamer Webs: The History and Techniques of Orenberg Lace Shawls by Galina Khmelev and Carol R. Noble (Loveland, CO: Interweave Press, 1998).

Handknit Skirts by Shirley MacNulty (Wilmington, NC: Self-published).

Head to Toe Knits: 24 Colorful Accessories for Your Child and Your Home by Zoe Mellor (North Pomfret, VT: Trafalgar Square, 1998).

How to Knit: The Definitive Knitting Course Complete with Step-by-Step Techniques, Stitch Libraries and Projects for Your Home and Family by Debbie Bliss (North Pomfret, VT: Trafalgar Square, 1999).

Kids Kids Kids: A Colorful Array of Fun-to-Wear Garments and Fanciful Toys to Knit for Children, edited by Ann. S. Regis (Sioux Falls, SD: XRX Books, 1999).

Knit Like Crazy by Poochie Myers (Letters Etcetera! Inc.).

Knitted Heirloom Lace II by Gloria Penning (Herman, MO: Heirloom Lace).

Knitted Heirloom Lace III by Gloria Penning (Herman, MO: Heirloom Lace).

Knitted Sweater Style: Inspirations in Color by Jo Sharp (Newtown, CT: Taunton Press, 1997).

Knitters Almanac by Elizabeth Zimmerman (New York, NY: Dover Books, 1985).

The Knitters Companion by Vicki Square (Loveland, CO: Interweave Press, 1996). A great reference manual.

Knitters Handbook: A Comprehensive Guide to the Principles and Techniques of Handknitting by Montse Stanley (Pleasantville, NY: Readers Digest, 1999).

Knitting Around by Elizabeth Zimmermann (Pittsville, WI: Schoolhouse Press, 1989).

Knitting Bazaar by Jo Sharp (Newtown, CT: Taunton Press, 1999).

Knitting Counterpanes by Mary Walker Phillips (Newtown, CT: Taunton Press, 1989).

Knitting from the Top by Barbara Walker (Pittsville, WI: Reprinted by Schoolhouse Press, 1997).

Knitting Ganseys by Beth Brown-Reinsel (Loveland, CO: Interweave Press, 1993).

Knitting in Plain English by Maggie Righetti (New York: St. Martin's Press, 1986).

The Knitting Sutra: Craft as a Spiritual Protection by Susan Gordon Lydon (San Francisco, CA: Harper, 1997).

Knitting Without Tears by Elizabeth Zimmermann (Pittsville, WI: Schoolhouse Press, 1971).

Lace from the Attic: A Victorian Notebook of Knitted Lace Patterns by Nancy Wiseman (Loveland, CO: Interweave Press, 1998).

The Lacy Knitting of Mary Schiffmann by Nancy Nehring (Loveland, CO: Interweave Press, 1998).

The Mary Thomas Book of Knitting Patterns by Mary Thomas (New York, NY: Dover Books, 1972).

The Mary Thomas Knitting Book by Mary Thomas (New York, NY: Dover Books, 1972).

Meg Swansen's Knitting by Meg Swansen (Loveland, CO: Interweave Press, 1999).

Mosaic Knitting by Barbara Walker (Pittsville, WI: Reprinted by Schoolhouse Press, 1997).

Nicky Epstein's Knitted Embellishments by Nicky Epstein (Loveland, CO: Interweave Press, 1999).

No Idle Hands: The Social History of American Handknitting by Anne L. Macdonald (New York, NY: Ballantine Books, 1988).

Old World Treasures by Gloria Penning (Herman, MO: Heirloom Lace).

Ribbon Knits by Judi Alweil (Newtown, CT: Taunton Press, 1998).

Sally Melville Styles: A Unique and Elegant Approach to Your Yarn Collection by Sally Melville (Sioux Falls, SD: XRX Books, 1999).

A Second Treasury of Knitting Patterns by Barbara Walker (Pittsville, WI: Reprinted by Schoolhouse Press, 1998).

Slip-Stitch Knitting: Color Pattern the Easy Way by Roxanna Bartlett (Loveland, CO: Interweave Press, 1998).

Socks, Socks, Socks: 70 Winning Patterns from Knitters Magazine Contests, edited by Elaine Rowley (Sioux Falls, SD: XRX Books, 1999).

Sweater Design in Plain English by Maggie Righetti (New York, NY: St. Martin's Press, 1990).

Traditional Lace Shawls by Martha Waterman (Loveland, CO: Interweave Books, 1993).

A Treasury of Knitting Patterns by Barbara Walker (Pittsville, WI: Reprinted by Schoolhouse Press, 1998).

Vogue Knitting Designer Knits by Vogue (Altoona, PA: Butterick Co., Inc.), 1998.

Craft Business Books

The Basic Guide to Selling Arts and Crafts by James Dillehay (Torreon, NM: Warm Snow Publishers, 1995).

Cash for Your Crafts by Wendy Rosen (Iola, WI: Krause Publications, 1999).

Crafting as a Business: Tools and Resources for Building a Profitable Craft Business by Wendy Rosen (Distributed by Chilton, Baltimore, MD: The Rosen Group, 1994).

Crafting for Dollars: Turn Your Hobby into Serious Cash by Sylvia Landman (Rocklin, CA: Prima Publishing, 1996).

The Crafts Business Answer Book & Resource Guide: Answers to Hundreds of Troublesome Questions About Starting, Marketing & Managing a Homebased Busi-ness Efficiently, Legally & Profitably by Barbara Brabec (New York, NY: M. Evans & Co., 1998).

The Crafts Supply Sourcebook: A Shop by Mail Crafts Supply Guide by Margaret Boyd (Cincinnatti, OH: Betterway Books, 1999).

Creative Cash: How to Profit from Your Special Artistry, Creativity, Hand Skills and Related Know-How by Barbara Brabec. Revised 6th edition. (Rocklin, CA: Prima Publishing, 1998).

Handmade for Profit: Hundreds of Secrets to Success in Selling Arts & Crafts by Barbara Brabec (New York, NY: M. Evans & Co., 1996).

Homemade Money: How to Select, Start, Manage, Market and Multiply the Profits of a Business at Home by Barbara Brabec. Revised 5th edition. (Cincinnatti OH: Betterway Books, 1997).

How to Publish, Promote, and Sell Your Own Book: The Insider's Guide to Everything You Need to Know About Self-Publishing, from Paste-up to Publicity by Robert Lawrence Holt (New York, NY: St. Martin's Press, 1985).

How to Sell What You Make: The Business of Marketing Crafts by Paul Gerhards (Harrisburg, PA: Stackpole Books, 1990).

How to Start Making Money With Your Crafts by Kathryn Caputo (Cincinnatti, OH: Betterway Books, 1995).

How to Write a Book Proposal by Michael Larsen. Revised edition. (Cincinnatti, OH: *Writer's Digest* Books, 1997).

Needlecrafter's Computer Companion: Hundreds of Easy Ways to Use Your Computer for Sewing, Quilting, Cross-Stitch, Knitting, & More by Judy Heim (Daly City, CA: No Starch Press, 1995).

Photographing Your Craftwork: A Hands-On Guide for Craftspeople by Steve Meltzer (Loveland, CO: Interweave Press, 1986).

Promoting and Marketing Your Crafts by Edwin M. and Selma G. Field (New York, NY: Macmillan, 1993).

Software Directory for Fiber Artists Includes: Weaving, Quilting, Needlework, Sewing and Industrial Artist Profiles and More by Lois Larson (Camrose, Alberta, Canada: Lois Larson, 1995).

Recommended Magazines and Newsletters

The following are knitting-related magazines that I recommend.

Knitting Magazines

Cast On

P.O. Box 1606, Knoxville, TN 37901-1606
Phone: (423) 524-2401
Toll-free phone: (800) 274-6034
Web site: www.tkga.com
E-mail: tkga@tkga.com

Published 5 times a year. The magazine of the Knitting Guild of America.

Family Circle Easy Knitting
Vogue Knitting

Publisher: Butterick Co.
P.O. Box 1072, Altoona, PA 16603
Toll-free phone: (800) 289-4304
Web site: www.vogueknitting.com
Published 3 times a year.

Interweave Knits

Publisher: Interweave Press
201 E. Fourth Street, Loveland,
CO 80537-5655

Toll-free phone: (800) 645-3675
Web site: www.interweave.com
E-mail: knits@interweave.com
Published 4 times a year.

Knit 'n Style

Publisher: All American Crafts
P.O. Box 173, Mt. Morris, IL 61054-9823
Toll-free phone: (800) 877-5527
Published bimonthly.

Knitting Digest

Publisher: House of White Birches
P.O. Box 9003, Big Sandy, TX 75755
Published bimonthly.

Knitter's Magazine

Publisher: XRX, Inc.
P.O. Box 1525, Sioux Falls, SD 57101-1525
Toll-free phone: (800) 232-5648
Web site: www.knittinguniverse.com
Published 4 times a year.

Knit Net

A quarterly magazine on the World Wide Web: www.KnitNet.com

Piecework

Publisher: Interweave Press
201 E. Fourth Street, Loveland, CO 80537-5655
Phone: (970) 669-7672
Toll-free phone: (800) 645-3675
Web site: www.interweave.com
Published bimonthly.

Knitting Newsletters

Knitters' News

Publisher: Mossom Publishing
P.O. Box 65004, 358 Danforth Avenue, Toronto, Ontario M4K 3Z2 Canada
E-mail: stp@interlog.com

Knitting News

P.O. Box 1612, Carolina Beach, NC 28412
Web site: www.craftassoc.com/knitting
.html
E-mail: country@isaac.net
Published quarterly.

Knitting Now

P.O. Box 543, Norfolk, MA 02056
Phone: (508) 528-3289
Web site: www.knittingnow.com
Published three times a year.

Pine Meadow Knitting News

P.O. Box 2375, Sun City, AZ 85372-2375
E-mail: joan_hamer@msn.com
Published quarterly.

Arts and Craft Magazines

Arts and Crafts

Publisher: Krause Publications
700 E. State Street, Iola, WI 54990-0001
Phone: (715) 445-2214
Toll-free phone: (800) 258-0929
Web site: www.krause.com
Published bimonthly.

Better Homes and Gardens Crafts Showcase

Publisher: Meredith Corporation
P.O. Box 37228, Boone, IA 50037-2228
Toll-free phone: (800) 688-6611
Published bimonthly.

Crafts

Publisher: Primedia, Inc.
P.O. Box 56015, Boulder, CO 80322
Toll-free phone: (800) 727-2387
Published 10 times a year.

Crafts 'N Things

Publisher: Clapper Publishing Co., Inc.
P.O. Box 5026, Des Plaines, IL 60017-5026
Toll-free phone: (800) 444-0441
Web site: www.clapper.com
E-mail: cntcs@clapper.com
Published 10 times a year.

Craftworks

Publisher: All American Crafts, Inc.
P.O. Box 413, Mt. Morris, IL 61054-9820
Toll-free phone: (800) 877-5527
Published 10 times a year.

Business Magazines

Craft and Needlework Age (this is for needlework trade)

Craft Supply Magazine (this is for professional crafters)

Publisher: Krause Publications
700 E. State Street, Iola, WI 54990-0001
Toll-free phone: (800) 258-0929
Web site: www.krause.com

Craft Marketing News

Publisher: The Front Room Publishers
P.O. Box 1541, Clifton, NJ 07015

Directed toward crafters interested in reaching craft shops, galleries, craft malls, and seasonal boutiques across the United States.

Craftrends

Publisher: Primedia Special Interest Publications, Inc.
741 Corporate Circle, Suite A, Golden, CO 80401
Phone: (800) 677-5212

A trade magazine for those in the craft, needlework, and sewing industries. Published monthly.

The Crafts Report

Publisher: The Crafts Report Publishing Company
300 Water Street, Wilmington, DE 19899
Toll-free phone: (800) 777-7098
Fax: (302) 656-4894
Web site: www.craftsreport.com

Published monthly. Contains business articles about craft shows for professional crafters.

Sunshine Artist

2600 Temple Drive, Winter Park, FL 32789
Phone: (407) 539-1399
Web site: www.sunshineartist.com

This monthly art and craft magazine lists craft shows all over the United States.

Craft Internet Malls

Arts and Crafts Internet Mall
Web site: www.artcraftmall.com

Coomers Global Gallery – online marketplace
Web site: www.coomers.com

Craft Mark – Internet craft sales
Web site: www.craftmark.com

Educational Opportunites on the Internet

The Knitting Guild of America online instructions
Web site: www.tkga.com

The Knitting Universe from Knitters Magazine
Web site: www.knittinguniverse.com

Knitting and Craft Associations

Arts and Crafts Network

Web site: www.acnshowguide.com (membership Internet site exclusively for craft exhibitors, promoters and suppliers)

Recommended Web Sites

In this section, you'll find Web sites that relate to knitting in one way or another. Happy surfing!

Chat Rooms

Artist Related Services: www.artistbiz.com

Barbara Breiter, Your About.Com Guide to Knitting: knitting.about.com

The Knit List: knitlist@kniton.com

KnitNet: www.knitnet.com

The Knitting Guild of America: www.tkga.com

The Knitting Universe: www.knitting universe.com.

Woolworks: www.woolworks.org

Craft Business Information

Barbara Brabec's Web site: www.crafter.com/brabec

Maria Nerius's Web site: www.procrafter.com/maria.htm

Professional Crafter, The: www.procrafter.com

Important Contact Numbers

The following are important contact numbers for many helpful areas.

Knitting, Craft, and Business Organizations

American Association of Home-Based Businesses

P.O. Box 10023, Rockville, MD 20849-0023
Toll-free phone: (800) 447-9710
Fax: (301) 963-7042
Web site: www.aahbb.org
E-mail: aahbb@crosslink.net

Craft Business Network, Country Sampler Group

Karen Slokum
707 Kautz Road, St. Charles, IL, 60174
Phone: (630) 377-8000 Ext. 250 and
(888) CRAFTER (888-272-3837)
Fax: (630) 377-8194
Web site: www.sampler.com
E-mail: karens@sampler.com

This organization invests in the future of craft professionals through local chapter participation.

Craft Yarn Council of America

P.O. Box 9, Gastonia, NC 28053
Phone: (704) 824-7838
Fax: (704) 824-0630
Web site: www.craftyarncouncil.com

The Knitting Guild of America

P.O. Box 1606, Knoxville, TN 37901-1606
Phone: (423) 524-2401
Toll-free phone: (800) 274-6034
Fax: (423) 524-8677

Web site: www.tkga.com
E-mail: tkga@tkga.com

The Knitting Guild of Canada

Box 444, Princeton, ON, Canada N0T 1V0
Phone: (519) 458-4440
Fax: (519) 458-4441
E-mail: bootsie.ckc@sympatico.ca

National Craft Association

1945 East Ridge Road, Suite #5178,
Rochester, NY 14622-2467
Phone: (716) 266-5472
Toll-free phone: (800) 715-9594
Fax: (716) 785-3231 and (800) 318-9410
E-mail: nca@craftassoc.com
Web site: www.craftassoc.com

The National Needlework Association (TNNA)

1100 H Brandywine Blvd., Zanesville, OH 43702
Phone: (740) 452-4541
Fax: (740) 452-2552

A trade association for the needlework industry.

The Professional Knitwear Designers Guild

c/o Diane Zangl, membership chairman, W-3090 Country Road Y, Lomira, WI 53048
E-mail: stitchwi@fdldotnet.com

Society of Craft Designers (SCD)

1100 H Brandywine Blvd., P.O. Box 3088, Zanesville, OH 43702-3088
Phone: (740) 452-4541
Fax: (740) 452-2552
E-mail: scd@offinger.com

Knitwear Designers and Producers

Charlene Anderson-Shea

P.O. Box 4780, Jackson, WY 83001-4780
Web site: www.andersonshea.com
E-mail: andersonshea@compuserve.com

Lisa G. Bennett

E-mail: lbennett@mayfield.hp.com

Mary Birenbaum

6509 Caballero Pkwy NW, Albuquerque,
NM 87107-5603
E-mail: challah@ix.netcom.com

Shirley Bailey Bowers

E-mail: sdbowers@webtv.net

Beth Brown-Reinsel

Knitting Traditions, P.O. Box 421,
Delta, PA 17314
Phone: (717) 456-7950
Web site: www.members.aol.com/
KnitTradit

Sally Crandall

5625 Green Turtle Lane, Wilmington,
NC 28409

Kimberley Derowin

E-mail: Rodeogal@ivillage.com

Bonita Edwards

995 Teaneck Road, Suite 2M, Teaneck,
NJ 07666
Phone: (201) 833-8570
E-mail: BEdw226624@aol.com

Shirley MacNulty

P.O. Box 1612, Carolina Beach, NC 28428
Phone: (910) 392-9469
Web site: www.craftassoc.com/knitting
.html
E-mail: country@isaac.net

Deborah Meyer

E-mail: MDeborah@aol.com

Poochie Myers

Knit Like Crazy, P.O. Box 1028,
Huntington, WV 25713
Phone (304) 522-3979
E-mail: poochie@prosperity.com

Sue Ordiway-Perri

E-mail: oberonmom@hotmail.com

Janet Rehfeldt

E-mail: kthreads@earthlink.net
Web page: www.home.earthlink.net/
~kthreads

Tina M. Sanders

E-mail: tsanders@cybertrails.com

Annmarie Signey

E-mail: knittinmama@yahoo.com

Joy Slayton

Joy Knits, Route 1, Box 1346, Cadet,
MO 63630
Web site: www.joyknits.com
E-mail: joyknits@joyknits.com

Janet Johnson Stephens

1025 Worton Park Drive, Mayfield Village,
OH 44143-3329
E-mail: knitjan@aol.com

Vanessa VanOrman

E-mail: bunniesnicker@hotmail.com

Diane Zangl

Stitch Witch Designs, W3090 Country Road Y, Lomira, WI 53048
E-mail: stitchwi@fdldotnet.com

Craft Suppliers

Following is contact information for a variety of craft suppliers.

Advertising and Printing Supplies

The Art of Photography

Toll-free phone: (800) 809-7947

This company makes postcards, business cards, catalogue sheets, brochures, and fine art prints.

Great American Printing Company

Toll-free phone: (800) 440-2368
Web site: www.gapco.com

This company makes full-color business cards.

Modern Postcard

1675 Faraday Avenue, Carlsbad, CA 92008
Toll-free phone: (800) 959-8365
Fax: (760) 431-9788
Web site: www.modernpostcard.com
E-mail: modern.cs@irisgroup.com

This company makes promo cards.

Pine Barrens Printing

351-1 Old Riverhead Road, Westhampton Beach, NY 11978
Phone: (516) 288-5200

Toll-free phone: (800) 414-0992
Web site: www.artistbiz.com
E-mail: pinebarrens@peconic.net

A full-service printing agency for artists by artists.

Business Supplies

Action Bag & Display

501 N. Edgewood Avenue, Wood Dale, IL 60191-1410
Phone: (630) 766-2881
Toll-free phone: (800) 824-BAGS (800) 824-2247
Fax: (800) 400-4451 or (630) 766-3548
Web site: www.actionbag.com
E-mail: info@actionbag.com

This company makes all kinds of bags and ribbons.

Fetpak Inc.

70 Austin Blvd, Commack, NY 11725
Toll-free phone: (800) 883-3872
Fax: (888) 329-4600
Web site: www.fetpak.com

This company makes pricing and tagging supplies, custom labels, rubber stamps, boxes, sign cards, and so on.

Craft and Show Supplies

Creative Canopies

4338 Austin Blvd., Island Park, NY 11558
Phone: (516) 431-4127
Web site: www.creativecanopies.com

Dealers Supply Inc.

P.O. Box 717, Matawan, NJ 07747
Toll-free phone: (800) 524-0576
Fax: (732) 591-8571
Web site: www.dlrsupply.com

This company makes display supplies, flame-retardant table covers, security supplies, hand trucks, and so on.

Elaine Martin Company

25685 Hillview Court, Suite E, Mundelein, IL 60060
Toll-free phone: (800) 642-1043
Web site: www.emartin.com

This company makes indoor booths, display systems, pedestals, tables, and so on.

Flourish Company

Toll-free phone: (800) 296-0049
Fax: (501) 677-3380
Web site: www.flourish.com
E-mail: info@flourish.com

This company makes canopies, indoor frames, flame-resistant fabrics, and so on.

Supply Source

P.O. Box 522-Forest Park, Dayton, OH 45405
Phone: (937) 274-4650 and (937) 274-4688
Fax: (937) 274-8143

This company makes canopies.

Knitting Software

Cochenille Design Studio

P.O. Box 234276, Encinitas, CA 92023-4276
Phone: (619) 259-1698
Web: www.cochenille.com
E-mail: cochenille@compuserve.com

Patternworks

P.O. Box 1690 Poughkeepsie, NY 12601
Phone: (914) 462-8000
Toll-free phone: (800) 438-5464
Fax: (914) 462-8074
Web site: www.patternworks.com
E-mail: knit@patternworks.com

Labels and Hangtags

Charm Woven Labels

2400 West Magnolia Blvd., Burbank, CA 91056-1758
Web site: www.charmwoven.com
E-mail: charm@charmlabel.com

Heirloom Woven Labels

P.O. Box 428, Moorestown, NJ 08057
Phone: (609) 722-1618
Fax: (609) 722-8905

Name Maker, Inc.

P.O. Box 43821, Atlanta, GA 43821
Toll-free phone: (800) 241-2890
Web site: www.namemaker.com
E-mail: cs@namemaker.com

Northwest Tag and Label

2435 SE Eleventh, Portland, OR 97214

Sterling Name Tape Co.

P.O. Box 939, Winsted, CT 06098
Phone: (888) 312-0113
Fax: (860) 379-0394
Web site: www.sterlingtape.com
E-mail: postman@sterlingtape.com

Stone House Traditions

247 W. State Street, Quarryville, PA 17566
Phone: (717) 786-6222 and (888) 221-VALU

This company makes custom-printed labels and tags, shopping bags, tissue paper, boxes, ribbon, and so on.

Mail-Order Yarn and Accessory Businesses

Aylin's Woolgatherer

7245 Arlington Blvd, Falls Church, VA 22042
Phone: (703) 573-1900
Toll-free phone: (800) 775-WOOL
Web site: www.aylins-wool.com

This company sells yarns, buttons, books, needles, accessories, and so on.

Bare Hill Studios/Fiber Loft

P.O. Box 327, Harvard, MA 01451
Toll-free phone: (800) 874-YARN

Bay Country Boutique

P.O. Box 1612, Carolina Beach, NC 28428.
Phone: (910) 392-9469
Web site: www.craftassoc.com/knitting
.html
E-mail: country@isaac.net

Betty Bornside Company

2733 Dauphine St., New Orleans, LA 70117
Toll-free phone: (800) 221-9276

Blackberry Ridge Woolen Mill

3776 Forshaug Road, Mt. Horeb, WI 53572
Phone: (608) 437-3762

Cherry Hill Tree Yarn

P.O. Box 254, East Montpelier, VT 05651
Phone: (802) 229-0831
Toll-free phone: (800) 739-7701
Fax: (802) 223-4792
Web site: www.cherryyarn.com
E-mail: orders@cherryyarn.com

Cotton Clouds

5176 South 14th Ave., Safford, AZ 85546-9252

House of Needlecraft

1314 N 4th Street, Coeur d'Alene, Idaho 83814
Phone: (888) 775-5648
Web site: www.ewekknit.com
E-mail: ewekknit@televar.com

Fiber Studio

9 Foster Hill Road, Henniker, NH 03242
Phone: (603) 428-7830
Web site: www.fiberstudio.com
E-mail: fiberstudio@connet.com

This company offers classes on weaving, spinning, and yarns.

Fiber Tech

248 Harbor Blvd., Belmont, CA 94002
Phone: (650) 610-0554
Fax: (650) 610-0557
This company sells wooden needles and Needles n' Things organizers.

Great Yarns

1208 Ridge Road, Raleigh, NC 27607
Phone: (919) 832-3599
Toll-free phone: (800) 810-0045
Web site: www.greatyarns.com
E-mail: greatyrn@gte.net

Halcyon Yarn

12 School Street, Bath, ME 04530
Phone: (207) 442-7909
Toll-free phone: (800) 341-0282
Fax: (207) 442-0633
Web site: www.halcyonyarn.com

Harrisville Designs

Center Village, P.O. Box 806, Harrisville,
NH 03450
Phone: (603) 827-3333
Toll-free phone: (800) 338-9415
Fax: (603) 827-3335
Web site: www.harrisville.com
E-mail: info@harrisville.com

Knitting by the Sea

P.O. Box Y-1, Carmel, CA 93921
Toll-free phone: (800) 823-3189

This company sells yarn, books, patterns,
accessories, finishing, buttons, and so on.

Knitting Traditions

P.O. Box 421, Delta, PA 17314
Phone: (717) 456-7950
Fax: (717) 456-5751
Web site: www.members.aol.com/
KnitTradit
E-mail: KnitTrad@aol.com

Knitworks of America

P.O. Box 95219, Seattle, WA 98145-2219

Phone: (888) 548-0910
Web site: www.knitworksofamerica.com

This company is a good source for fashion
yarns.

Marr Haven

772 39th Street, Allegan, MI 49010
Phone: (616) 673-8800
Web site: www.accn.org/~mhyarn

Mary Maxim, Inc.

P.O. Box 5019, 2001 Holland Avenue,
Port Huron, MI 48061-5019
Toll-free phone: (800) 962-9504
Fax: (810) 987-5056
Web site: www.marymaxim.com

The Needlepoint Joint

241 Historic 25th Street, Ogden, UT 84401
Phone: (801) 394-4355
Toll-free phone: (800) 660-4355
Web site: www.needlepointjoint.com

This company sells all types of knitting,
spinning, and weaving accessories, and
beads, buttons, and so on.

The Needlework Attic

4706 Bethesda Avenue, Bethesda,
MD 20814
Phone: (301) 652-8688
Toll-free phone: (800) 654-6654

This company offers yarns, books,
needlepoint, cross-stitching, and finishing
accessories.

Northwest Peddlers

Toll-free phone: (800) 764-YARN
(800-764-9276)
Web site: www.nwpeddlers.com

This company offers sewing kits.

Patternworks

P.O. Box 1690 Poughkeepsie, NY 12601
Phone: (914) 462-8000
Toll-free phone: (800) 438-5464
Fax: (914) 462-8074
Web site: www.patternworks.com
E-mail: knit@patternworks.com

This company offers yarn, needles, books, buttons, and so on.

Personal Threads Boutique

8025 West Dodge Road, Omaha, NE 68114-3413
Phone: (402) 391-7288
Toll-free phone: (800) 306-7733
Fax: (402) 391-0039
Web site: www.personalthreads.com
E-mail: carolyn@personalthreads.com

This company sells accessories for knitting, weaving, spinning, and needlepoint.

Ram Wools

143 Smith Street, Winnipeg, MB Canada R3C 1J5
Toll-free phone: (800) 263-8002
Web site: www.gaspard.ca/ramwools.htm
E-mail: ram@gaspard.com

This company will send you a free catalogue.

Schoolhouse Press

Pittsville, WI 54466
Phone: (715) 884-2799
Toll-free phone: (800) YOU-KNIT (800-968-5648)

This company sells books, videos, yarn, and so on.

School Products Co., Inc.,

1201 Broadway, New York, NY 10001
Phone: (212) 679-3516
Web site: www.schoolproducts.com
E-mail: berta@schoolproducts.com

Velona Needlecraft

5753 D Santa Ana Canyon Road, Anaheim Hills, CA 92807
Phone: (714) 974-1570
Toll-free phone: (800) 972-1570
Fax: (714) 693-3131
Web site: www.velona.com
E-mail: info@velona.com

This company sells books and yarns.

The Weaver's Loft

308 S. Pennsylvania Ave., Centre Hall, PA 16828
Toll-free phone: (800) 693-7242
Web site: www.knitters-underground.com
E-mail: yarnshop@aol.com

This is the home of the Knitters' Underground.

Web.sters

11 N. Main Street, Ashland, OR 97520
Toll-free phone: (800) 482-9801

This company will send you a free color catalogue.

WEBS

America's Yarn Store, P.O. Box 147, Service Center Road, Northampton, MA 01061-0147
Phone: (413) 584-2225
Fax: (413) 584-1603

Web site: www.yarn.com
E-mail: webs@yarn.com

This company sells popular brands of yarn at discounts.

Woodland Woolworks

P.O. Box 400, Yamhill, OR 97148-0400
Phone and Fax: (503) 662-3641
Toll-free phone: (800) 547-3725
E-mail: woolworks@teleport.com

This company sells yarn, books, accessories, videos, and so on.

Woolstock

4848 Butler Road, Glyndon, MD 21071
Phone: (410) 517-1020
Toll-free phone: (800) 242-5648
Fax: (410) 517-1021
Web site: www.woolstock.com

This company sells yarns, needles, videos, books, patterns, blockers, and so on.

Wool Connection

34 East Main Street, Old Avon Village N, Avon, CT 06001
Phone: (860) 678-1710
Toll-free phone: (800) 933-9665
Fax: (860) 677-7039
Web site: www.woolconnection.com
E-mail: wool@tiac.net

Wooly Knits

6728 Lowell Avenue, McLean, VA 22101
Phone: (703) 448-9665
Toll-free phone: (800) 767-4036
Web site: www.woolyknits.com
E-mail: donna@WoolyKnits.com

This is a designer-yarn superstore.

Yarn Barn (of Andersonville)

Route 3, P.O. Box 8945, Dillwyn, VA 23936
Phone: (804) 983-1965
Toll-free phone: (800) 850-6008
Web: www.yarnbarn.com
E-mail: pkirtland@yarnbarn.com

Yarn Barn

930 Massachusetts, Lawrence, KS 66044
Toll-free phone: (800) 468-0035
Web site: www.yarnbarn.com

Yarns By Design

247 E. Wisconsin Avenue, Neenah, WI 54956
Phone: (920) 727-0530 and (888) 55-YARNS (888) 559-2767
Web site: www.yarnsbydesign.com
E-mail: yarns@juno.com

Yarns International

5110 Ridgefield Rd, Suite 200, Bethesda, MD 20816
Phone: (301) 913-2980
Toll-free phone: (800) YARNS 2U (800) 927-6728
E-mail: YARNS2U@aol.com

This company sells Shetland yarn.

Yarn and Accessory Manufacturers and Distributors

Please check with these companies for the name of the retail store nearest you.

Anny Blatt USA, Inc.

7796 Boardwalk, Brighton, MI 48116
Phone: (248) 486-6160

Bartlettyarns, Inc.

P.O. Box 36, Harmony, ME 04942
Phone: (207) 683-2251

Bergere De France

8238 NW 16th Street, Coral Springs,
FL 33071
Toll-free phone: (800) 236-6140

Bernat, Brunswick and Coats Patons Yarn

c/o Spinrite Yarns, 320 Livingston
Avenue, South, Listowel, ON N4W 3H3,
Canada

Berroco, Inc.

P.O. Box 367, Uxbridge, MA 01569
Phone: (508) 278-2527

Bouton D'Or

R. Massamiri & Co., P.O. Box 5040,
San Clemente, CA 92674
Phone: (949) 492-4242

Brown Sheep Company, Inc.

100622 Country Road 16, Mitchell,
NE 69357
Phone: (308) 635-2198
Web site: www.brownsheep.com

Classic Elite Yarns

12 Perkins Street, Lowell, MA 01854
Phone: (978) 453-2837

Coats and Clark

P.O. Box 1530, Albany, GA 31702
Web site: www.coatsandclark.com

Coats Patons Yarns

c/o Spinrite Yarns, 320 Livingston
Avenue, South, Listowel, ON N4W 3H3,
Canada

Colinette Yarns

c/o Unique Kolours, 1428 Oak Lane,
Downingtown, PA 19335
Phone: (610) 280-7720

Crystal Palace

3006 San Pablo Ave., Berkeley, CA 94702
Web site: www.straw.com/cpy

Dale of Norway

N 16 W 23390 Stoneridge Dr., Suite A,
Waukesha, WI 53188
Toll-free phone: (800) 441-DALE

JCA (Reynolds and Unger Yarns)

35 Scales Lane, Townsend, MA 01469
Phone: (978) 597-8794

K^1C_2 Innovative Solutions

2220 Eastman Avenue #105, Ventura,
CA 93003
Phone: (805) 676-1176
Toll-free phone: (800) 607-2462
E-mail: K1C2@ix.netcom.com

Knitting Fever, Inc.

35 Debevoise Avenue, Roosevelt,
NY 11575
Toll-free phone: (800) 645-3457

Lane Borgosesia

P.O. Box 217, Colorado Springs, CO 80903

Lion Brand Yarn

34 W. 15th Street, New York, NY 10011
Phone: (212) 243-8995
Toll-free phone: (800) 258-YARN
Web site: www.lionbrand.com

Louet Sales

P.O. Box 267, Ogdensburg, NY 13669
This company sells 100% linen yarn.

Marr Haven

722 39th Street, Allegan, MI 49010
Phone: (616) 673-8800

Muench Yarns and Buttons

285 Bel Marin Keys Boulevard, Novato,
CA 94949
Phone: (415) 883-6375
E-mail: muenchyarn@aol.com

Phildar/Pingouin

P.O. Box 217, Colorado Springs, CO 80903

Plymouth Yarn Company

P.O. Box 28, Bristol, PA
Phone: (215) 788-0459
Web site: www.Plymouthyarn.com

Prism

2595 30th Avenue North, St. Petersburg,
FL 33713
Phone: (727) 327-3110

Reynolds Yarn

c/o JCA, 5 Scales Lane, Townsend,
MA 01469
Phone: (978) 597-8794

Rowan Yarns

c/o Westminster Fibers, 5 Northern Blvd.,
Amherst, NY 03031
Phone: (603) 886-5041

Schaefer Yarns

Toll-free number: (800) FOR-YARN
(800) 367-9276
E-mail: schaefer@epix.net

Skacel Collection

P.O. Box 88110, Seattle, WA 98138-2110
Phone: (253) 854-2710
Web site: www.skacelknitting.com

Spinrite Yarns

320 Livingston Avenue, South, Listowel,
ON N4W 3H3, Canada

Stacy Charles Collection, Filatura Di Crosa

1059 Manhattan Avenue, Brooklyn,
NY 11222

Swedish Yarn Imports

126A Wade Street, P.O. Box 2069,
Jamestown, NC 27282
Phone: (336) 883-9939

Tahki Yarns

11 Graphic Place, Moonacchie, NJ 07074
Phone: (201) 807-0070

Trendsetter Yarns

16742 Stagg Street, #104, Van Nuys, CA
91406
Phone: (818) 780-5497
Toll-free phone: (800) 446-2425
E-mail: Trndstr@aol.com

Unger Yarns

c/o JCA, 35 Scales Lane, Townsend, MA
01469
Phone: (978) 597-8794

Unique Kolours

1428 Oak Lane, Downington, PA 19335
Phone: (610) 280-7720
Web site: www.colinette.com

This company sells colinette yarns.

Westminster Fibers

5 Northern Blvd., Amherst, MA 03031

This is a distributor of Rowan yarns.

Art/Craft Shows and Malls

There are so many arts and crafts shows that I can only list a few of them. For complete listings and information, I suggest you subscribe to *Sunshine Artist* and/or *The Crafts Report* magazines.

Retail Craft Shows

Arts and Crafts Festivals, Inc. (NY, CT)

P.O. Box 227, Granby, CT 06060-0227
Phone: (860) 653-6671
Toll-free phone: (800) 784-9744
Web site: www.HandMadeinAmerica.com

Castleberry Fairs and Festivals
(CT, MA, NH)

P.O. Box 307, Farmington, NH 038335
Phone: (603) 755-2166
Fax: (603) 755-2647
Web site: www.castleberryfairs.com
E-mail: info@castleberryfairs.com

Christmas Gift and Craft Shows
(CA, NE, UT)

Phone: (702) 798-4944
Fax: (702) 798-4945
E-mail: nyfinc@aol.com

Columbia Sunday ARTS & CRAFTS

The New City Arts & Crafts Shows,
P.O. Box 247, Kingsville, MD 21087
Phone: (410) 679-2288
Fax: (410) 679-6919

Cord Shows Ltd. (NY, CT)

4 Whippoorwill Lane, Armonk, NY 10504
Phone: (914) 273-4667
Fax: (914) 273-4656
Web site: www.cordshows.com
E-mail: Cordshows@aol.com

Country Folk Art Shows, Inc
(AZ, CA, CO, CT, FL, IN, MI, MN, NJ, NY)

8393 E. Holly Road, Holly, MI 48442
Phone: (248) 634-4151
Fax: (248) 634-3718
E-mail: cfas@tir.com

Country Peddler Shows (NE, OH, TX)

American Country Shows, P.O. Box 1129,
Fredericksburg, TX 78624
Toll-free phone: (800) 775-2774
Fax: (830) 997-0453
E-mail: peddler@ktc.com

Harvest Festival (NV, CA, AZ)

601 North McDowell Blvd., Petaluma,
CA 94954
Phone: (707) 778-6300
Toll-free phone: (800) 321-1213
(outside California)
Fax: (707) 763-5346
Web site: www.harvestfestival.com

High Country Art and Craft Guild
(NC and TN)

P.O. Box 2854, Asheville, NC 22802
Phone: (828) 252-3880

Holiday Fantasy

Coastal Crafts Originals, c/o Frances
Bowen, 606 Otter Creek Landing, Carolina
Beach, NC 28428

Held annually in October at Trask
Coliseum, UNC-Wilmington, Wilmington,
NC. I have participated in this show for
several years.

Huff Promotions, Inc. (FL, NY, OH, PA)

4275 Fulton Road NW, Canton, OH 44718
Phone: (330) 493-4130
Fax: (330) 493-7607

International Art Resource (Florida)

22191 Martella Ave., Boca Raton, FL 33433
Phone: (561) 451-4485
Fax: (561) 451-1502

National Christmas Show
(and other shows around DC and VA)

Home Office, P.O. Box 11565, Winston
Salem, NC 27116
Phone: (336) 924-4359

Sugarloaf Craft Festivals
(GA, MD, MI, NJ, PA, VA)

Sugarloaf Mountain Works, Inc.,
200 Orchard Ridge Drive, #215,
Gaithersburg, MD 20878
Phone: (301) 990-1400
Toll-free phone: (800) 210-9900
Fax: (301) 253-9620
Web site: www.sugarloafcrafts.com

Vermont Craft Workers Inc.

P.O. Box 8139, Essex, VT 05451
Phone: (802) 878-4786 and (802) 879-6837
Fax: (802) 878-5778 and 879-1370

Craft Malls

American Craft Malls

American Craft Malls, Inc., P.O. Box 799,
Azle, Texas 76098-0799
Phone: (817) 221-1099
Toll-free phone: (800) 335-2544
Fax: (817) 221-4556
Web site: www.procrafter.com/craftmal
.html

Cape Cod Crafters of New England

Toll-free phone: (800) 321-6240
Web site: www.capecodcrafters.com

Coomers Craft Malls

6012 Reef Point Lane, Suite F, Ft. Worth,
Texas 76135
Phone: (817) 237-4588 and
(888) DO-CRAFTS (888-362-7238)
Fax: (817) 237-4875
Web site: www.coomers.com

Craftworks

Phone: (888) CWORKS7 (888-296-7577)
Web site: www.craftworksonline.com

Homespun Crafter's Mall

Phone: (888) HMESPUN (888-463-7786)
Web site: www.homespuncrafters.com

Sterling Craft Mall

101 Cape Fear Blvd, Carolina Beach,
NC 28428
Phone: (910) 458-4429
Fax: (910) 458-0399
E-mail: askcojc@aol.com

Internet Craft Malls

Arts and Crafts Internet Mall
Web site: www.artcraftmall.com

Craft Mark: Internet Craft Sales
Web site: www.craftmark.com

Index

About the Author

SHIRLEY MACNULTY, certified professional knitwear designer, master knitter, and professional crafter, knitted her first pair of argyle socks in seventh grade and has been designing and teaching others to knit ever since. Shirley edits her own newsletter, *Knitting News*; has published numerous articles in *Cast On Magazine*; and has self-published eleven knitting leaflets. She teaches and judges knitting and crafts for many organizations. Shirley operates Bay Country Boutique, a needlework mail order business, and has sold her own design handknits plus other craft items for over forty years. Shirley enjoys all forms of needlework and sewing, plus gardening, cooking, and being involved in community organizations. She and her husband, Brad, divide their time between their homes in Beech Mountain and Wilmington, NC.

About the Series Editor

BARBARA BRABEC is one of the world's leading experts on how to turn an art or craft hobby into a profitable home-based business. She regularly communicates with thousands of creative people through her Web site and monthly columns in *Crafts Magazine* and *The Crafts Report*.

To Order Books

Please send me the following items:

Quantity	Title	U.S. Price	Total
_____	Decorative Painting For Fun & Profit	$ 19.99	$ _____
_____	Holiday Decorations For Fun & Profit	$ 19.99	$ _____
_____	Woodworking For Fun & Profit	$ 19.99	$ _____
_____	Knitting For Fun & Profit	$ 19.99	$ _____
_____	Quilting For Fun & Profit	$ 19.99	$ _____
_____	Soapmaking For Fun & Profit	$ 19.99	$ _____
_____	_____	$ _____	$ _____
_____	_____	$ _____	$ _____

Subtotal	$ _____
Deduct 10% when ordering 3–5 books	$ _____
7.25% Sales Tax (CA only)	$ _____
8.25% Sales Tax (TN only)	$ _____
5% Sales Tax (MD and IN only)	$ _____
7% G.S.T. Tax (Canada only)	$ _____
Shipping and Handling*	$ _____
Total Order	$ _____

*Shipping and Handling depend on Subtotal.

Subtotal	Shipping/Handling
$0.00–$29.99	$4.00
$30.00–$49.99	$6.00
$50.00–$99.99	$10.00
$100.00–$199.99	$13.50
$200.00+	Call for Quote

**Foreign and all Priority Request orders:
Call Customer Service
for price quote at 916-632-4400**
This chart represents the total retail price of books only
(before applicable discounts are taken).

By Telephone: With American Express, MC, or Visa,
call 800-632-8676 or 916-632-4400. Mon–Fri, 8:30–4:30.
www.primapublishing.com
By E-mail: sales@primapub.com
By Mail: Just fill out the information below and send with your remittance to:
Prima Publishing · P.O. Box 1260BK · Rocklin, CA 95677

Name _____

Address _____

City _____ State _____ ZIP _____

MC/Visa/American Express# _____ Exp._____

Check/money order enclosed for $ _____ Payable to Prima Publishing

Daytime telephone _____

Signature _____